AVIS AU COMMERCE

*Cette Méthode avec texte Anglais ne peut se vendre en Angleterre que par l'entremise de nos seuls Agents W. HAWKES and C°*

# COMPLETE METHOD

FOR THE

## CONTRE-BASSE

(Double-Bass)

BY

## G. BOTTESINI

*IN TWO PARTS*

*1st Part. The Contre Basse in the Orchestra*

*2nd Part. The Contre Basse as a Solo Instrument*

nett Price...... 18 *Schillings*


Propriété des Editeurs Henry LEMOINE et Cie à Paris.

*London RIVIÈRE et HAWKES 28 Leicester Square.*

*The English adaption of this Method by F. CLAYTON.*




17947. H.

# A Note On This Publication

A typical part of a double bass student's development is to study the Bottesini Method, presented usually as a series of short exercises in a small book with no accompanying text to explain each exercise. When I first studied the method I was unaware that Bottesini had originally written any text in his Method as I was working from a later edition. I continued to work through the exercises as I progressed until I stumbled upon a copy of Bottesini's original Method in French. In this, I was surprised to find paragraphs written by Bottesini describing the exercises and of his experiences performing on the double bass.

I was a little confused as to why this detail had been lost from later publications and why, when the most famous double bass virtuoso of the time was asked to write a method book, that the later editors would remove content that is integral to his style of playing. Initially I assumed that the Method would have been published only in Italian and French and that it was just bad luck that it was never translated into English. I did wonder whether it would be advantageous to translate Bottesini's Method into English to make it more accessible to a wider audience; however this would have been a significant task and I thought it would be best to save that project until time permitted. It was only later, when I was completing other research in the British Library, that I stumbled upon three versions of the Bottesini Method in Italian, French and, more unusually, in English! This suggests there may have been far fewer copies of the English translation printed, representing a significant loss to the double bass community.

After discovering this, I decided to take it upon myself to bring back these methods for other bassists to see and study so that we can get a greater insight into how the genius Bottesini performed. However, as the Method was produced over a hundred years ago the original printing plates were no longer in existence and so it would be impossible to reprint copies from these. Secondly, from searching the world library catalogue, there seem to be only five copies left of the English translation in libraries across the entire world. In light of this, the British Library and Hal Leonard (Ricordi) have supported my project by allowing me to republish all three original Methods from the originals in the British Library's collection.

### *Creating the new edition*

Thanks to the British Library archival team, the three Methods were photographed in high resolution allowing me to create this facsimile re-print. Each page from the three translations has been edited individually to correct perspective and remove unnecessary colour from the original paper. The image below taken from page 5 in the Method shows how the colour has been removed on the left hand side:

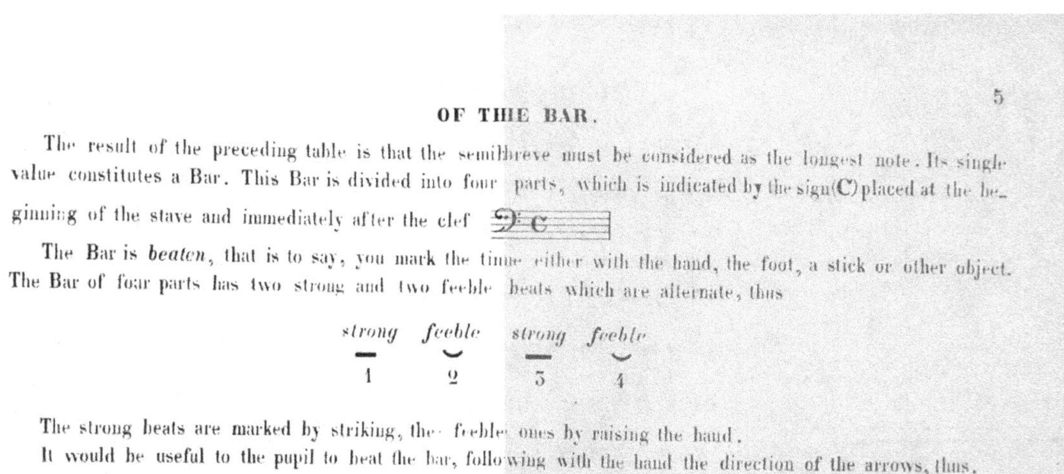

5

OF THE BAR.

The result of the preceding table is that the semibreve must be considered as the longest note. Its single value constitutes a Bar. This Bar is divided into four parts, which is indicated by the sign(C) placed at the beginning of the stave and immediately after the clef

The Bar is *beaten*, that is to say, you mark the time either with the hand, the foot, a stick or other object. The Bar of four parts has two strong and two feeble beats which are alternate, thus

*strong* *feeble* *strong* *feeble*
1 2 3 4

The strong beats are marked by striking, the feeble ones by raising the hand.
It would be useful to the pupil to beat the bar, following with the hand the direction of the arrows, thus.

Figure 1 Showing how colour has been removed on the left hand side. (*1*)

As the printing of the original Method was made by pressing ink onto a page, any malformation of characters has been caused by a lack of ink on the original plate when first pressed onto the paper, rather than the clarity being lost in the editing process. The malformation of letters before and after editing is shown in the next picture:

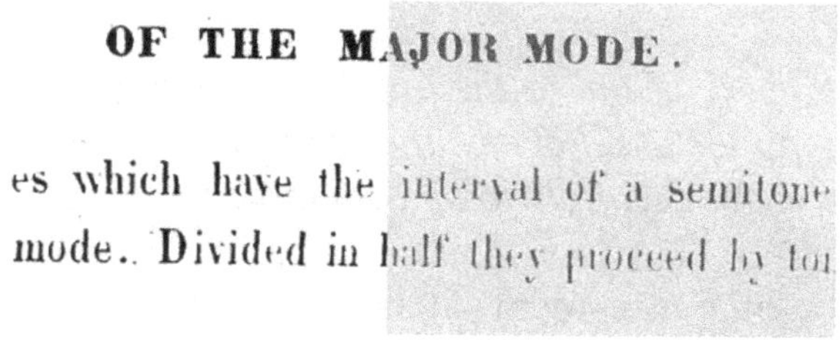

OF THE MAJOR MODE.

es which have the interval of a semitone
mode.. Divided in half they proceed by ton

Figure 2 Showing malformation of letters. (*1*)

Each page has been digitally enhanced individually to counteract any malformed characters in the original print by adjusting levels and contrast in each image to thicken the text. The next image shows how much thicker and clearer the text has become after processing:

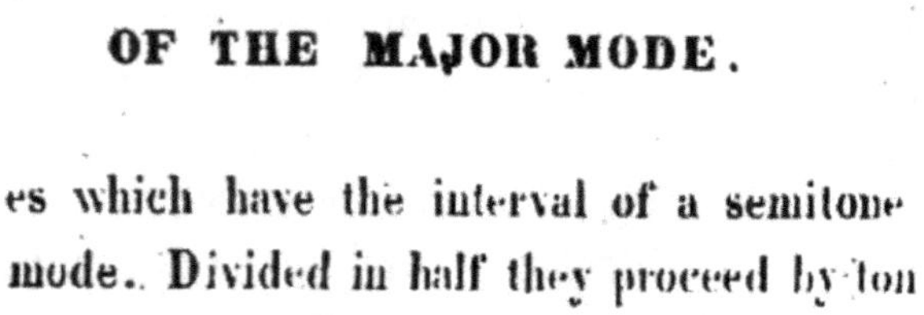

OF THE MAJOR MODE.

es which have the interval of a semitone
mode.. Divided in half they proceed by ton

Figure 3 Showing how text has been made clearer by editing. (*1*)

The entire Method and musical examples could be re-typeset to overcome the malformation of any text; however I wanted to retain the charm and character of the original publication. If demand is sufficient re-type setting could be a future project. The purpose of this publication is to preserve the information and make it available again as soon as possible to bass players.

### *Bottesini's Teaching Method*

Reading the Method has given me a fascinating insight into both the man behind the instrument and how he negotiated his way around it. One of the most amusing things to read in the book is how forthcoming Bottesini is with his opinions. He does mention himself in the preface:

> *I hasten to foreworn who might accuse me of a certain exclusiveness, more apparent than real, that I have every respect for the opinion of others, whilst I frankly state my own.* [1]

This frankness is most apparent in his discussion of the Dragonetti bow of which he says:

> *This position, as one can see, is not very elegant. Although at first sight it may appear favourable to a good attack on the strings, it has the great disadvantage of dulling sounds seeing that the hair of the bow in this manner stays too long on the string and impedes its vibration.* [2]

---

[1] G.Bottesini, *Complete Method for the Contre-basse* (London: Rivière et Hawkes/Hawkes and Co, 1872), Preface page.

[2] *Ibid., 3.*

It is clear to see that Bottesini approached music not just from being an instrumentalist but also as a master of harmony, composition and arranging, drawn from his studies at Milan Conservatoire. Bottesini takes his time to talk about the fundamentals of scales and harmony, which have been left out in most recent republications, but these are details that are obviously important to Bottesini to make the pupil a more skilled musician. In Bottesini's own words:

> *I believe it will be very useful to the pupil that he should have some slight knowledge of that art (harmony) or at all events that he should understand the meaning of certain words which one ought certainly to be acquainted with.*[3]

Unlike most other styles of music today, it is usual for 'Classical' musicians to be either players or composers. There are always exceptions to this rule, but rarely does a classical musician get a chance to excel at both skills. However, it is through this special combination that Bottesini managed to achieve so much on the double bass.

In his exercises, Bottesini gives away a few secrets to the way he manages to play certain sections of his own pieces. Throughout the book, each study has been meticulously fingered with great detail as to how he would play certain passages and various string crossings he would use. Something that is very apparent from early on is that Bottesini gets the pupil shifting up and down a string (page 27) (*1*) by writing exercises that practice shifts up an individual string at a time. This is slightly different to other methods such as Simandl (*2*), which deals with each position as a block. Simandl keeps exercises mostly within a position, working across strings until the student is ready to move a semitone up to the next position. In contrast I presume that Bottesini did not want the pupil to be afraid of shifting and to develop some useful habits of avoiding unnecessary string crossing that can be achieved by playing up and down a string. Although Bottesini's Method is written for using fingers one-three-four, all the exercises can of course be played with the one-two-four technique instead. Bottesini however does not always strictly use one-three-four in a position; his method opens and closes the left hand with some semitones being played first and then fourth finger rather than always first and then third finger. I think this technique was developed to avoid the fatigue he mentions frequently in the book, especially in the lower positions.

Bottesini's choice of fingering in his exercises often suggest a *bel canto* style of playing, shown as one of the techniques he discusses on page 81 (*1*) by making the use of *portamento* to connect positions. Bottesini himself calls it the 'carrying' of one note tied to another without removing the hand from the string, insinuating that he did not take the weight out of the string when shifting. He achieves this by shifting to the next position using the same finger he has in the previous position and is shown in the Method by writing more than one note on one particular finger. He goes on to describe how to use this technique by saying:

> *This passing must be made with a certain rapidity in order to avoid falling into a dragging or exaggerated sliding, which would be always in bad taste.*[4]

Two other techniques that became apparent in re-discovering this Method are that when Bottesini performed in the area of harmonics he would either pinch the string between the first finger and the thumb or strongly push against the string if there was a note that did not fall on to natural harmonics. He doesn't mention what direction the string should be pushed (I presume it is to the left) but it seems he used this manner to alter the pitch of a natural

---

[3] *Ibid., 15.*

[4] *Ibid., 81.*

harmonic, and that he chose to pinch the string when he needed to create a stopped note that didn't fall onto either a natural harmonic or the length of the fingerboard.

Bottesini shows in two exercises on page 116 (*1*) that the student should push against the string to alter the C natural harmonic on the D string to become a C sharp to fit a D major scale. In the next exercise he instructs the pupil to pinch the string to achieve an A sharp on the first string, again not falling on a natural harmonic or on the length of the fingerboard. Bottesini's fingerings on harmonic passages also show he favoured moving towards the bridge to play higher harmonics rather than creating them with 'false harmonics' lower down the instrument. I think this explains many of the amusing illustrations in newspapers of Bottesini clambering over his bass.

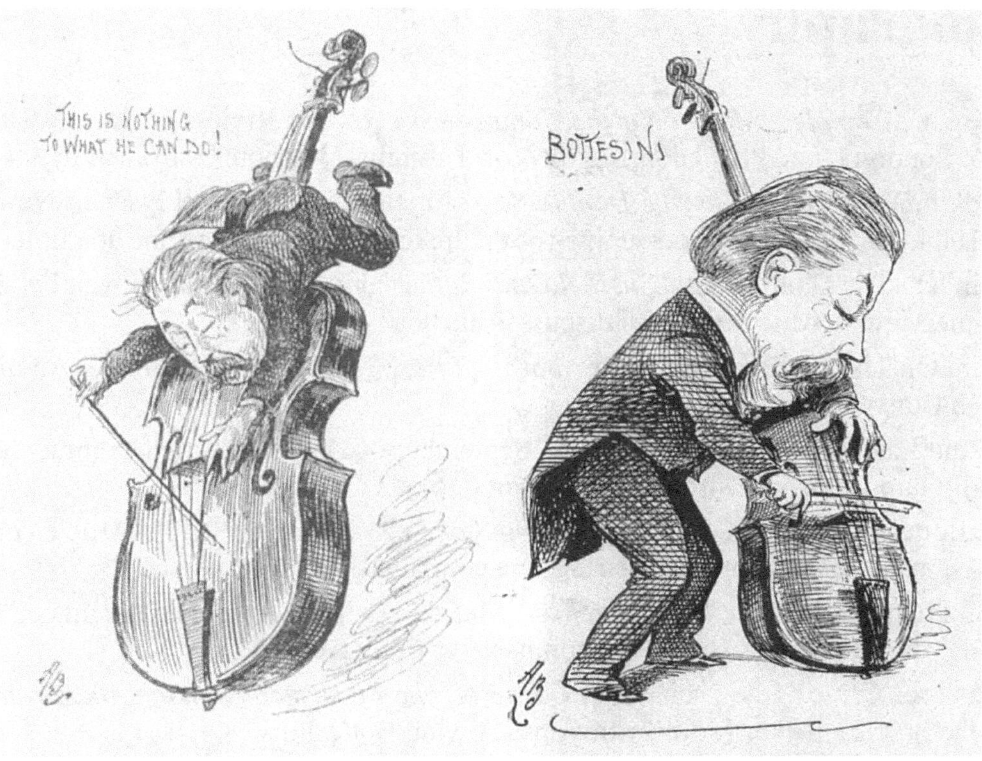


Figure 4 *The Illustrated Sporting And Dramatic News*, October 23rd 1886, page 159. (*8*)

Bottesini also gives us an insight into the equipment he used and preferred. His choice of an 'over hand' bow made like a cello bow, preferring black hair (page 20) (*1*) and having a preference for three over four strings[5]. In the Method and from contemporary interviews, Bottesini is very disparaging of the Dragonetti or German bow type. He also mentions that double bass bows varied much more in length than the rest of the string family. Measurements of between 21 ½ (55 cm) and 27 ½ inches (70 cm) in length are given in the book.[6] In an interview with the *Sheffield Independent* from Monday 21st November 1887 in an article named 'Bottesini on the double bass', he informs the journalist that he tried many different lengths of bow until he found his preference, thus giving some rationale to the measurements in this method (*1*) (*3*) (*4*). It is also interesting to hear Bottesini's reasoning for a three string bass over four; however he suggests that the pupil should first learn on a three string bass and if it is really called for, to move on to a four string instrument once he has mastered the three (*1*)[7]. The Method mentions that the third and fourth strings of four string basses were often

[5] *Ibid., 2.*

[6] *Ibid., 20.*

[7] *Ibid., 2.*

metal covered; however Bottesini writes that he prefers a 'plain string' though exactly what the plain string was made out of is not identified *(1)* *(5)* *(6)* *(7)*[8].

I'm sure that you will agree with me that there is much that has been lost in removing Bottesini's original writing from the original publication. I am also sure that the longer time spent with the Method, the more there will be uncovered about how he played. I hope that you enjoy the opportunity to learn more about Bottesini, as much as I have through studying this edition.

Stephen Street

# Bibliography

1. Bottesini, G. *Complete Method for the Contre-basse,* 1st ed.; Rivière et Hawkes/Hawkes and Co: London United Kingdom, 1872; Vol. 1, English Version Translated by F.Clayton.
2. Simandl, F. *New Method For the Double Bass,* First Edition ed.; Carl Fischer: New York USA, 1904; pp 7,8,11,14, For examples of the treatment of positions one at a time.
3. Bottesini On The Double Bass. *Sheffield and Rotherham Independant,* November 21, 1887, 8, An interview in which Bottesini discusses his bow.
4. Bottesini On The Double Bass. *Knaresborough Post,* November 26, 1887, 2, An interview in which Bottesini discusses his bow.
5. Third And Last Concert. *Liverpool Mail,* September 01, 1849, 3, Article comments on how unusually thin Bottesini's strings are compared to other bassists.
6. Signor Bottesini's Concert. *London Evening Standard,* June 18, 1884, 3, Article comments on how unusually thin Bottesini's strings are compared to other bassists.
7. Musical Phenomenon. *Leeds Intelligencer,* May 31, 1851, 4, Article comments on how unusually thin Bottesini's strings are compared to other bassists.
8. Our Captious Critic at the Promenade Concerts. *The Illustrated Sporting And Dramatic News,* October 23, 1886, 159, Illustrations showing Bottesini.



[8] *Ibid., 3.*

These editions have been reproduced by kind permission of:
Hal Leonard Europe S.r.l. – Italy (Ricordi); (Italian Edition)
Éditions Musicales Alphonse Leduc (French Edition); (formerly Heugel and Escudier)
Henry Lemoine and Boosey and Hawkes (English Edition).

# PREFACE.

It is not so easy, as one might suppose at a first glance, to write a method for the Contre-Basse (an instrument played in so many different styles) to propound and explain with clearness a system of rules, examples and progressive exercises, which, without too much fatigue to the pupil, shall facilitate his first studies, and conduct him by the best road to a perfect command of this Instrument — as difficult as it is important.

Thus I should not hastily have undertaken this work; I have only determined to do so at the request of those who, knowing with what kindness the public have always welcomed me, have believed that it was my duty to put forth, for the benefit of youth, the little experience I have acquired in playing the Contre-Basse.

In carrying out the wishes of those who have prompted me to write this method, I am enabled at the same time, to produce a work which I believe will be profitable to all who would learn to play this Instrument; and I cannot do better than place it under their patronage.

I hasten to forewarn those who might accuse me of a certain exclusiveness, more apparent than real, that I have every respect for the opinions of others, whilst I frankly state my own.

Discarding every trifling disputation I have followed but one threefold guide in the composition of this method: Truth for science; — Beauty for art; — Usefulness for the pupil.

G. BOTTESINI.

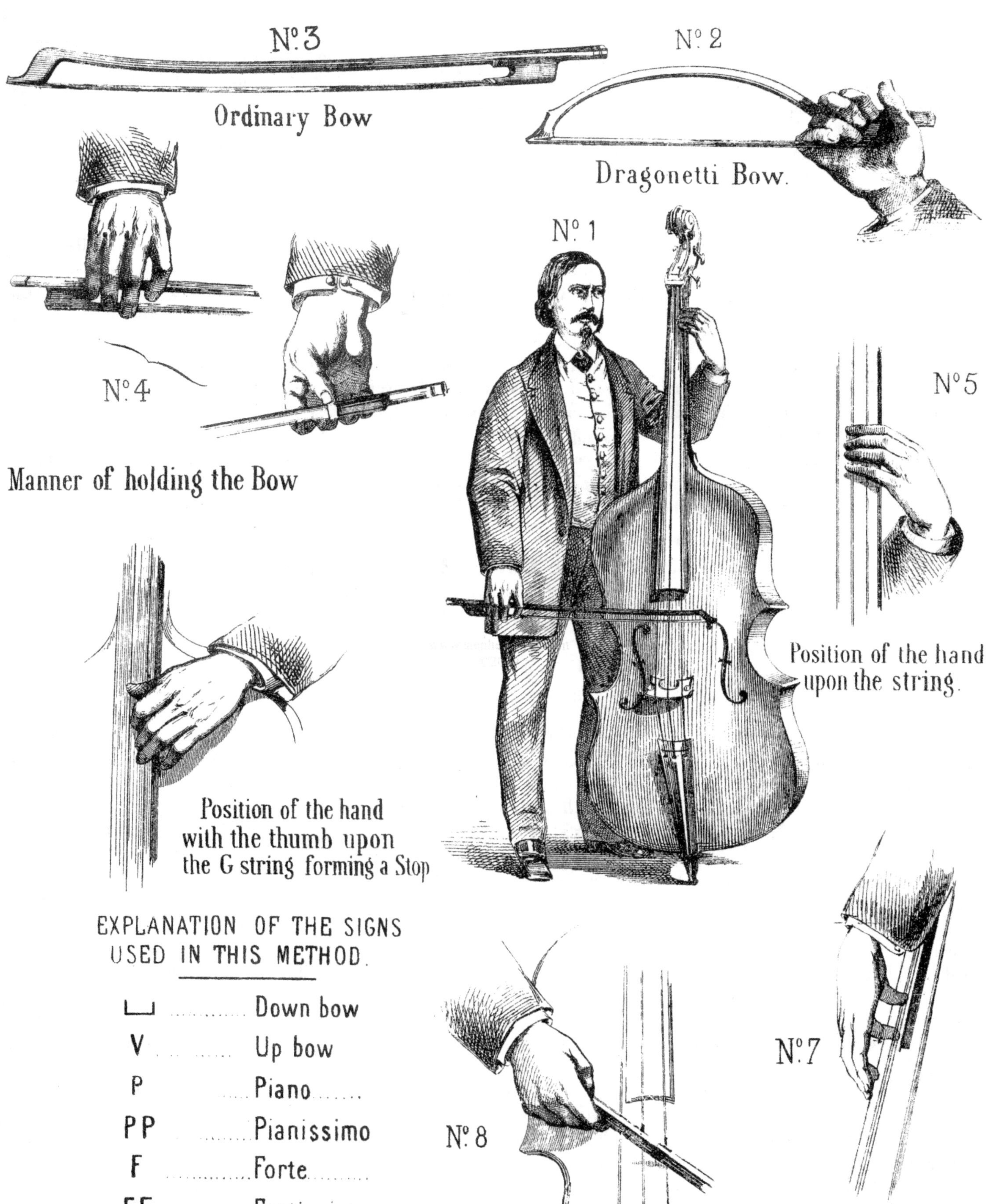


EXPLANATION OF THE SIGNS USED IN THIS METHOD.

|  |  |
|---|---|
| ⊔ | Down bow |
| V | Up bow |
| P | Piano |
| PP | Pianissimo |
| F | Forte |
| FF | Fortissimo |
| MF | Mezzo-Forte |

# OF THE CONTRE BASSE
## (commonly called in England The Double Bass)

Without entering into an useless enumeration of the advantages and inconveniences of this instrument as used with four strings in preference to three; without discussing the mechanism of the fingering and the various qualities of tone which this fourth string gives to the Contre Basse, considered as the fundamental part of the Orchestra; finally, without enlarging too much upon the form and size of the Bow, upon the different ways of holding and managing it, and upon the different kinds of the sounds which result from the form of the Bow and the use which is made of it; I commence by speaking of the Contre Basse itself — of that which by the ease and certainty of the fingering as well as by the neatness and roundness of its tones is complete with only three strings.

I will mention, further on, the reasons for this assertion, which at first sight might seem arbitrary and gratuitous.

The Reader may be at once assured that I have, so to speak, compiled this method according to the excellent traditions of the most competent and best of the Italian Contre Bassists — Of this number are Dragonetti, Andreoli, etc, and above all Louis Rossi, my regretted master, who was Professor of the Contre Basse at the Conservatoire of Milan.

It must not be thought that it is a very easy matter to learn to play this Instrument according to the Rules. In like manner as for the Violin, one must have not only a natural disposition for it, but also great firmness of hand. The Artist wanting in this last quality, is to an equal extent burdened by so much preoccupation with respect to the mechanism as to prevent his freely rendering his ideas and inspiriting his audience.

This firmness of hand, this complete dominion over the strings, can only be acquired by long practice. In order, then, to obtain that mastery it is absolutely necessary to have time, patience and perseverence.

Knowing as I do the numerous obstacles which the pupil must overcome before attaining his purpose, I must recommend him to begin the study of this Instrument at an early period of life — at 14 years old for example That is the age most favorable to the developement of the physical and intellectual faculties.

## On the study of the Contre Basse with 3 strings as facilitating that of the 4 string instrument.

### PRELIMINARY OBSERVATIONS
#### UPON THE NATURE OF THE INSTRUMENT.

No one who is acquainted with the nature of the Contre Basse can deny that the extra string has been added for the sole purpose of giving to the Instrument some additional lower notes. This is doubtless of some importance to the Composer, and is to a certain extent, useful, particularly in sustained notes.

But if the Contre Basse gains, by this fourth string, a greater extension of the deeper notes, this extension cannot be obtained without detriment to quality of tone, which naturally becomes impaired as the strings are increased in number

Those who doubt this fact need only make the experiment upon the Instrument — this I have myself done over and over again. The question had for some years seemed to me of sufficient importance to induce me to experiment upon the effect of the fourth string on the best Contre Basses that passed through my hands, particularly those of the celebrated Gaspar da Salo, who, in my opinion and in the opinion of all connaisseurs was the best maker of Contre Basses. The result was always the same and always bad — all those instruments without exception, lost with the fourth string that clear and sonorous quality so necessary especially in the low notes. Hence we are led to this conclusion; that it is much better to sacrifice a few low notes to the perfect clearness and sonorousness of the Contre Basse, than to sacrifice those qualities to the slight advantage of four lower notes obtained by the addition of a string.

Besides, in England, where Classical music is in great favor and admirably executed, the want has never been felt, to my knowledge of adding a fourth string to the Contre Basse.

It must not by any means be believed that the study of the Contre Basse with four strings necessitates a different method from that of the Three stringed instrument. It would be impossible to gain a knowledge of the resources of the fourth string, — to make use of it — to bring out its powers — without having become master of the first three strings by force of study, labour and very numerous progressive exercises.

This assertion is not due simply to my experience — it is corroborated by the example and confirmed by the testimony of the best Contre Bassists who have decided to add the fourth string only after having, for a long time, worked upon the Instrument with three strings.

I will confine myself to mentioning the principal reasons for this distinction.

1. By using the three plain strings we avoid the great inconvenience of two wire covered strings which by the very nature of their heterogeneous envelope allow of less pressure, and present more difficulties to the attack of the Bow. If the use of these strings is so troublesome to Virtuosi and Musicians of the Orchestra, imagine what it must be to a young pupil who commences the study of an Instrument so little proportioned to his size!

2. The strings must be some distance apart to give vibration and allow of the inflexion of the Bridge, so that the bow can work freely on each string; it therefore follows that the neck of the instrument, in accordance with the number of strings and the space between them, is disproportionate to the hand of a young pupil: I have just said that the study of this Instrument should be commenced at about the age of fourteen.

3. Passages upon the fourth string, the sounds of which attain the greatest depth, always fail in clearness and may easily deceive the pupil's ear — thence arises the fault of inaccuracy — the worst of all faults.

I repeat it then: To arrive at a thorough knowledge of the Contre Basse, and to play it with neatness and elegance, it is not only useful but necessary to practise it at first with three strings.

## OF THE BOW.

Two sorts of bows are used for the Contre Basse. The first called the "Dragonetti Bow" is very short and curved like an arch. (see plate fig: 2)

This position, as one can see, is not very elegant.

Although at first sight it may appear favorable to a good attack on the strings, it has the great disadvantage of dulling the sounds seeing that the hair of the Bow used in this manner stays too long on the string and impedes its vibration.

Besides, the very form of this bow and its shortness are little adapted to the production of sounds of long duration (sostenuti); wherefore slurred or bound notes are almost impossible.

At the same time this Bow has one advantage — that of an excellent attack in staccato passages. It is much used in England and in a few Towns in Italy.

The English have however, of late years, adopted a modification of the Dragonetti Bow — it is much straighter and very slightly curved until near the head.

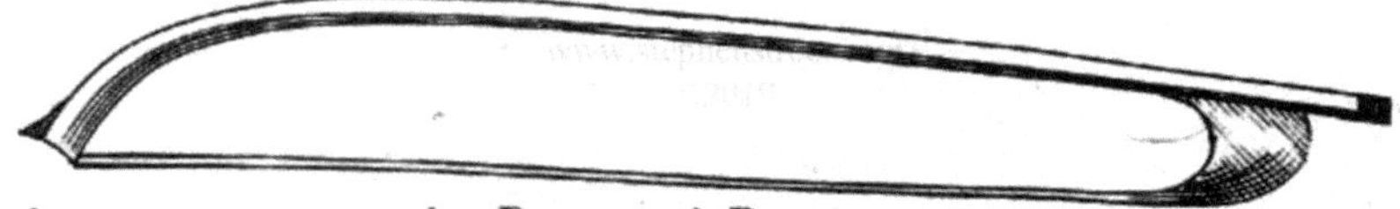

It is held nearly in the same manner as the Dragonetti Bow.

The other Bow, more generally in use, is longer and of quite another shape; it is the Bow I myself use. (see plate fig: 3)

This Bow, except in its size, much resembles the Violoncello Bow, and is held in the same manner.

I shall speak more fully as to this Bow, when I come to mention the various positions of the hand, in relation to the strings it has to attack.

Although I assume that the pupil can read music I think it will be useful to explain the elementary principles of the study of Notation for those who may not already have acquired a knowledge of musical writing.

## SYSTEM OF NOTATION.

The notes are seven in number and are named after the first seven letters of the alphabet, *A, B, C, D, E, F,* and *G*.

In Italy and France the notes are named *Do, Ré, Mi, Fa, Sol, La, Si*. These syllables are almost as familiar to the English as the Alphabetical nomenclature. The Italian names however, as above expressed, correspond with the notes which we should call *C. D. E. F. G. A. B.* / *do. ré. mi. fa. sol. la. si.* — It is not necessary for our purpose to explain the origin of these syllables or letters as expressing musical sounds, nor why the first Italian syllable is identical with the letter *C* and not with the first letter of the alphabet. Suffice it to say that *Do* and *C* are synonimous and are arbitrary terms, and that the remaining notes succeed in the rotation we have mentioned; namely:

*C. D. E. F. G. A. B.*
*Do. Re. Mi. Fa. Sol. La. Si.*

The notes thus disposed form the Gamut or Scale.

There are 24 different Scales.

The notes are written upon five parallel lines and in the four spaces which are the result of those five lines, thus.

5th line.
4th space.
4th line.
3rd space.
3rd line.
2nd space.
2nd line.
1st space.
1st line.

These five lines form what is called a Stave.

The stave is always preceded by a Clef _ There are seven clefs; each clef serves to indicate the extent of one sort of Instrument or voice. The study of the *F.* Clef (called also ***the Bass Clef***) is sufficient for the Contre Basse pupil. The Clef is placed at the head of the stave, thus.

The three dots of this sign palpably indicate the line upon which a particular note is placed: that note is called ***F***.

The duration, longer or shorter, of the sound constitutes what is called the value of the note. As in a Book we have the ordinary marks of punctuation, the full stop, the comma, et cætera, to indicate certain stoppages, so in music we must have marks to denote a suspension of sound for a definite time, longer or shorter, and according to the different values of notes _ these are called rests.

The following table gives the form of each note according to its duration (value) with the corresponding rest and the name of each.

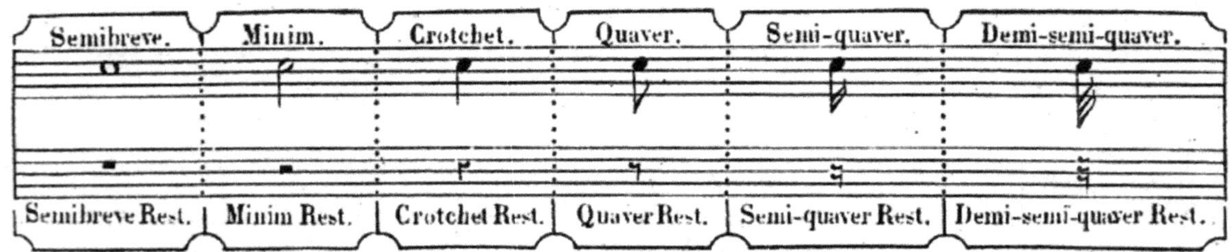


To form an exact idea of the relative values of notes the pupil should make himself acquainted with the following table.

## COMPARATIVE TABLE
### of the different values of notes.

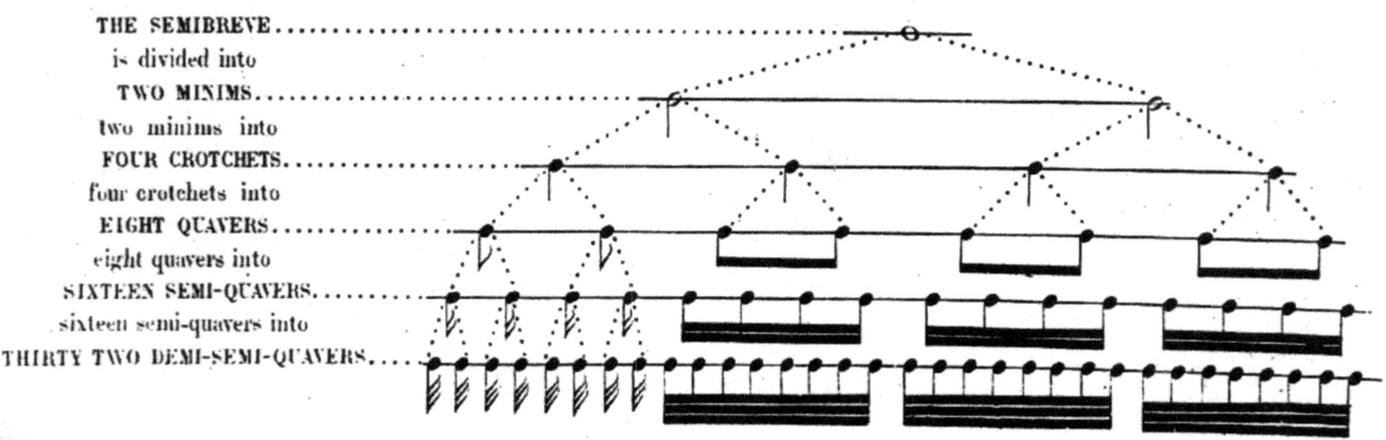

## OF THE BAR.

The result of the preceding table is that the semibreve must be considered as the longest note. Its single value constitutes a Bar. This Bar is divided into four parts, which is indicated by the sign (C) placed at the beginning of the stave and immediately after the clef

The Bar is *beaten*, that is to say, you mark the time either with the hand, the foot, a stick or other object. The Bar of four parts has two strong and two feeble beats which are alternate, thus

| *strong* | *feeble* | *strong* | *feeble* |
|---|---|---|---|
| — | ‿ | — | ‿ |
| 1 | 2 | 3 | 4 |

The strong beats are marked by striking, the *feeble* ones by raising the hand.

It would be useful to the pupil to beat the bar, following with the hand the direction of the arrows, thus.

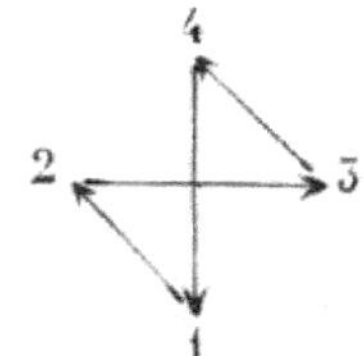


## SCALE IN C MAJOR.

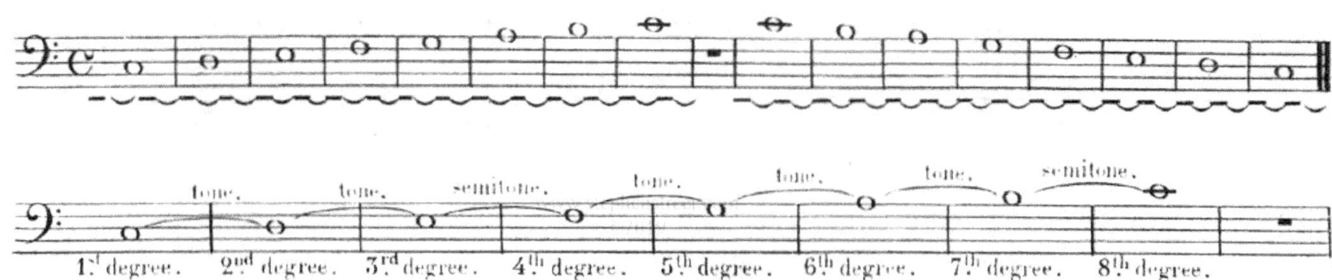


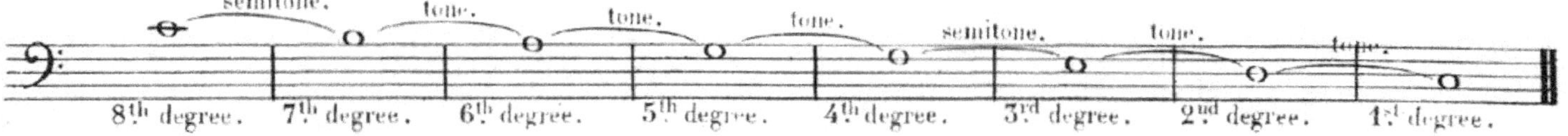


All the scales which have an interval of a semitone between the third and fourth, and the seventh and eighth degrees are in the major mode.

The distance which separates two notes constitutes what is called in harmony *an interval*.

In a scale the interval betwen two notes next to each other, as *C, D.* is called the interval of a second; *C, E* forms the interval of a third; *C, F* a fourth, and so on up to an octave.

There are numerous other intervals enabling alterations by means of *accidentals* which are introduced for the purpose of modulation but we will speak of those subsequently.

## EXERCISES UPON INTERVALS.

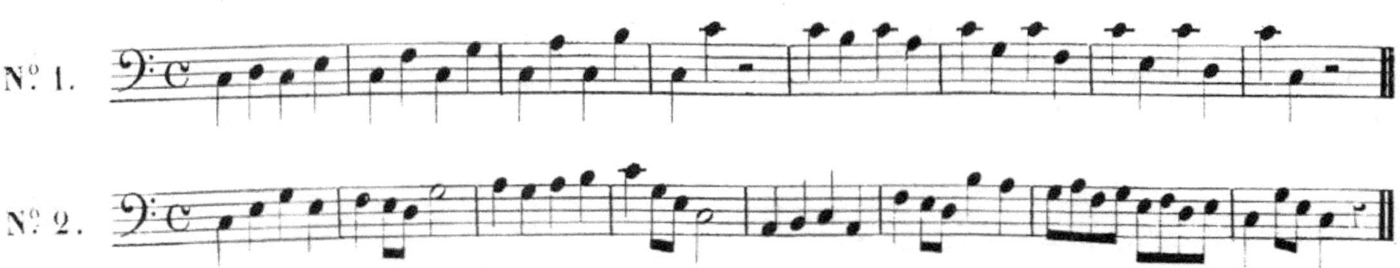

## DOTTED NOTES.

The dot placed after a note increases its value by one half. Thus, for example, a dotted minim (𝅗𝅥.) is equal to three crotchets (♩♩♩) or rather a minim and a crotchet (𝅗𝅥 ♩). In the same way it follows that a dotted crotchet (♩.) is equal to three quavers (♪♪♪) or more properly speaking a crotchet and a quaver (♩♪) The following example will better explain the effect of the dot.

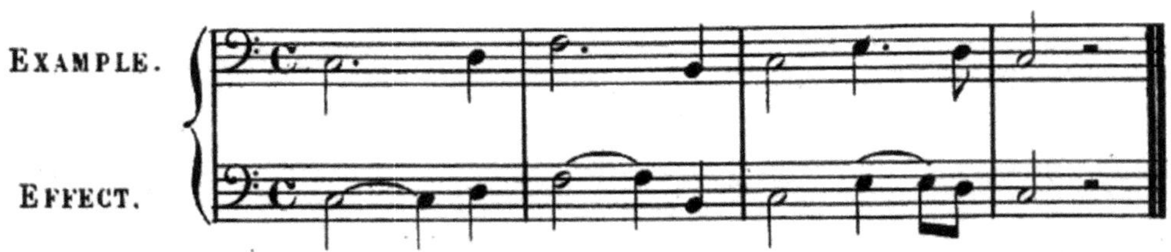


When we add two dots to a note the second one is equivalent to half the first one. Thus, for example, a minim followed by two dots (𝅗𝅥..) is equal to seven quavers, or rather, a minim, a crotchet, and a quaver (𝅗𝅥 ♩ ♪).

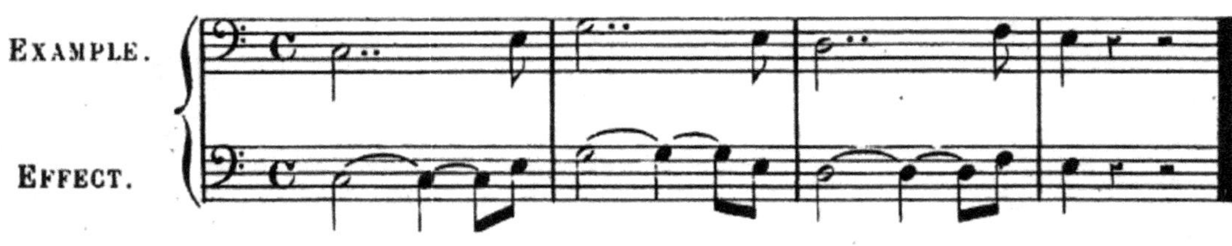


## OF THE MAJOR MODE.

As we have just seen all the scales which have the interval of a semitone between the 3rd and 4th and the 7th and 8th degrees, are of the major mode. Divided in half they proceed by tone and semitone in the same order.

EXAMPLE.

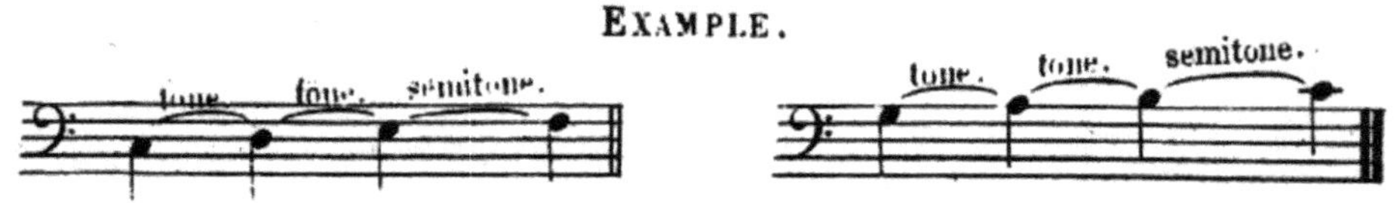


The major scales proceed by fifths ascending or descending.

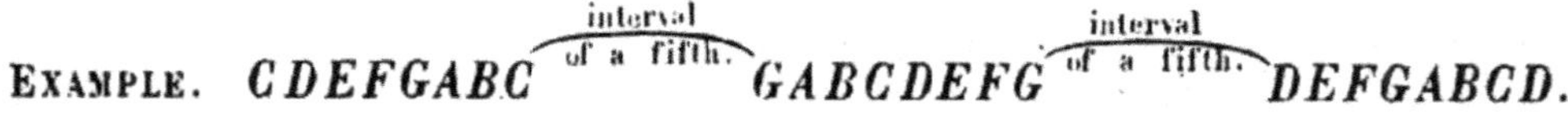


It therefore follows that the perfect fifth of any major scale whatever may be considered as the first degree also of the major scale *relative* to the preceding scale. In other words the relative scale has for its first moiety the second half of the preceding scale.

EXAMPLE.

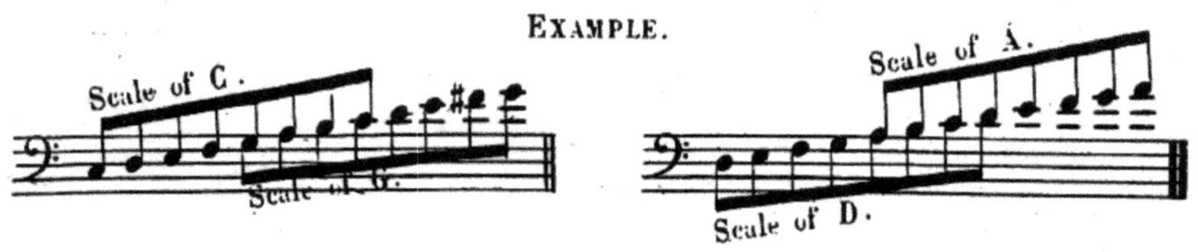

Thus the scale of *G* is relative to that of *C*, for the former commences with the second moiety of the latter. At the same time so that the scale of *G* may be composed of two moieties exactly equal with those of the scale of *C* it is necessary to raise the *F* a semi-tone. To raise a note a semi-tone we must place before it the sign ♯ called a sharp.

On the contrary when a note has to be lowered a semitone we must place before it the sign ♭ called a flat.

If we wish to restore the altered note to its natural tone we must place before it the sign ♮ called a natural.

If instead of raising a note a semitone we desire to raise it a whole tone we must place before it the sign x called a double sharp — In the same way when it has to be lowered a whole tone we use double flat 𝄫.

Finally to restore the note so raised a whole tone to its natural state, we must place before it the double sign ♮♯, or else this one ♮♭ when we would restore the note which has been lowered a whole tone by the double flat 𝄫.

## MAJOR SCALES.

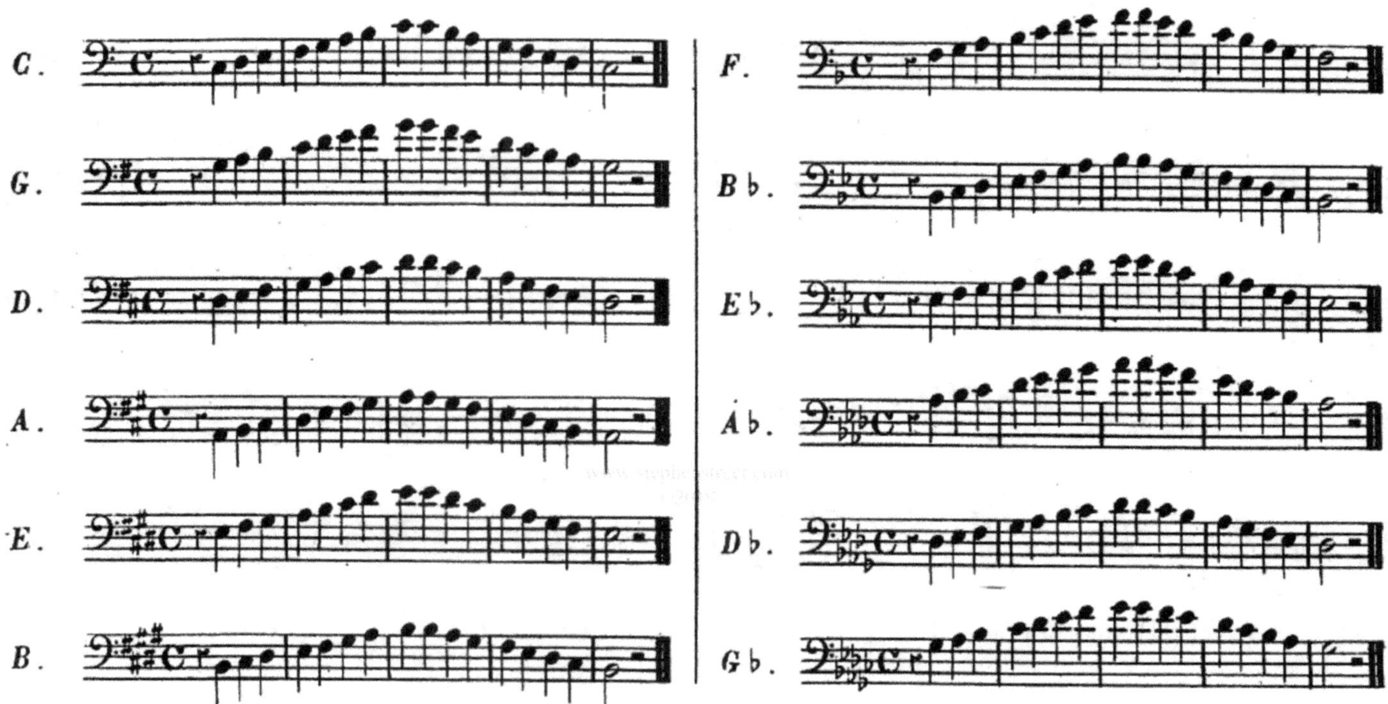


The scales of *G*♭ and of *F*♯ are the same, as also are those of *C*♯ and *D*♭.

## OF THE MINOR MODE.

The minor scale differs from the major by the 3$^{rd}$ and the 6$^{th}$ which are lowered half a tone.

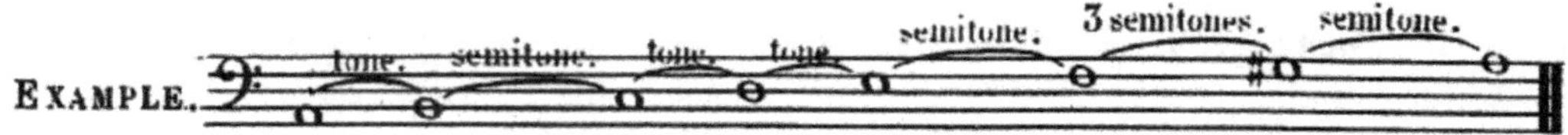


Such would be, really, the minor scale. But, seeing the difficulty which we encounter in getting over the interval of a tone and a half between the sixth and seventh degrees, we must adopt the following modification.

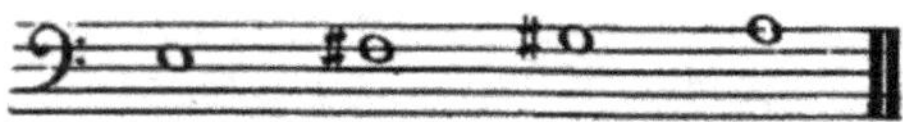

It will be seen that the alteration of the sixth by sharpening it facilitates the passing to the seventh. In descending, we must reverse the process and bring down the 7$^{th}$ degree to the 6$^{th}$.

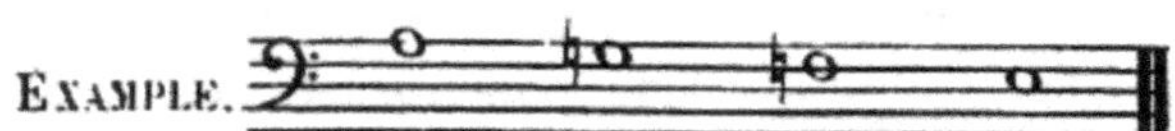

COMPLETE MINOR SCALE.

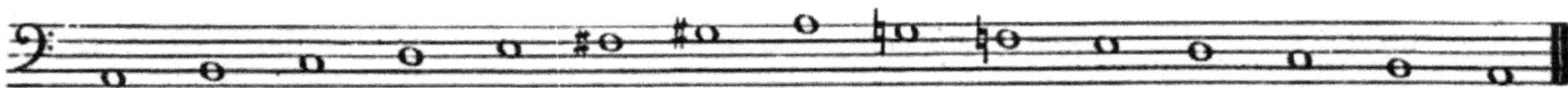

The sharp placed before the *G* in the ascending scale must not be put at the clef, seeing that it is very often suppressed and that in consequence it must be considered as an accidental.

We proceed now to the minor scales.

MINOR SCALES.

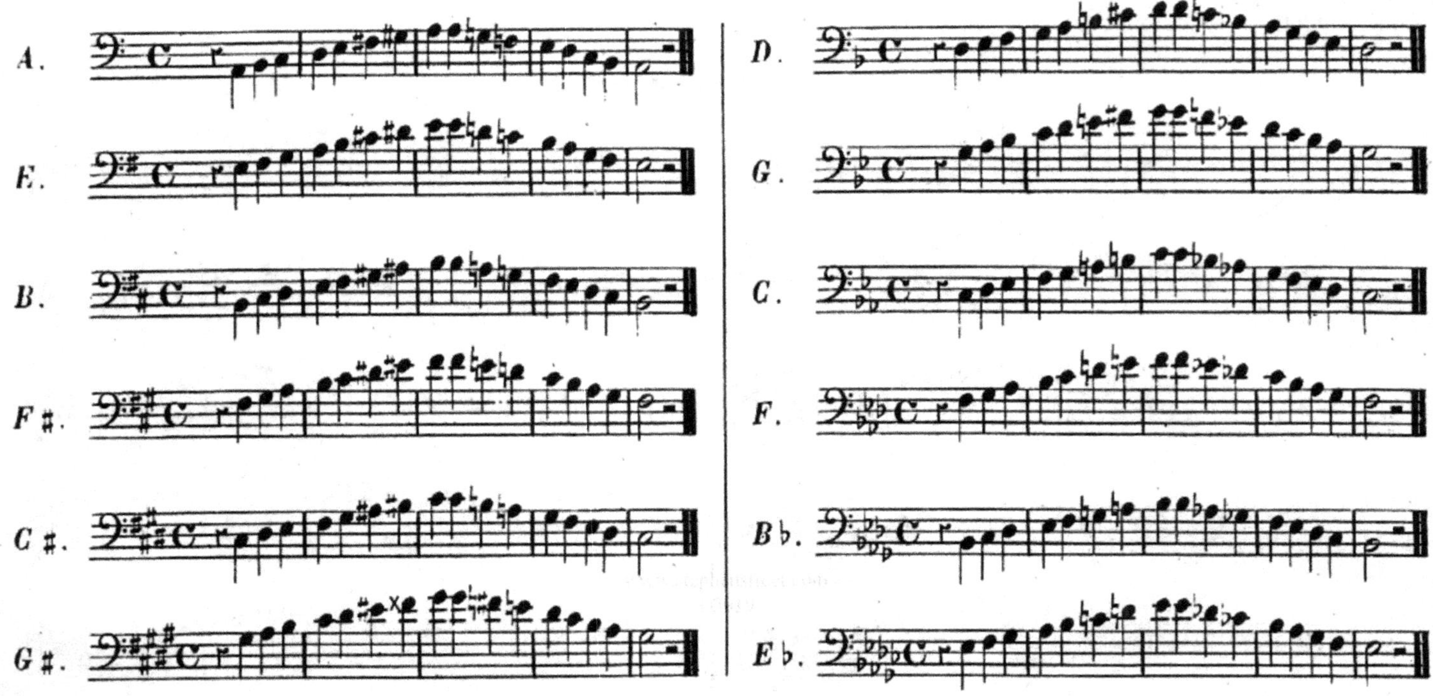


The scales of *E*♭ and *D*♯ are alike, as also are those of *A*♭ and *G*♯.

# OF MOVEMENT.

We understand by "movement" that gradual variety of slowness or rapidity which is comprised between the two extremes, and which is appropriate to the due execution of a piece, so as to give it the true character or sentiment intended by the composer. These movements are numerous. We will only mention the principal ones:

| | | | |
|---|---|---|---|
| **Largo.** | _ very slow. | **Moderato.** | _ moderately quick. |
| **Larghetto.** | _ not quite so slow. | **Allegretto.** | _ a little faster. |
| **Adagio.** | _ slow and expressive. | **Allegro.** | _ gay and rather fast. |
| **Andantino.** | _ not too slow. | **Vivace.** | _ lively. |
| **Andante.** | _ not quite so slow as Andantino. | **Presto.** | _ quick. |
| | | **Prestissimo.** | _ very quick. |

When an entire passage is to be gradually retarded or accelerated, the word *ral_len_tan_do* or *ac_ce_le_ran_do* is written above. This embraces the whole phrase and finishes at the note where its action is intended to cease. When the rallentando or accelerando is of short duration we use *rall: acc:* _ When it is required to gradually increase or diminish the force of a passage we adopt in the same manner the words *crescendo* _ *diminuendo* _ or else the marks *cres.* *dim.*

# OF TIME.

There are two sorts of time: Common and Triple. The first is divisible in twos as we have already seen. the other is divisible in threes. Examples:

## COMMON TIME.

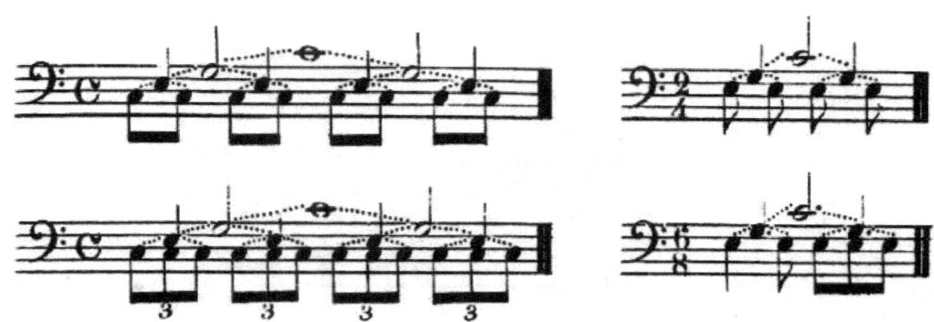

## 4 CROTCHET TIME.

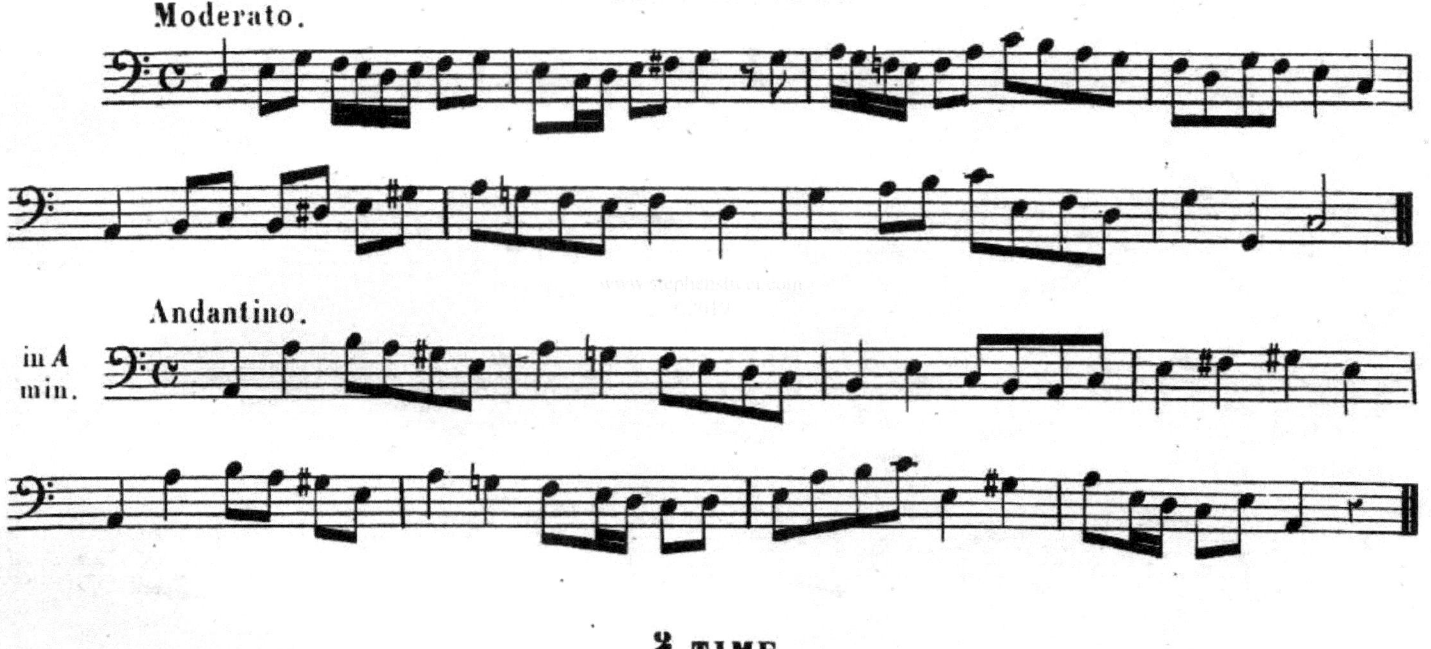


## $\frac{2}{4}$ TIME.

The mark $\frac{2}{4}$ is written at the commencement of the piece after the clef. It is beaten thus.

2

1

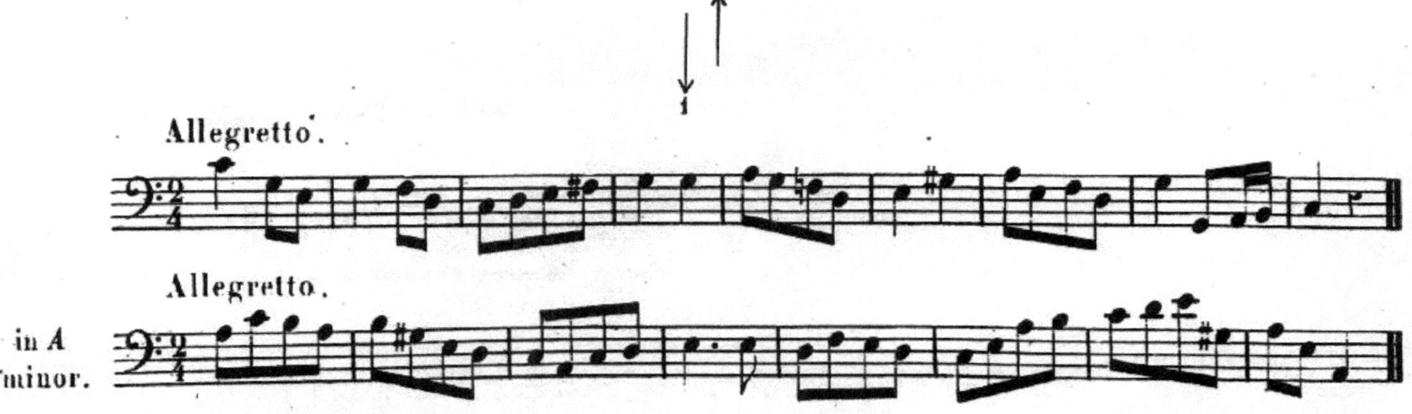

## $\frac{12}{8}$ TIME.

EQUAL TO TWELVE QUAVERS.

The sign ⁀ placed over two or more notes, signifies that those notes must be continued in the same stroke of the Bow; the notes are said to be "bound" when they are the same sound — "slurred" when they are different.

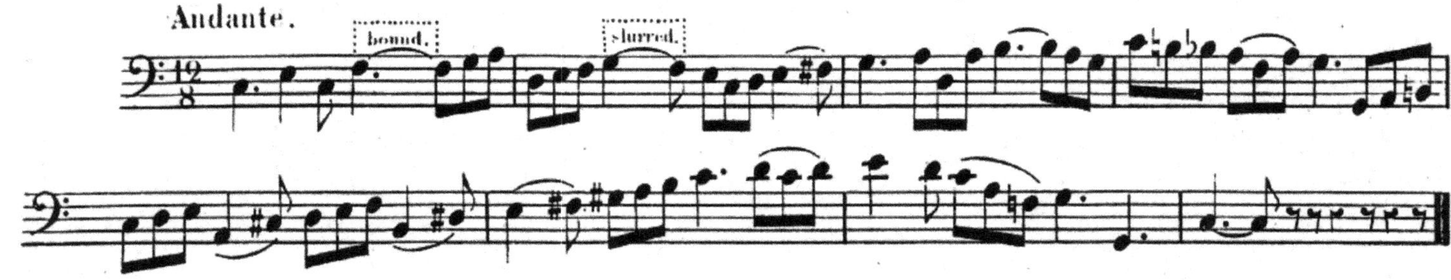


## $\frac{6}{8}$ TIME.

EQUAL TO SIX QUAVERS.

Allegretto.

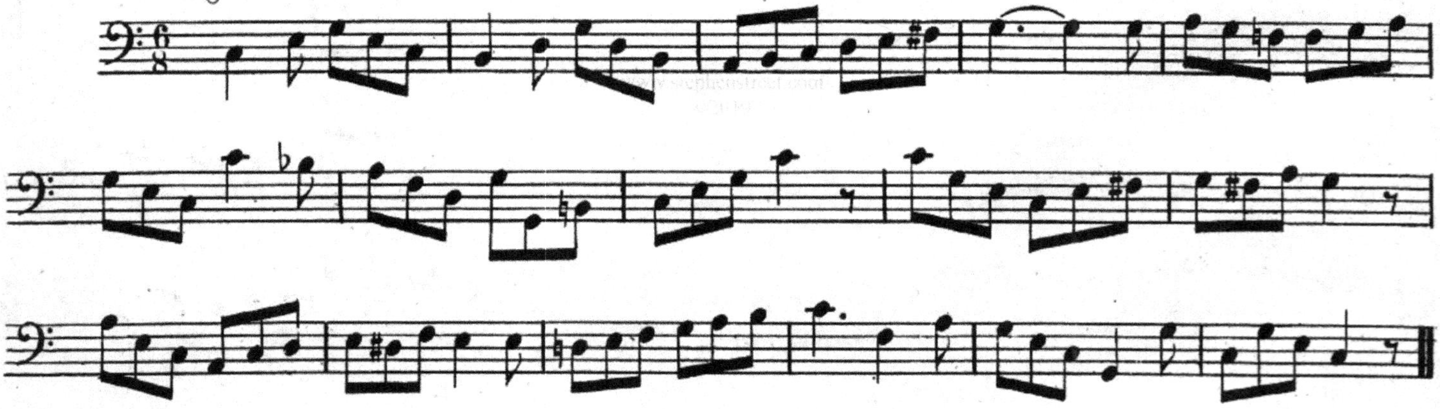

## $\frac{3}{4}$ TIME.

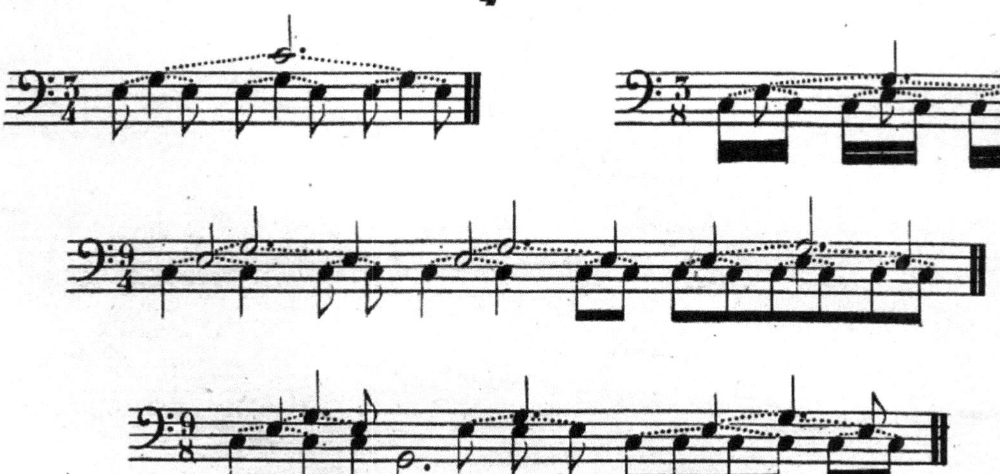

Le temps à $\frac{3}{4}$ se bat comme ci-après:

$\frac{3}{4}$ time is beaten in this manner:

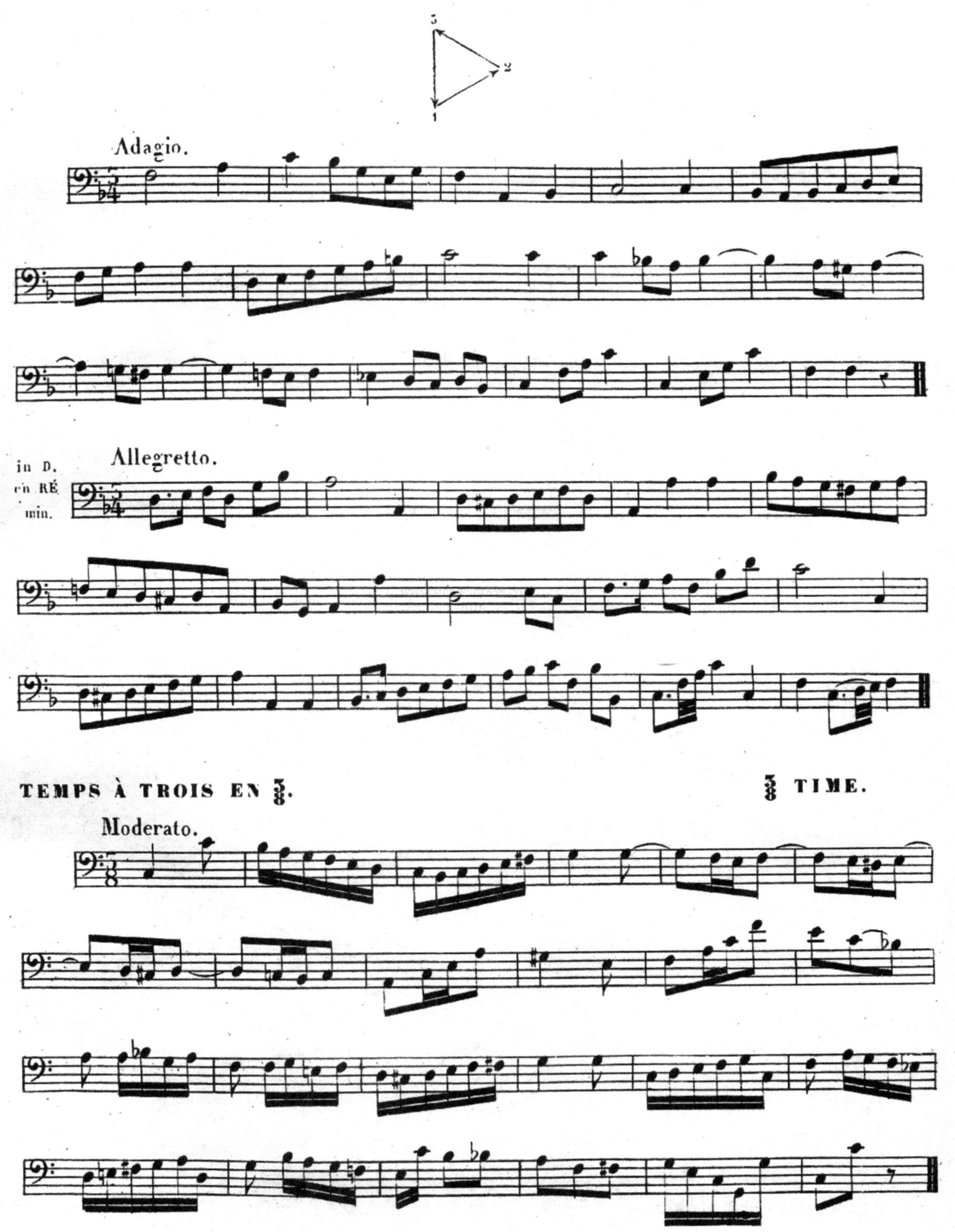

## 9/8 TIME.

Adagio.

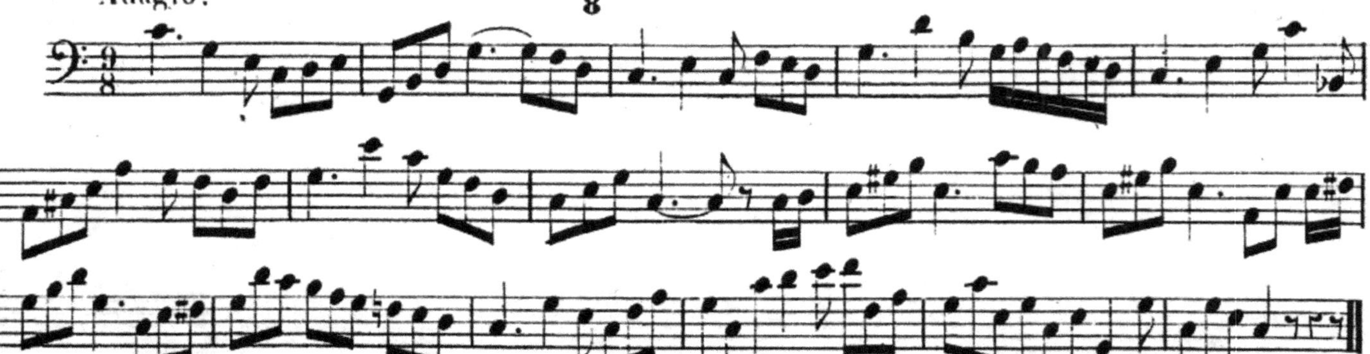

Moderato.

in A min.

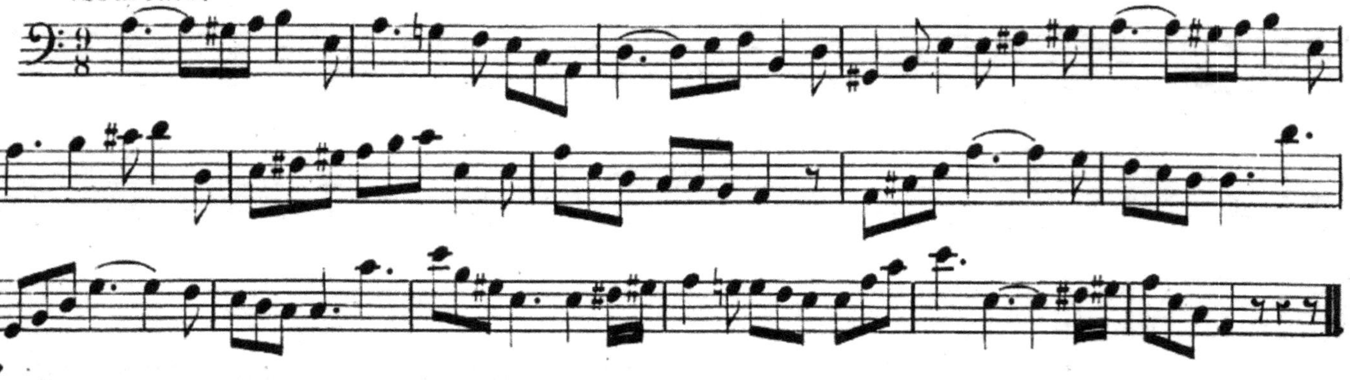

## OF TRIPLETS AND SIXES.

It sometimes happens that we meet with bars of common time containing small groups of notes divided into threes or sixes, and which might lead us to suppose that the time indicated at the Clef is altered. These small groups are only *accidental*: (that is, occasional alterations). They consist of three or six notes, and are called ***Triplets*** or ***Sixes***. The triplets are marked by a 3 over the notes, and the others by a 6. These figures indicate that the presence of these groups do not alter in any manner the fundamental measure of the piece. Example:

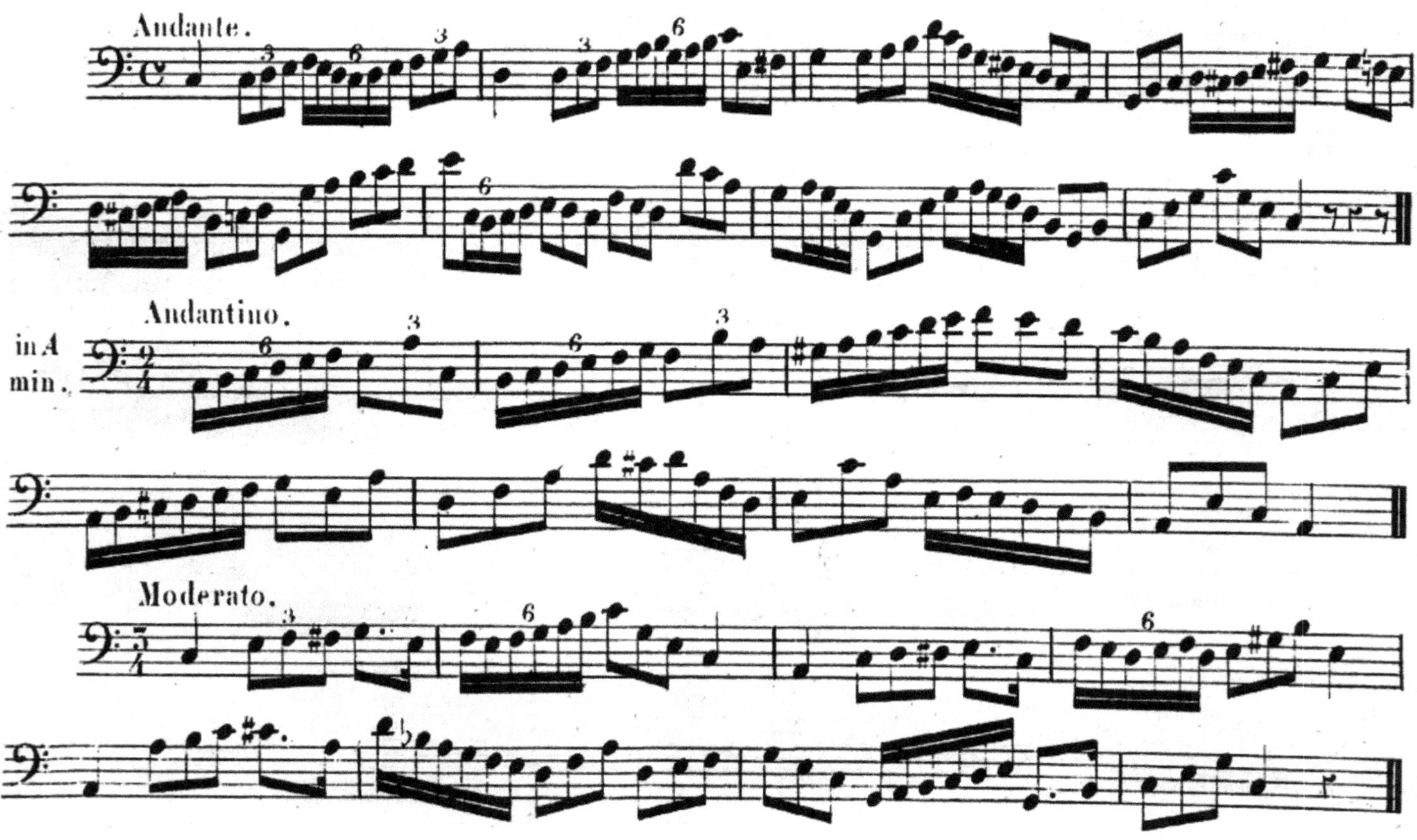

## SYNCOPATION.

Syncopation is the prolongation into an accented note of a sound commenced upon an unaccented note. Example.

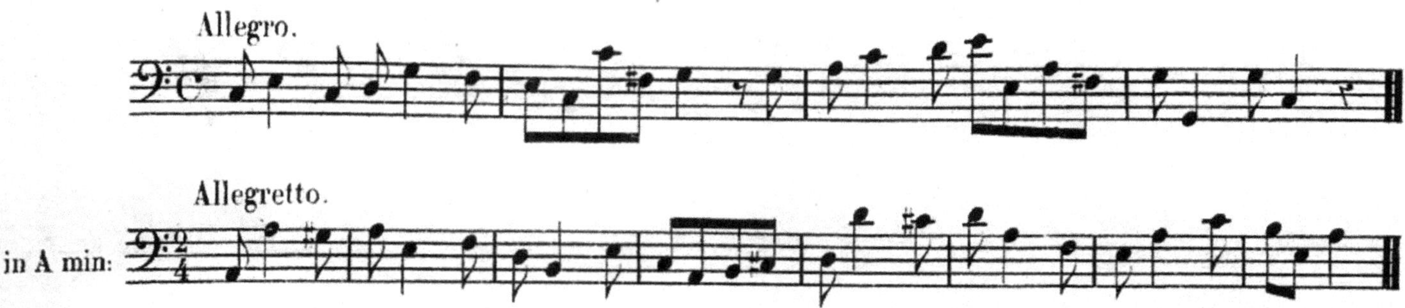


When the last note of one bar and the first note of the next are syncopated the sign ⌒ called a *bind* or *tie* is marked over them. This indicates that the two notes are to be played with the same Bow.

Adagio.

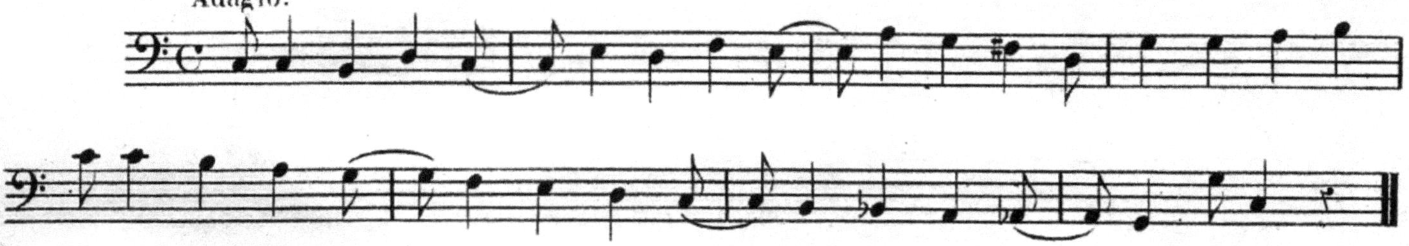

Moderato.

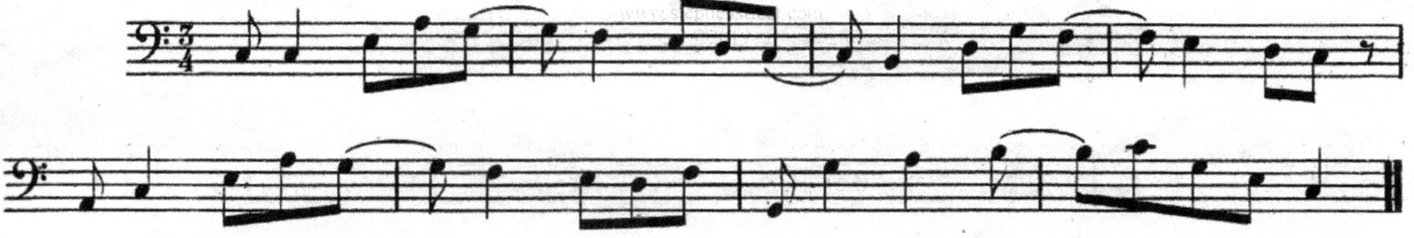

## EXERCISES ON DOTTED NOTES.

Andantino.

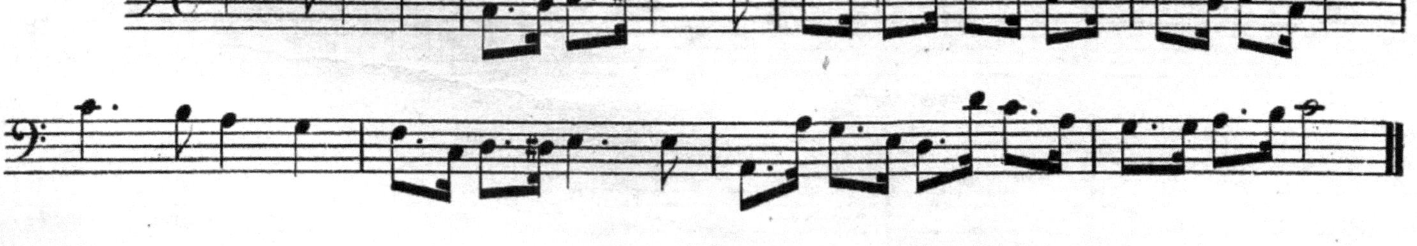

Moderato.

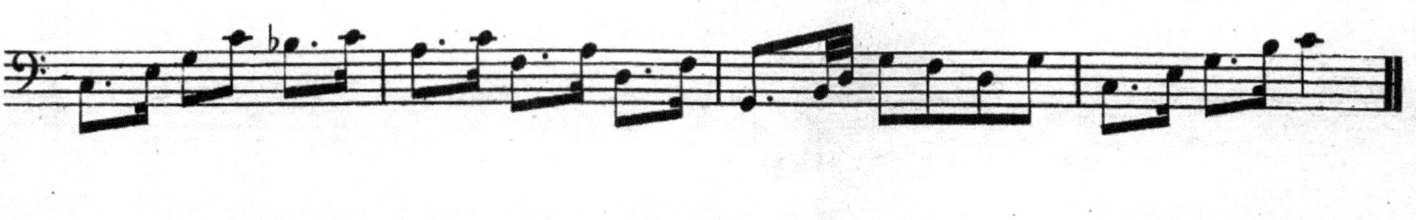

## RÉSUMÉ.

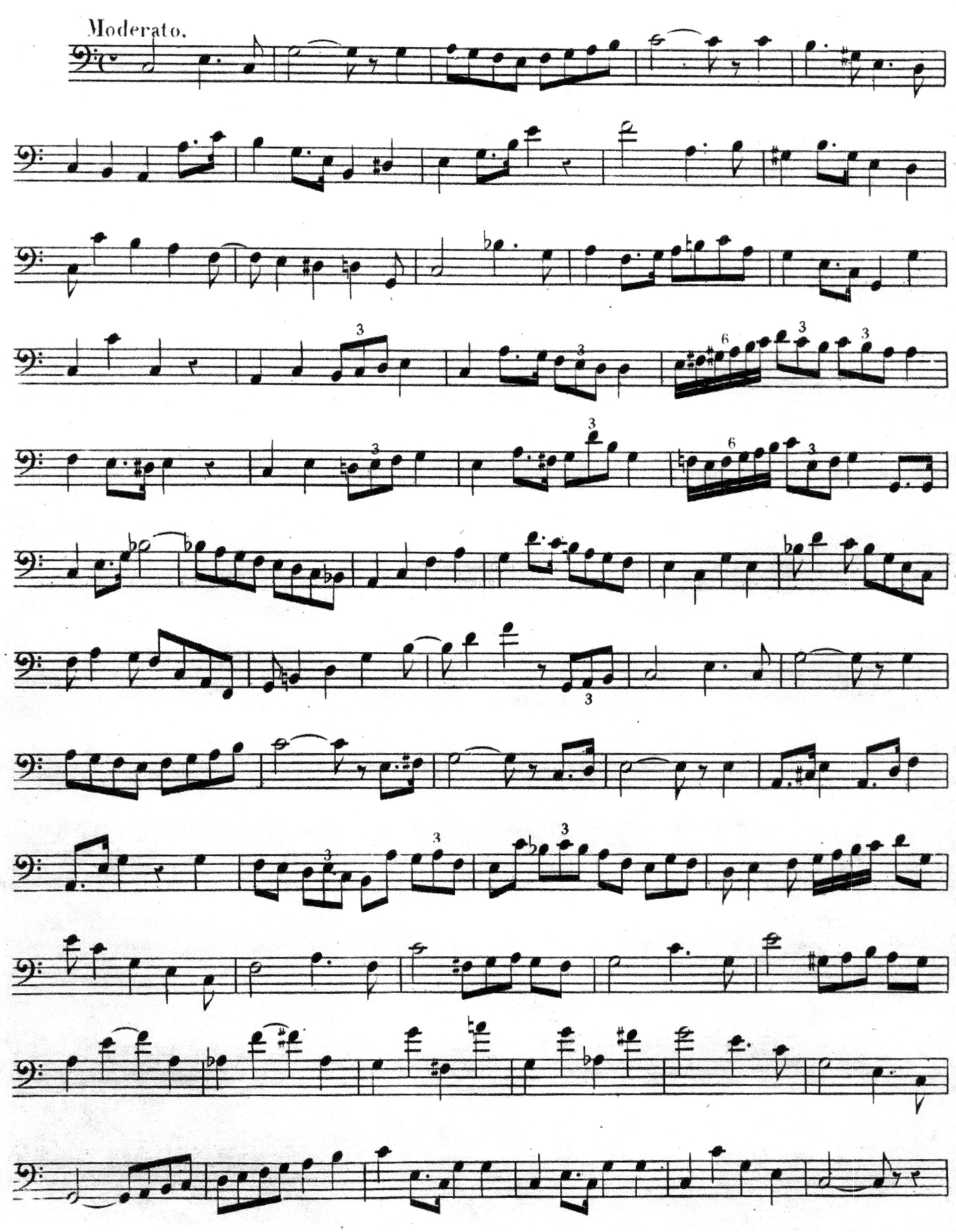

## OF THE MEANING OF CERTAIN TERMS USED IN HARMONY.

Although it is not absolutely necessary that a Contre Bassist should understand harmony, I believe it will be very useful to the pupil that he should have some slight knowledge of that art, or at all events that he should understand the meaning of certain words which one ought certainly to be acquainted with, in studying music.

Harmony is an art which teaches the knowledge of chords and the different ways of combining them so as to render them agreeable to the ear; such chords taken separately, being simply in music what words are in a discourse.

A succession of harmonies always in the same key would very soon become monotonous. Thus, *modulation*, the art of passing properly from one key to another, considerably enriches the harmony of numerous combinations, of which each one produces a different effect.

## OF THE ALTERATION OF THE INTERVALS.

For simplifynig the rules figures are substituted in harmony for the names of the notes. Thus the fundamental note of any key whatever is called the *Tonic*, and the other notes of the scale are called the second, third, fourth, fifth, sixth, seventh, octave As we have already seen, in speaking of intervals they may be altered, that is to say, augmented or diminished. It is precisely these alterations which we have now to discuss: The alteration of an interval is always effected by the accidental presence of a sharp ♯ or a flat ♭ which augments or diminishes it.

The interval of the 2nd may be *minor, major* or *augmented*. — minor. major. augmented.

3rd *minor, major* or *augmented*. — minor. major. augmented.

4th *diminished, perfect* or *augmented*. — diminished. perfect. augmented.

5th *diminished, perfect* or *augmented*. — diminished. perfect. augmented.

6th *minor, major* or *augmented*. — minor. major. augmented.

7th *minor, major* or *augmented*. — minor. major. augmented.

8th *diminished, perfect* or *augmented*. — diminished. perfect. augmented.

9th *minor, major* or *augmented*. — minor. major. augmented.

## OF CONCORDS AND DISCORDS.

Intervals are either *consonant* or *dissonant*. In other words *concords* or *discords*. The *concords* are of two sorts: *perfect* or *imperfect*. The *perfect concords* are: the *perfect fourth*, the *perfect fifth* and the *octave*. They are called *perfect concords* because they cannot be altered without ceasing to be consonant. The *imperfect concords* are: the *major third*, the *minor third*, the *major sixth* and the *minor sixth*. They are called imperfect because they can be used both in major and minor without thereby ceasing to be consonant.

The other intervals are discords.

Intervals are reckoned from below upwards. In saying C. G. we have the interval of a *fifth*. If on the contrary we say G. C., reversing the order we have the interval of a fourth. Example:

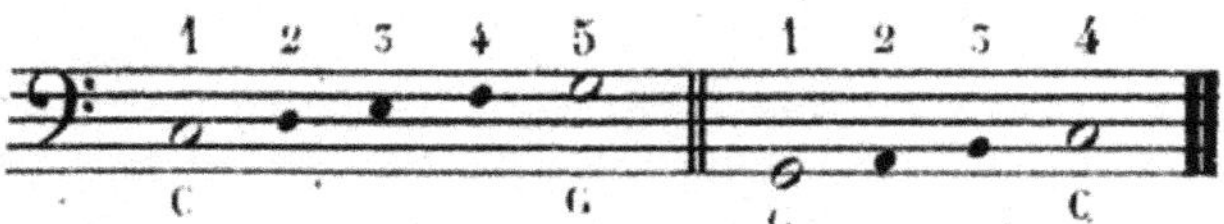


A lower note carried to the octave above, or an upper note taken an octave lower, forms what is called an *inversion*; in the preceding example G. C. is the inversion of C. G., and the interval of a *second* inverted becomes the interval of a *seventh*.

The key note of any scale is called the *tonic*: the perfect fourth is called the *subdominant*; the perfect fifth is called the *dominant*. These three degrees give their names to the three *fundamental chords*, which comprise the scale.

## OF MOTION.

Motion means the direction taken by two or more notes proceeding from one interval to another. There are three kinds of motion viz. similar, contrary and oblique. Similar motion is that in which the parts, whatever the intervals may be, follow the same direction, in ascending as well as descending. Example.

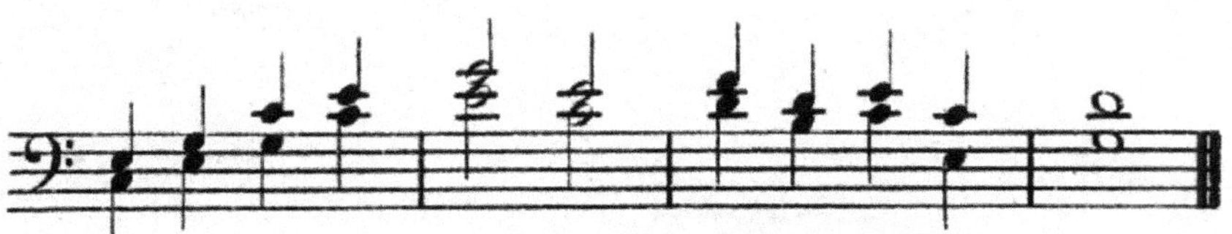

Contrary motion is one part ascending while the other descends. Example.

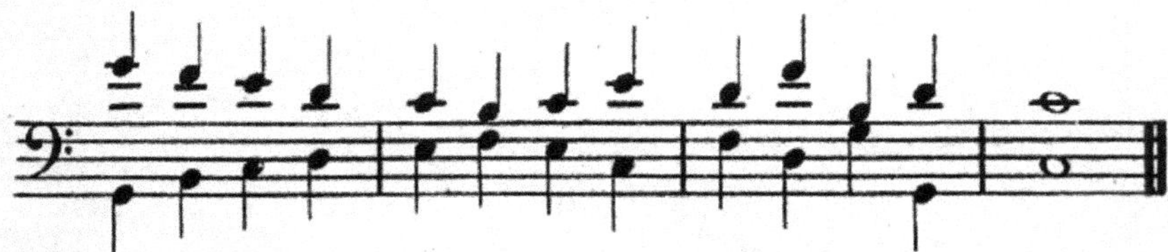

Oblique motion is, one part remaining stationary while the other ascends or descends. Example.

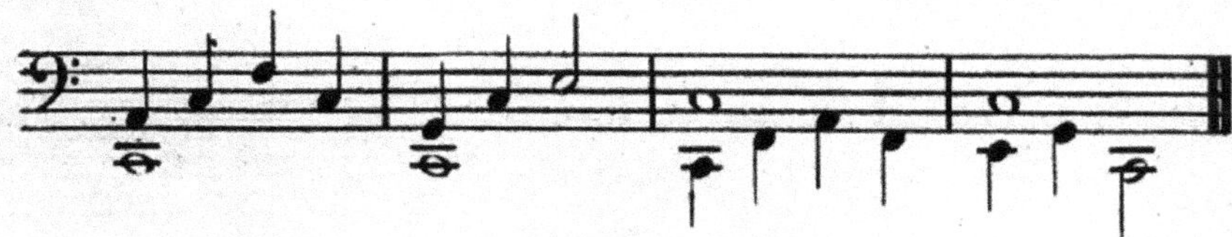

## OF THE FIRST FUNDAMENTAL CHORD.

*(CALLED THE COMMON CHORD)*

The first fundamental chord consists of a Bass note to which are added its third, fifth, and frequently the octave. That is a full *common chord*. By extending its parts by means of octaves, higher or lower, we obtain for this chord a great number of positions. Examples.

1st position. 2nd position. 3rd position. With the fifth suppressed. With the third doubled. With the fifth doubled.

With the parts extended.

These positions are limited by the stretch of the hand upon the key-board of the Piano forte; but in the orchestra this chord is capable of more extended positions. When the upper parts of a chord change places with each other upon the same bass, the intervals remain the same; the result is a simple change of position which must not be confounded with *inversion*. That is obtained by taking as the bass note the intervals which compose the original chord. Example:

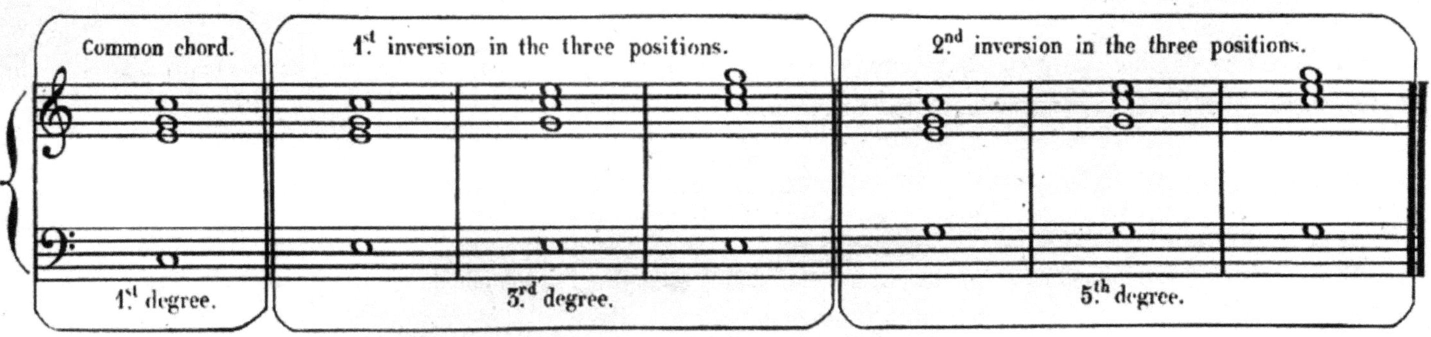


The *first inversion*, having the 3rd degree for a Bass, with its third and sixth, is called the chord of the sixth, and is marked with a 6.

The *second inversion*, which has the 5th degree for a Bass, accompanied by its fourth and sixth, is called the chord of the fourth and sixth, and is marked $\genfrac{}{}{0pt}{}{6}{4}$.

The chord of the tonic is the only one that can be said to be perfect; all the degrees of the scale bear a chord of the third and fifth, but the idea of perfection results only from this chord made upon the first degree.

## OF THE SECOND FUNDAMENTAL CHORD

COMPOSED OF FOUR SOUNDS.

The second fundamental chord composed of four sounds has for its bass the *dominant* of the key, that is to say, the fifth, and is composed of its *major third, perfect fifth* and *minor seventh.* This chord, called also the *dominant seventh* not only occupies with the common chord the first place of its kind but it is also the first key for modulation.

The chord of the dominant seventh admits of three inversions.

We here give the degrees upon which they are placed, as well as the intervals of which they are composed.

| Chord of the dominant seventh of C in its direct state. | Its first inversion chord of the fifth and sixth marked $\begin{smallmatrix}6\\5\end{smallmatrix}$ | Its second inversion chord of the third and fourth marked $\begin{smallmatrix}4\\3\end{smallmatrix}$ | Its third inversion chord of the second and fourth marked $\begin{smallmatrix}4\\2\end{smallmatrix}$ |
|---|---|---|---|
| 7 | $\begin{smallmatrix}6\\5\end{smallmatrix}$ | $\begin{smallmatrix}4\\3\end{smallmatrix}$ | $\begin{smallmatrix}4\\2\end{smallmatrix}$ |
| 5th degree for a bass with its major third, perfect fifth and minor seventh. | 7th degree *(called also the leading note*)* for a bass with its minor third, diminished fifth and minor sixth. | 2nd degree for a bass with its minor third, perfect fourth and major sixth. | 4th degree for a bass with its major second, augmented fourth and major sixth. |

(*) The major seventh of the scale is called *"The leading note"* because it leads so evidently to the tonic or key note.

The chord of the seventh being slightly dissonant provokes a resolution; that is to say, it seems to ask for a consonant chord which gives the idea of repose. The natural resolution of each of the parts composing this chord, whether in its direct state or in its inversions, is always the same.

G (dominant) whether in the lower, or middle or upper part of the chord, is always consonant. The resolution takes place upon one of the notes of the tonic. Example.

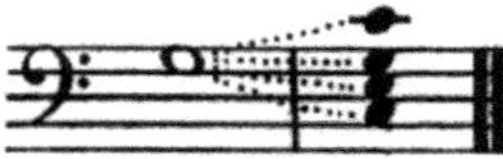

B, the third of the chord (leading note of the scale) when it is placed for a bass, must never be added to the upper parts; it resolves itself to the tonic. Example.

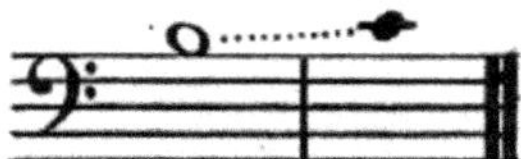

D, the fifth of the chord (second degree of the scale) ascends or descends by conjoint degrees. Example.

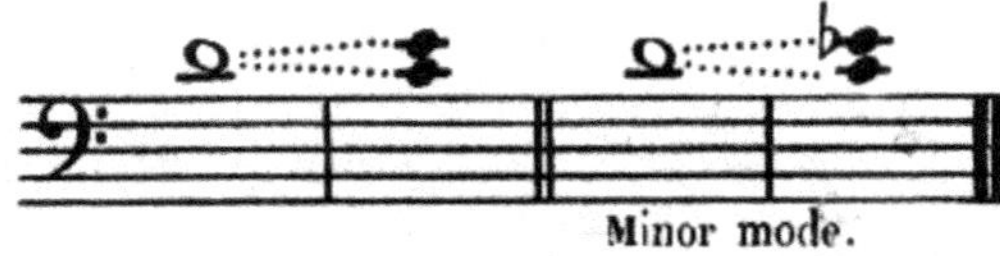


F, the seventh, dissonant (fourth degree of the scale) remains always dissonant in the three inversions. It must always descend a semitone in major keys, and a whole tone in minor keys. Example.

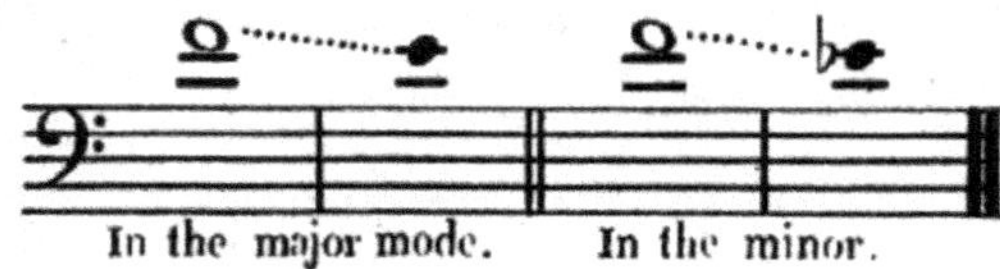

In the chord of the seventh, taken in its direct position it is not absolutely necessary to sound all the notes of which it is composed: the fifth may be omitted and the bass note doubled. Example.

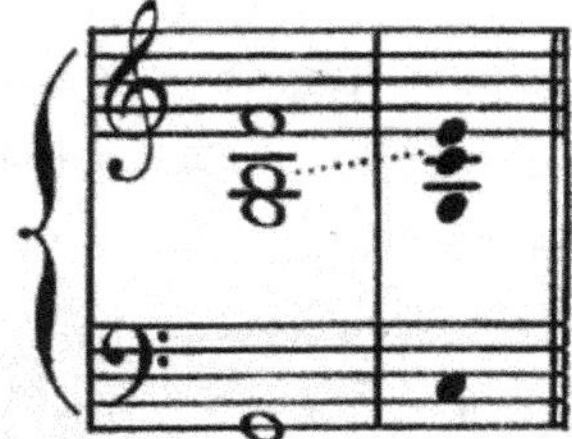

After placing the four parts which constitute the chord if we would increase its power we must in preference double the fundamental note.

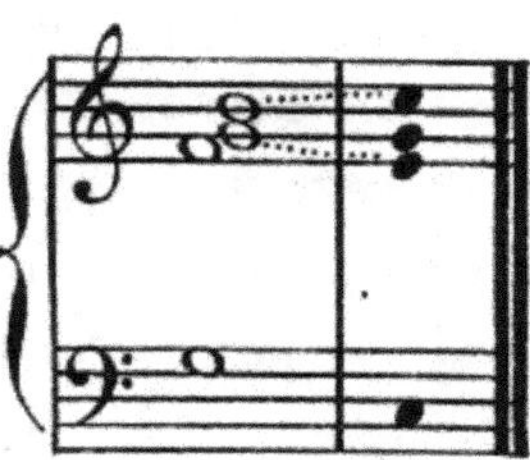

There would still be much to say, if we intended to enter fully into the elements of harmony; but, as a treatise comprising the fundamental rules of that art, however compressed it might be, would carry us beyond the proper limits of this method for the Contre Basse, we will stop at this point. We will finish then this short dissertation by explaining succinctly what is understood by the terms *diatonic, chromatic* and *enharmonic*.

## EXPLANATION OF THE WORDS DIATONIC CHROMATIC AND ENHARMONIC.

A major or minor scale is called *diatonic* when its degrees succeed each other by tones and semitones. A piece belongs to the diatonic style whenever it proceeds almost entirely upon the notes of the diatonic scale.

The notes accidentally altered, which do not arise from the key, are called *chromatic*. A progression by semitones constitutes the *chromatic scale*. When a piece abounds in accidentals, it belongs to the *chromatic style*.

The word *enharmonic* signifies the repetition or prolongation of the same sound under the form of two different notes. Example.

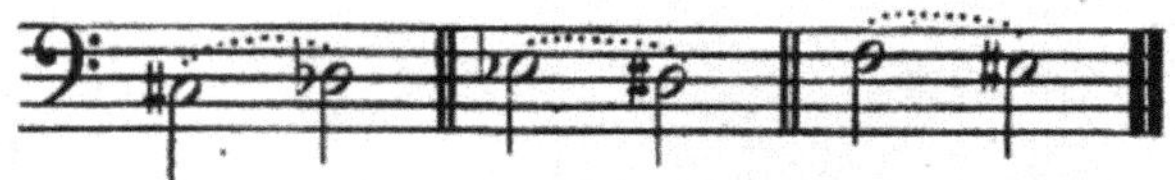

The following keys are enharmonic. The black points indicate the relative minors to the major keys.

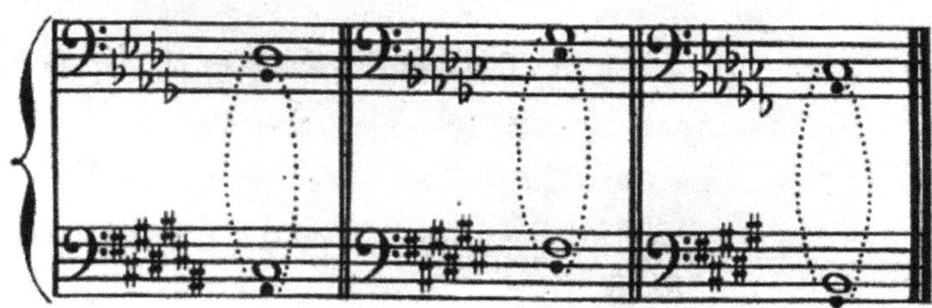

These keys only differ from each other by the manner of writing them.

D ♭ and C ♯ are the same note on the Piano forte key board; they are therefore enharmonic.

# CHARACTER OF THE CONTRE BASSE

Before undertaking the practical part of this instrument, it will be proper to say a few words upon its nature, in order to gain a precise idea of it. The Contre Basse cannot aspire to the advantages of other solo instruments; it has against it the irregularity of its mechanism, and the depth of its tones; but it is the base and, as it were, the pedestal of the orchestra. It is the last of the family of stringed instruments; it is required to extend the low notes of the Bass Viol which by its medium position continues those of the Violin. The sole end and purpose of the contre basse ought then to be the giving of the fundamental notes in the orchestra. Let us make no mistake on this subject; you do not learn to play the Contre Basse for the purpose of executing brilliant "morceaux" with purety of tone, elegance of coloring and lightness of bow. If uncommon talent, seconded by rare gifts and long studies can attain exceptional results, such attainments are not generally acquired. Hence, in this method, we have abstained from writing exercises too difficult, which only make a display of science at the expense of the pupil. There are however a few of those more difficult studies for violin and violoncello which can be performed also upon the Contre basse, but the result obtained compensates neither the labour of the player nor the attention of the listener. The simple scale of C well executed, is sufficient to prove that the pupil has followed good principles. This Method, it is believed, whilst preserving for the instrument its true character, smoothens the difficulties of execution; and if we encounter here and there a few of the more difficult passages (and which it has been impossible to avoid) they must be laid to the charge of certain keys not very favorable to the instrument. It being however absolutely necessary that the pupil should learn to play all the scales thoroughly well, he will in the end, with patience and labour, overcome all difficulties.

## MANNER OF HOLDING THE CONTRE BASSE.

The pupil must hold himself erect, slightly leaning to the right. He must hold the instrument not quite vertically, but insensibly inclined towards himself. Supposing him to have the proper height for playing the contre basse, he must so arrange that the upper rib of the instrument leans against his left side, and that the angle of the lower rib touches the ball of the knee. In this way the instrument stands upright without the assistance of the arm. (see plate, figure 1)

## MANNER OF HOLDING THE BOW.

The Bow generally used for the Contra Basse of the orchestra should be about 21½ inches in length, and its weight should be proportionate with the thickness of the strings. The hair may be white or black. I prefer the black, as being more solid. The bow of the soloist may be 27½ inches in length, but no fixed rule can be established; every soloist has his own. It is not very easy to express exactly the manner of holding the bow; I shall therefore confine myself to the following directions: the hand not too near the nut, nor too far from it; the middle finger, the third finger and the little finger firmly placed against the nut in such a way that the middle finger adapts itself to the place where the hair commences; the forefinger must hook upon the stick and press it strongly; the thumb on the other side of the nut and always opposite the middle finger, pressing from the right side and a little obliquely the edge of the groove in the nut (see plate, fig: 4) The fingers thus placed ought to hold the bow so as to use it with power, whilst allowing the fore arm and the wrist great flexibility and full liberty of action. In conclusion let us add that the nearer the bow is to the bridge the stronger are the sounds: the farther from the bridge, the softer the sounds.

## COMPASS AND TUNING OF THE CONTRE BASSE.

The A in the first space which is the lowest note of the instrument, corresponds in sound to the A of an octave lower and it is the same with the other notes. The position of an octave higher than the real sound has been generally adopted so as to avoid too great a number of ledger lines below the stave. This is the system followed in this first part. In the second part the note will be found in its own place. We shall see the advantages of this notation.

The Contre Basse is tuned by fourths as follows.

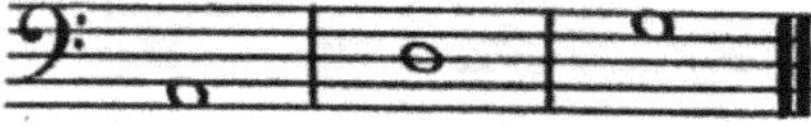

Tuning by fifths, as is done in some countries, is absurd. It causes a harshness of tone and a continual changing of position, which renders the execution difficult, uncertain and disconnected. The compass of the Contre Bass considered as an orchestral instrument, as we treat of it in the first part of this method, is as follows.

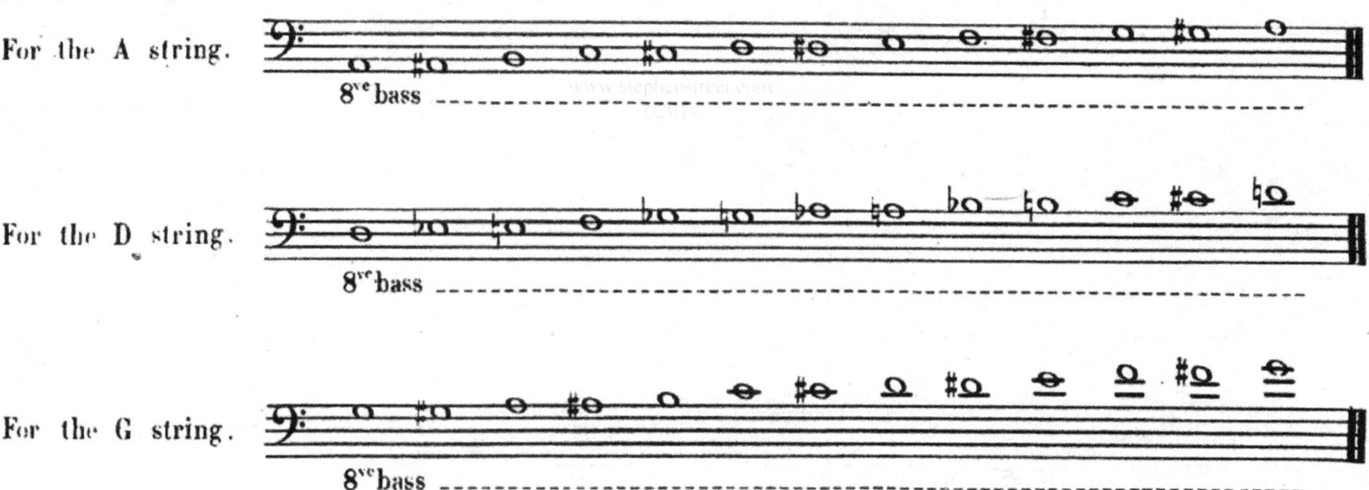

## EXERCISES FOR THE MANAGEMENT OF THE BOW UPON THE OPEN STRINGS.

The first difficulty in the management of the Bow, caused by the stiffness of the hand, is the width of the strings. It frequently troubles the pupil, especially when the wrist is near the finger board. This must be avoided; for this purpose it is best to play the note lightly at first, gradually increasing the sound both in drawing and pushing the bow.

After each note the pupil should stop, so that the teacher may rectify the position of the arm, hand and fingers.

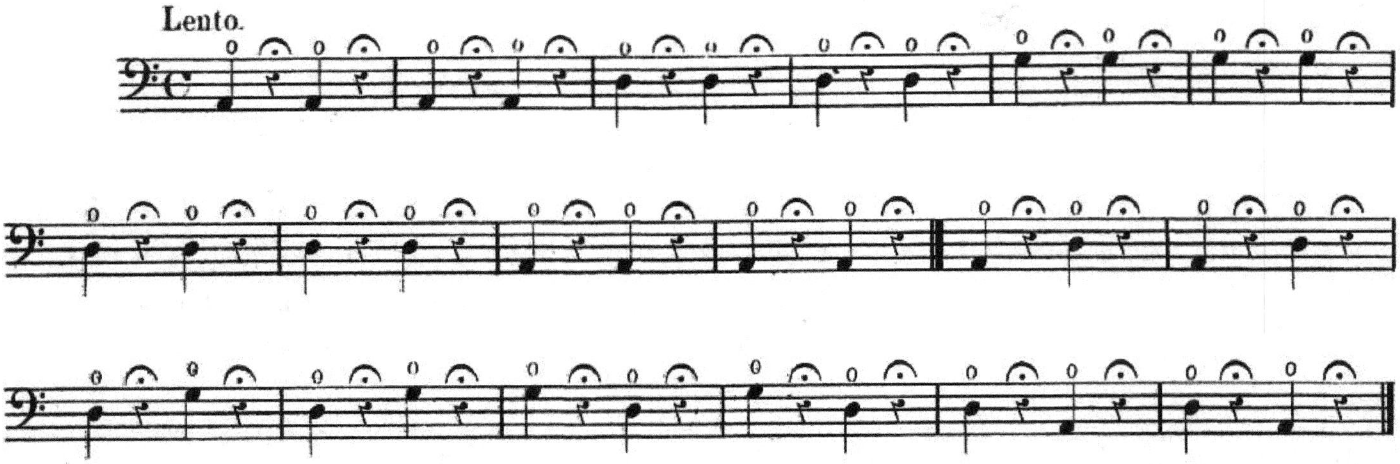

Lento.

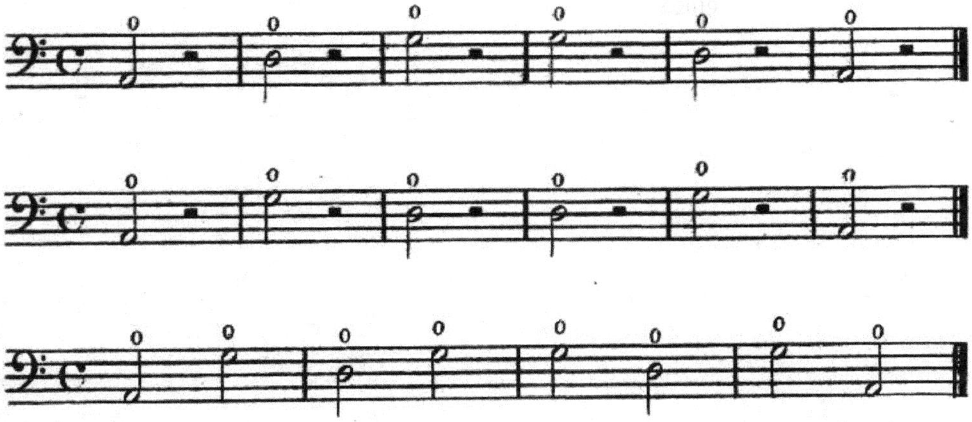

## FIRST EXERCISES FOR THE LEFT HAND.

The fingers must not be too near the string to be played on, nor too far from it. There should be sufficient space to allow of vibration and produce the note with facility and precision. (see plate fig. 7)

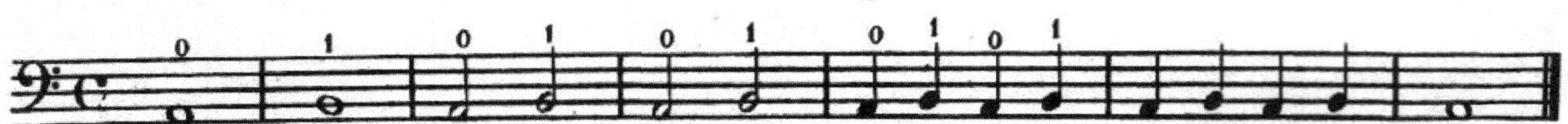

## THE SAME EXERCISE UPON THE TWO OTHER STRINGS.

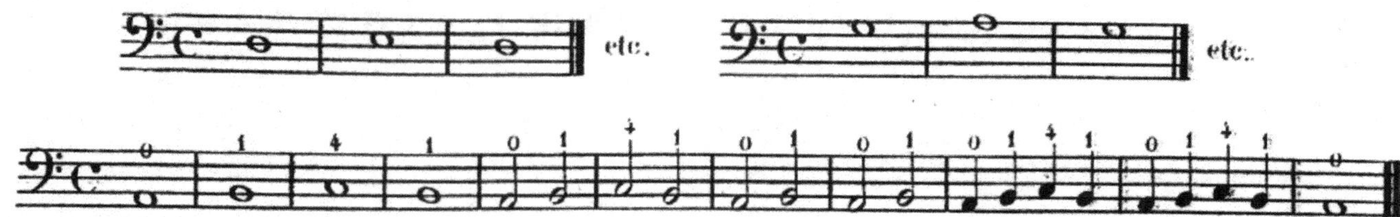


## ANOTHER EXERCISE.

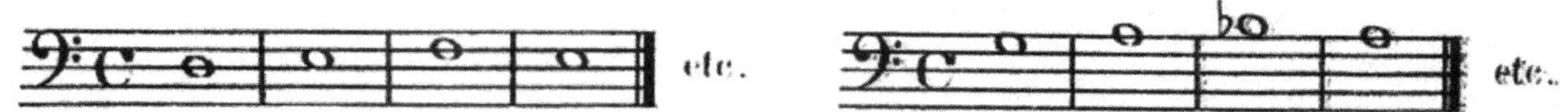


Whenever the pupil sees the sign ⊔ over a note he must play it by *drawing* the bow, when he sees the sign V the bow is to be *pushed*.

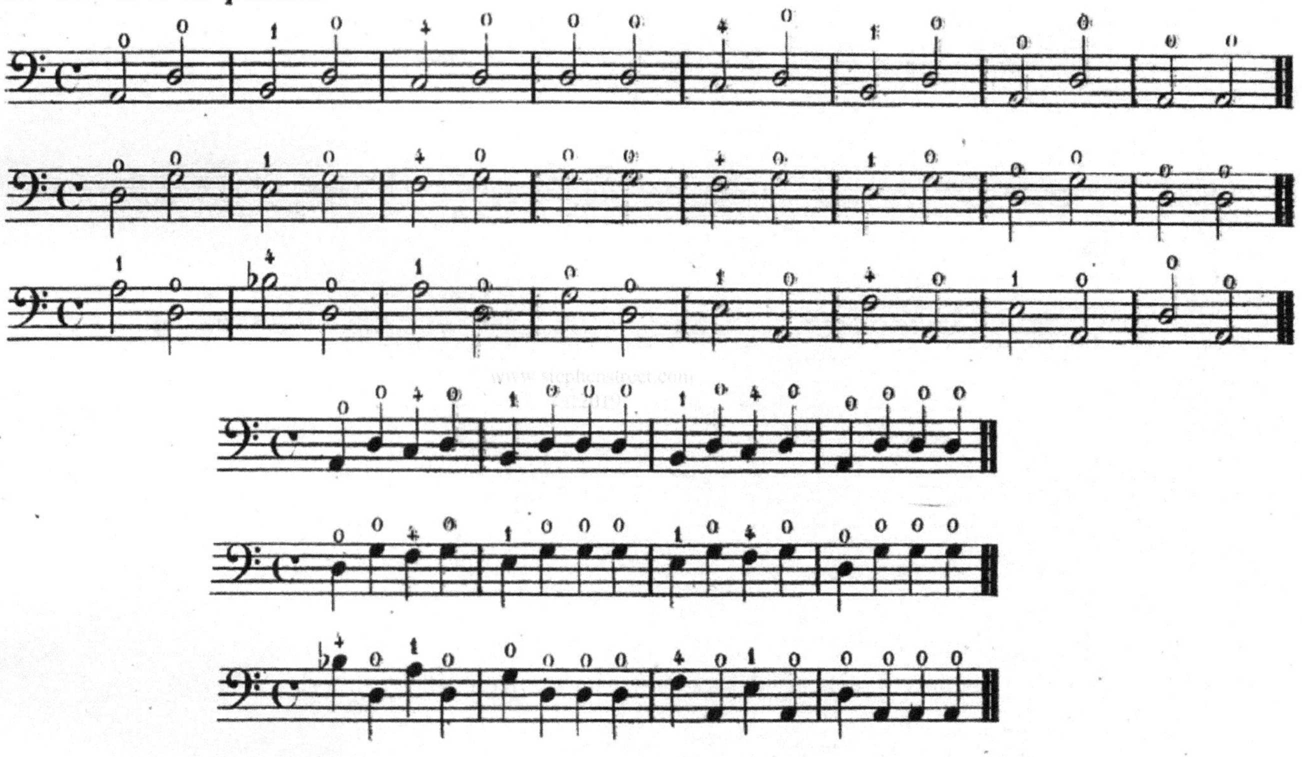

And now we must accustom the left hand to the first position.

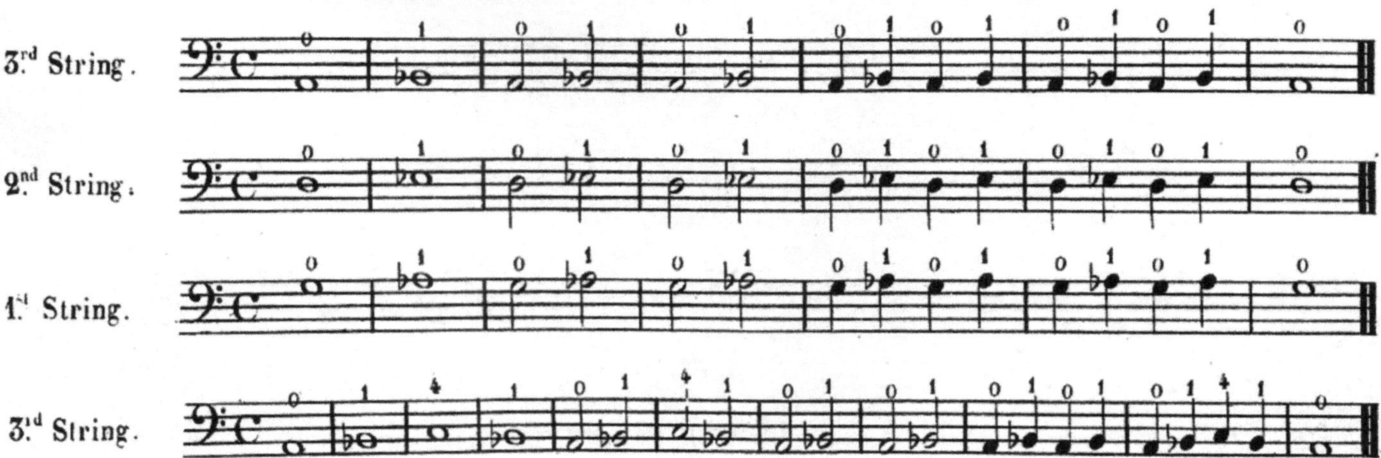

## THE SAME EXERCISE UPON THE TWO OTHER STRINGS.

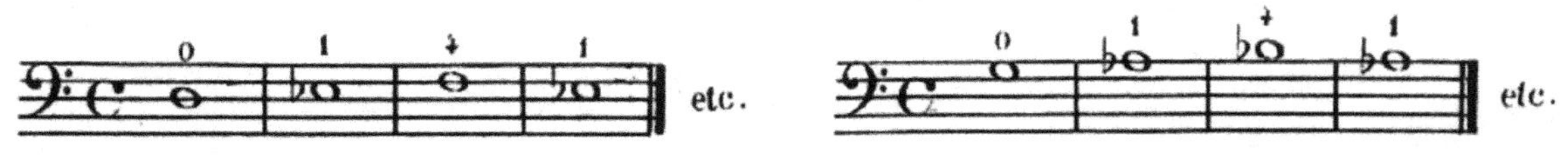

etc. etc.

1.

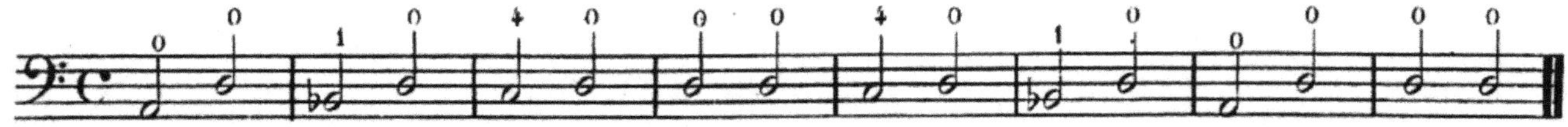

2.

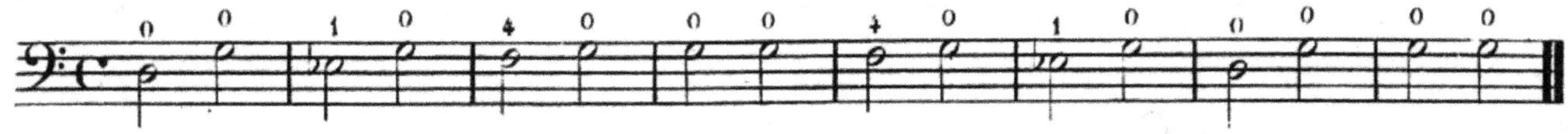

3.

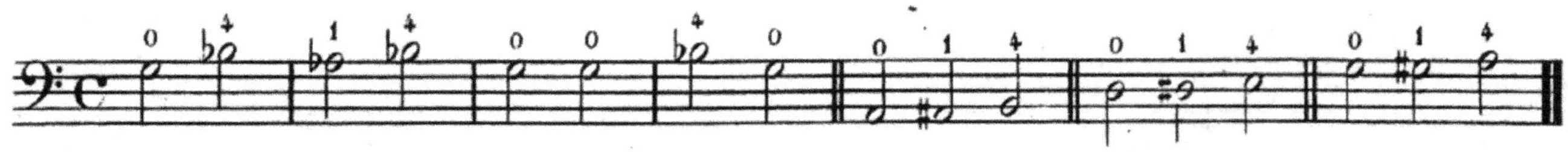

4.

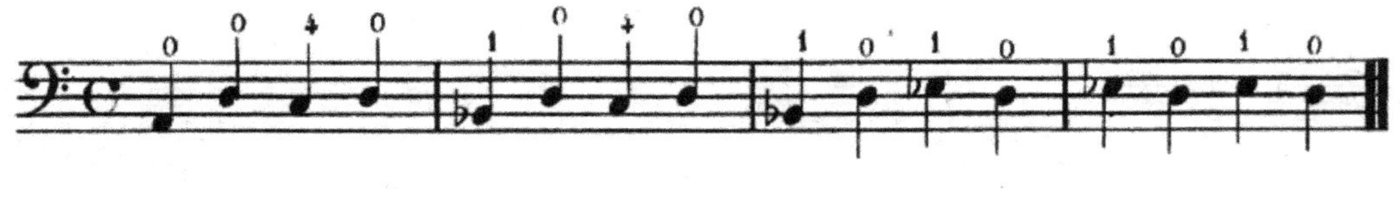

5.

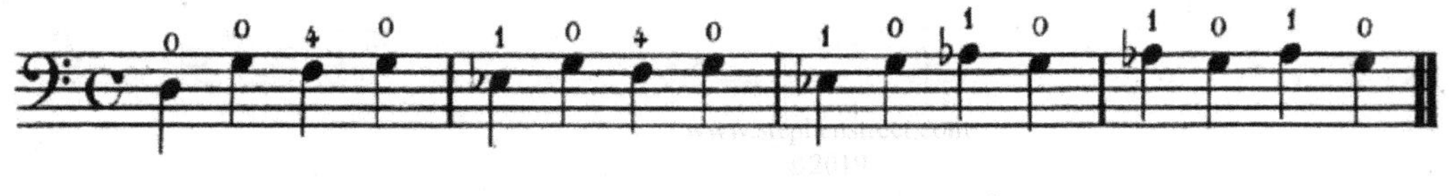

6.

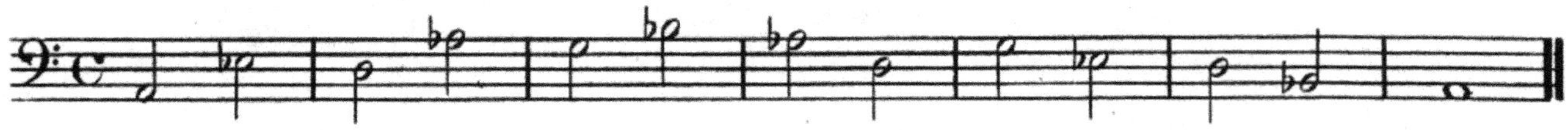

As the instrument itself offers so many inconveniences, among others that of frequently changing the position, the following examples will facilitate the passing from the 1st to the 2nd position.

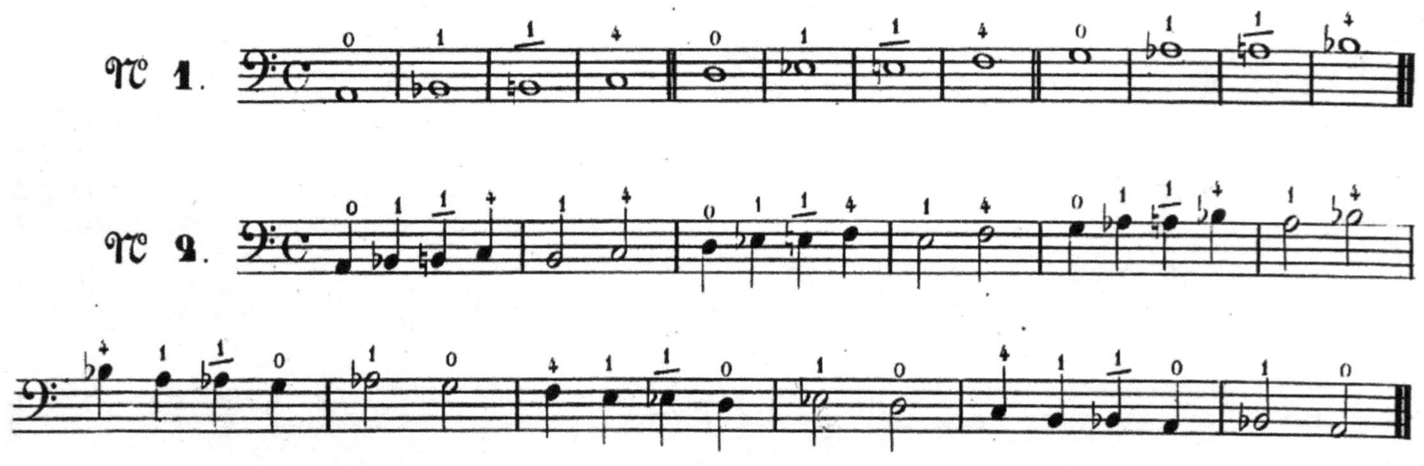


With these exercises we shall gradually attain all the positions necessary to the management of the Contre Basse.

## OF SUSTAINED SOUNDS.

Before commencing the practice of the scale, we will speak of a fault against which the pupil must be on his guard: it is that nervous trembling which the pupil feels in sounds held on for each stroke of the Bow and which is caused by impatience to commence another note before having fully completed the former one.

## SCALES WITH SHORT STROKES OF THE BOW.

Strike the Bow sharply but firmly leaving it quite at rest after each note.

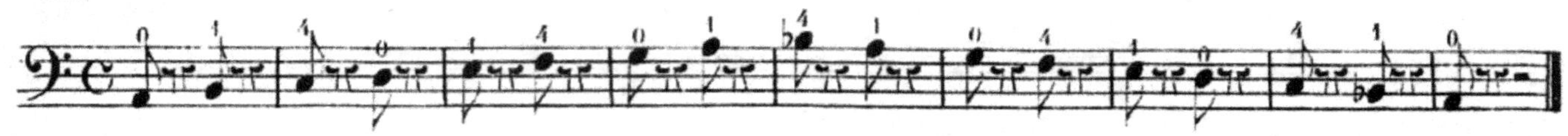

## C. POSITION.

These preliminary exercises must be played very slowly, keeping on the note without raising the Bow, unless so indicated.

## EXERCISES IN ALL THE KEYS.

C Major.

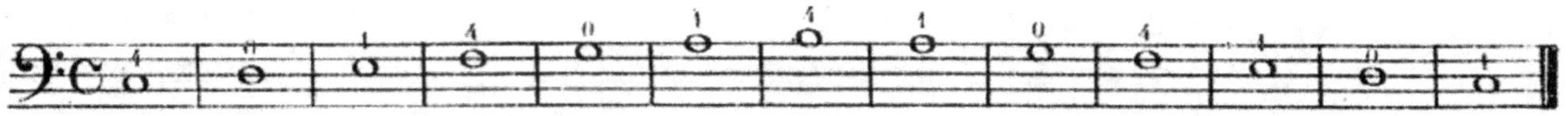

A Minor.

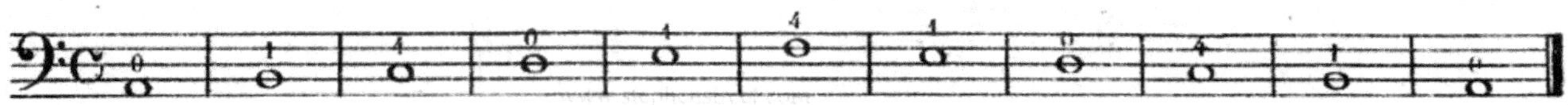

G Major.

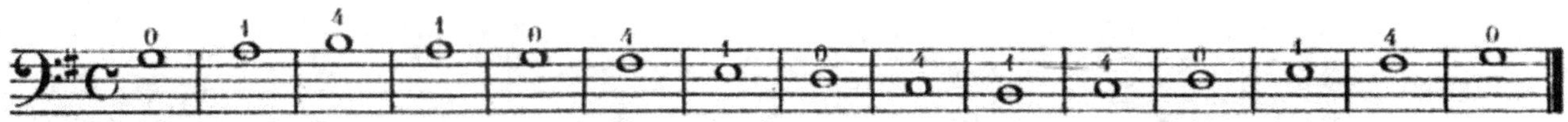

E Minor.

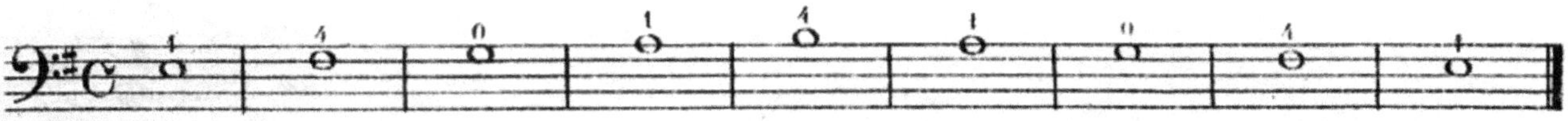

D Major.

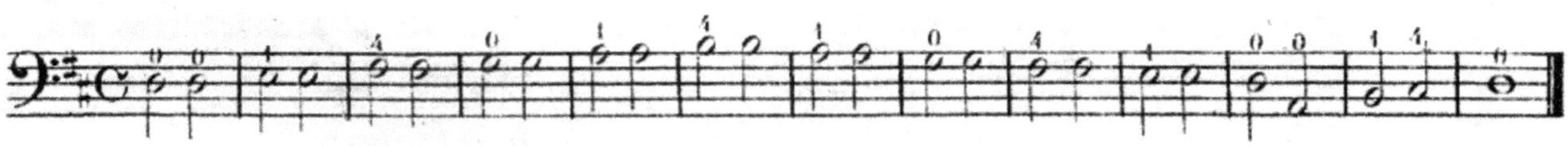

B Minor.

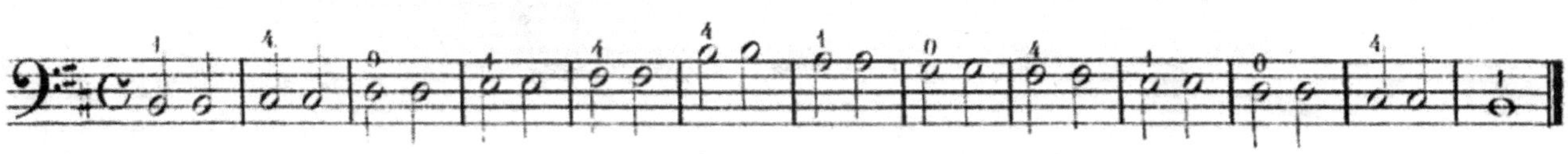

A Major

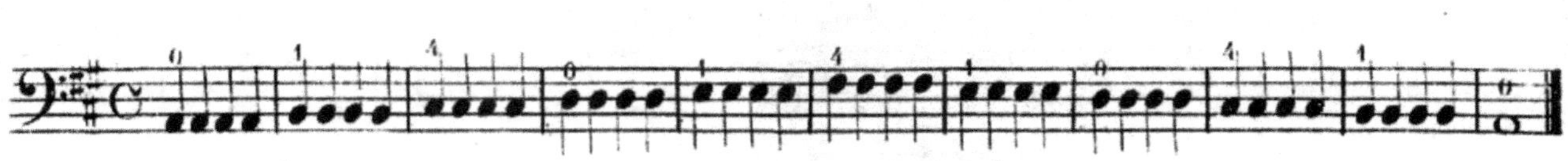

F♯ Minor.

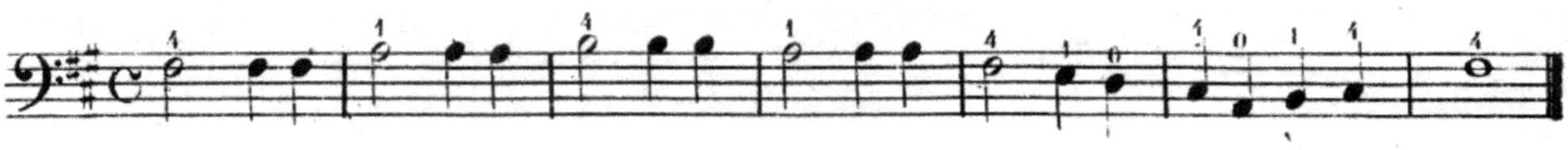

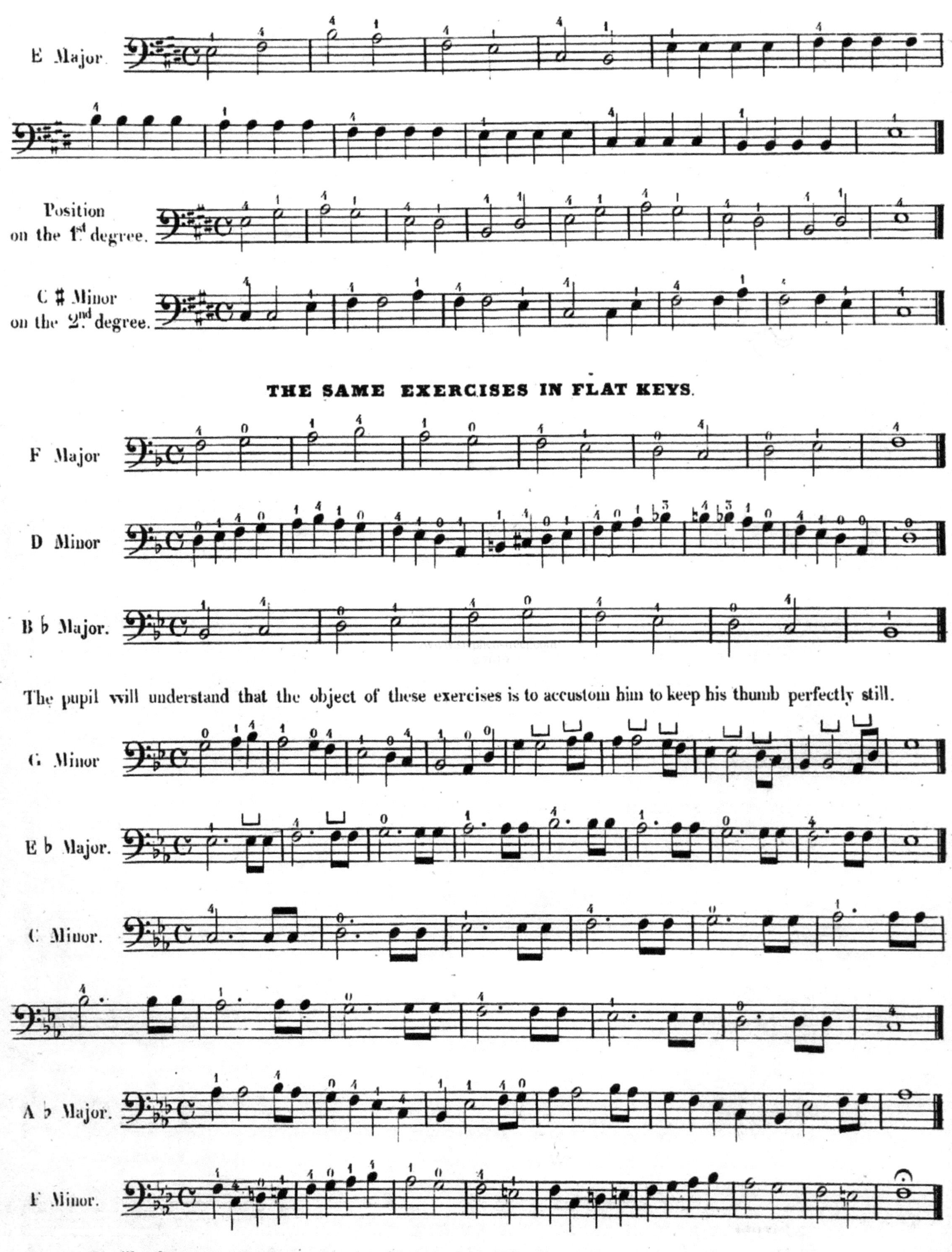
E Major.
Position on the 1st degree.
C # Minor on the 2nd degree.
THE SAME EXERCISES IN FLAT KEYS.
F Major
D Minor
B ♭ Major.
The pupil will understand that the object of these exercises is to accustom him to keep his thumb perfectly still.
G Minor
E ♭ Major.
C Minor.
A ♭ Major.
F Minor.
The pupil will take care not to move his thumb in getting the A ♭ on the G string.

Before proceeding to other exercises which the non-melodious character of the instrument would render monotonous the pupil must learn all the different ways of changing position. Let us use the G string which is least fatiguing to the hand and is best for all sorts of exercises. So soon as the pupil acquires power over that string he will perform the same exercises upon the other two. These exercises develope the flexibility of the hand, and facilitate the knowledge of all the degrees of the scale, before even the Method brings them before the pupil. When he finds a minim surmounted with the figure 1 underlined he should wait a moment so as to well understand the change of position.

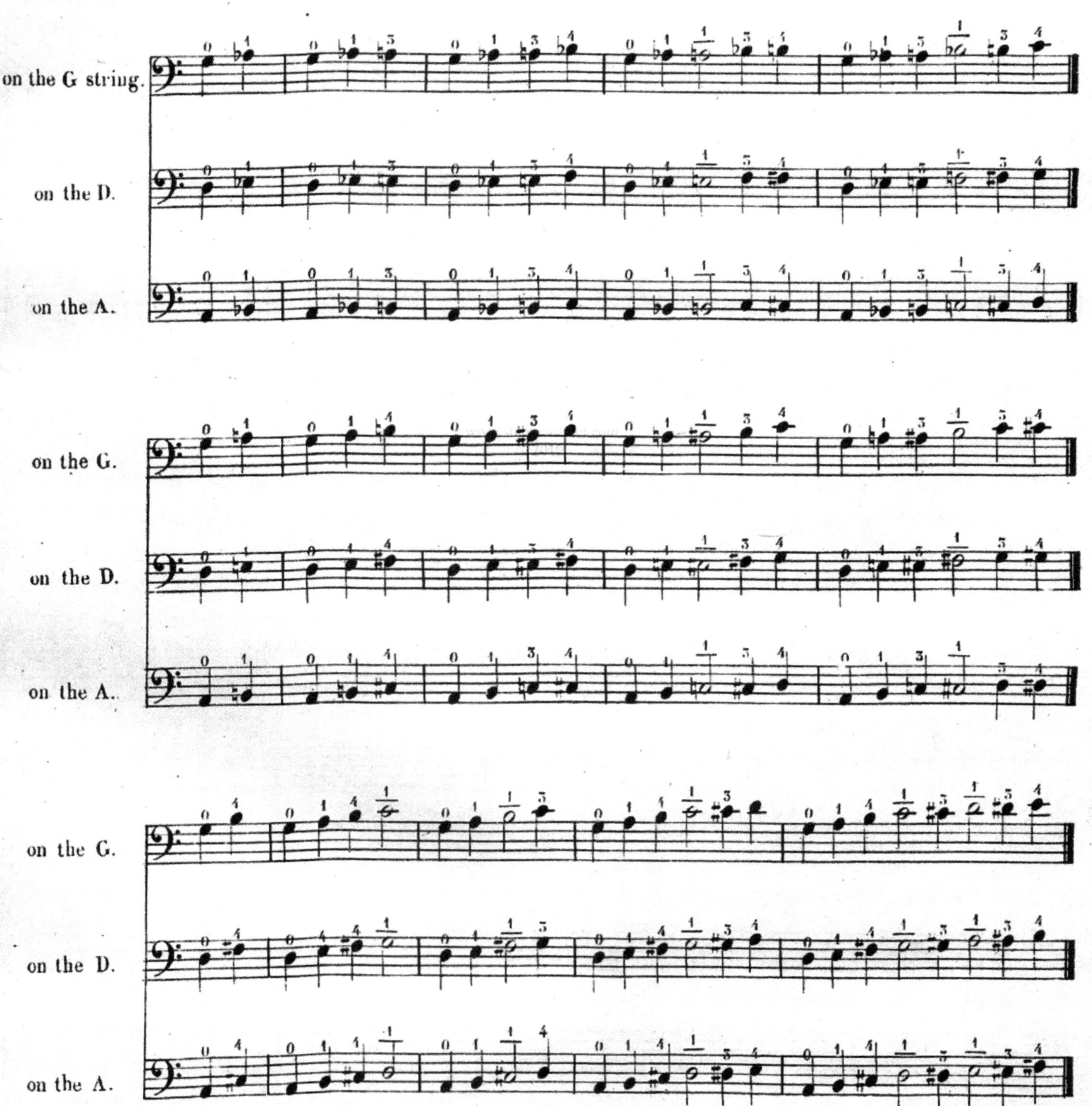

on the G.

on the D.

on the A.

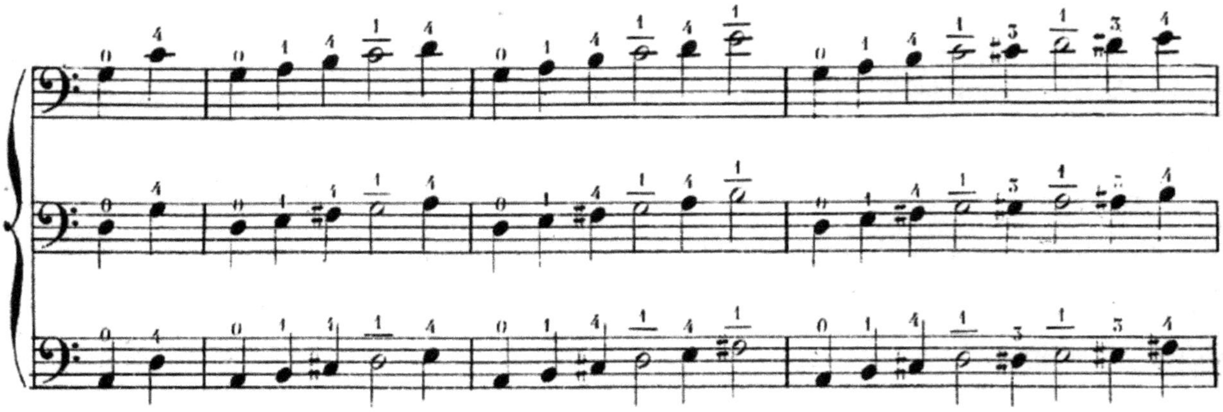

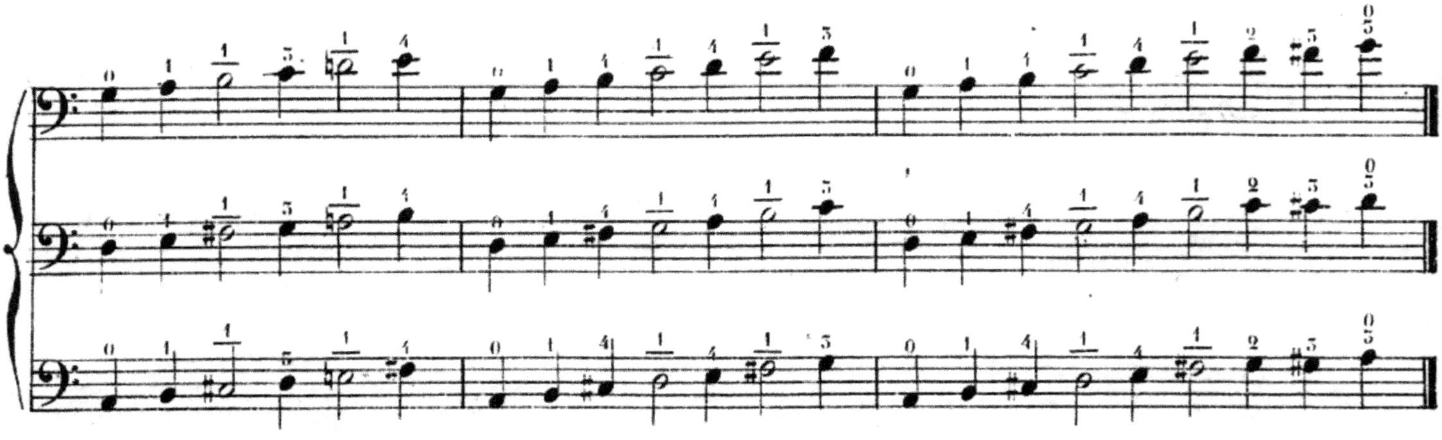

These exercises will gradually facilitate the positions for the chromatic scale.

**EXAMPLE.**

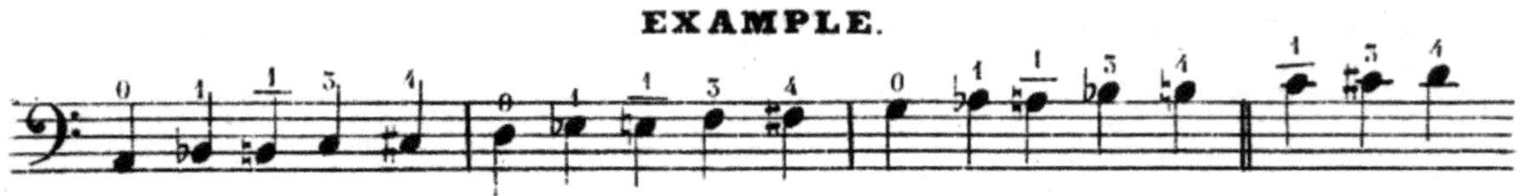

In passing from one string to another always avoid raising the Bow.

INTERVALS OF THIRDS.

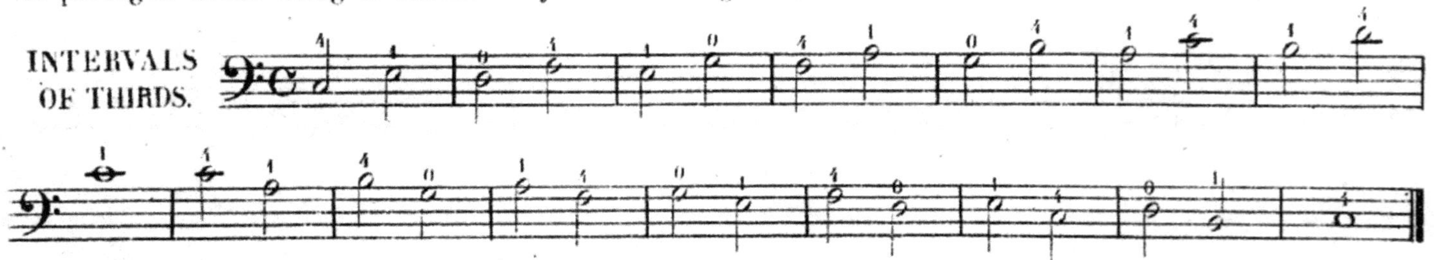

The pupil must accustom himself to the abrupt change of position from A to C and from B to D.—Further on we shall see a position much more useful.

INTERVALS OF FOURTHS.

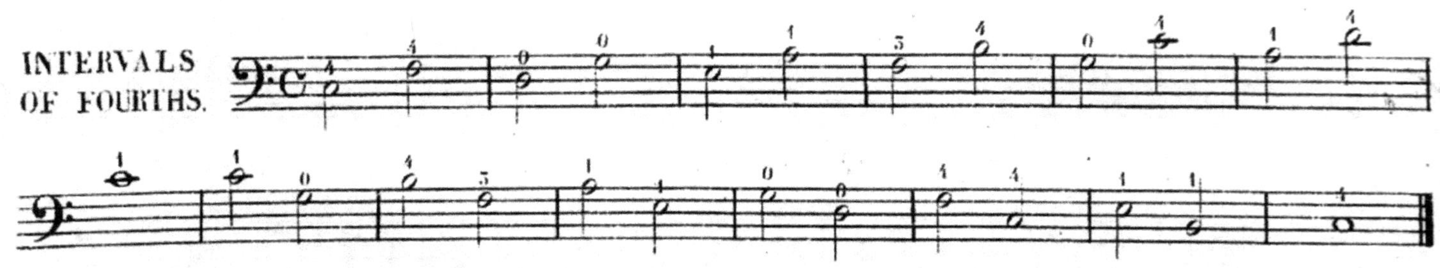

Here also we must leap to the D after the C on the first string. Pay attention to the position of the F with the 3.rd finger and the B with the 4.th both in going up and down.

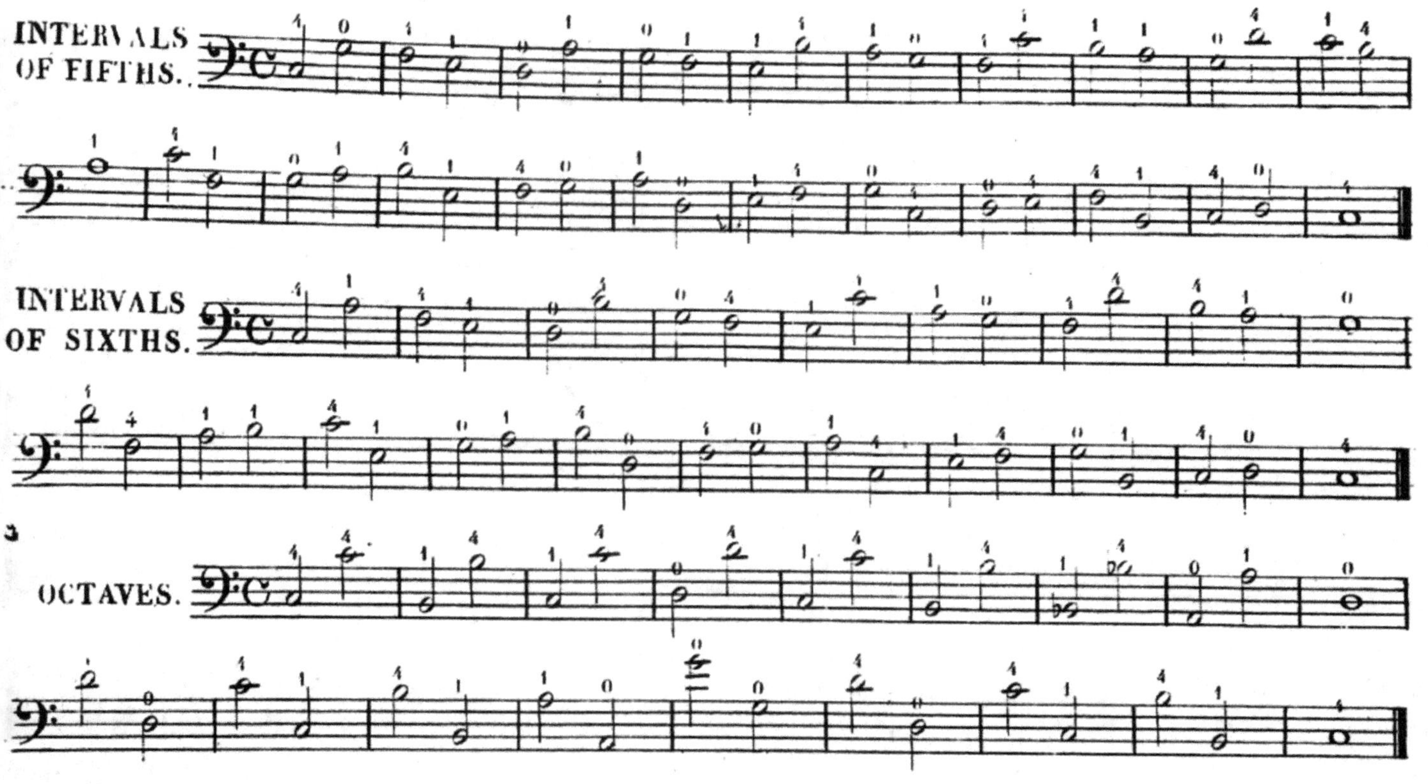


## SCALE OF C MAJOR.

The following scales are written in *Crotchets;* this is done to occupy less space. The pupil can play them at his own time giving to the notes what value he pleases.

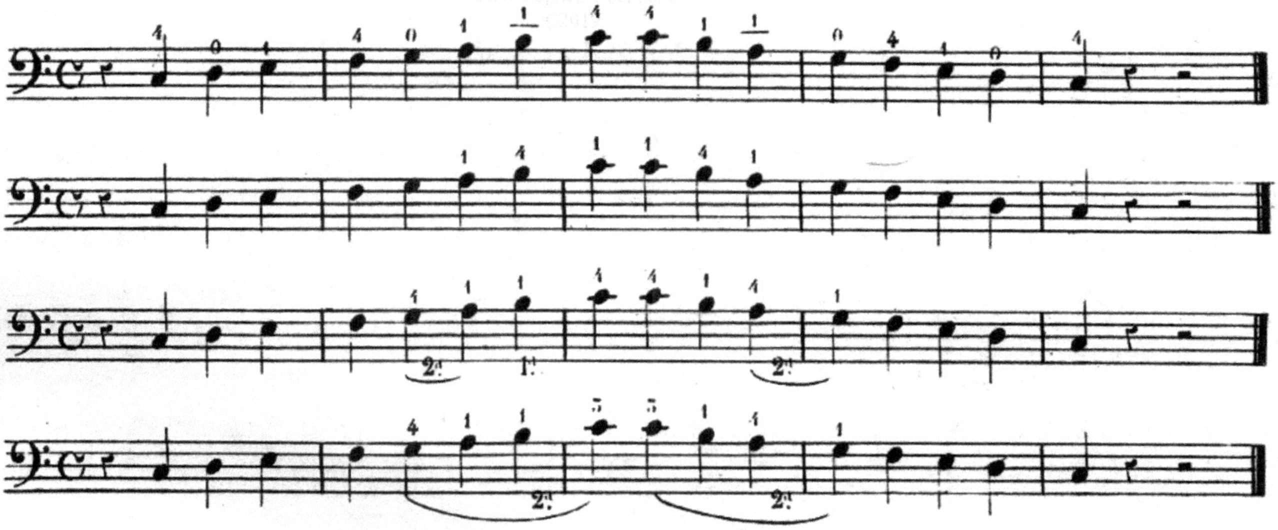

### TO REACH D.

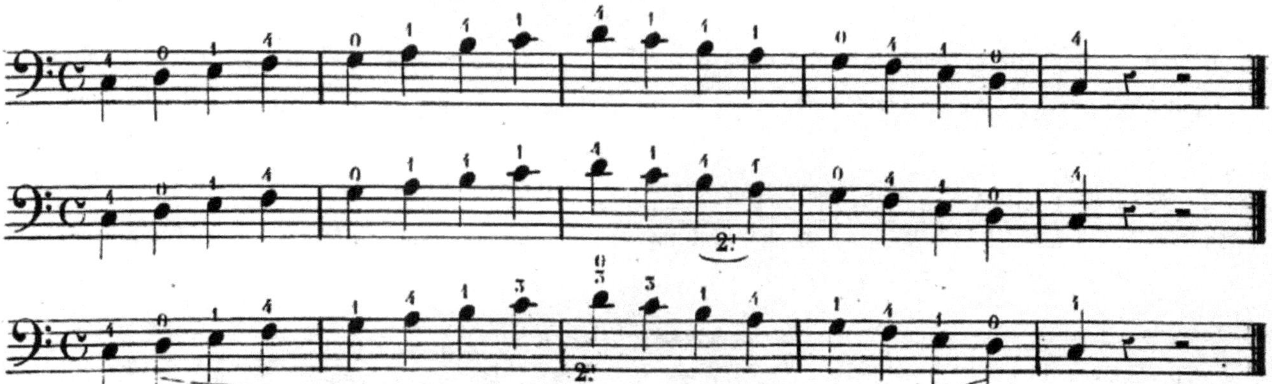

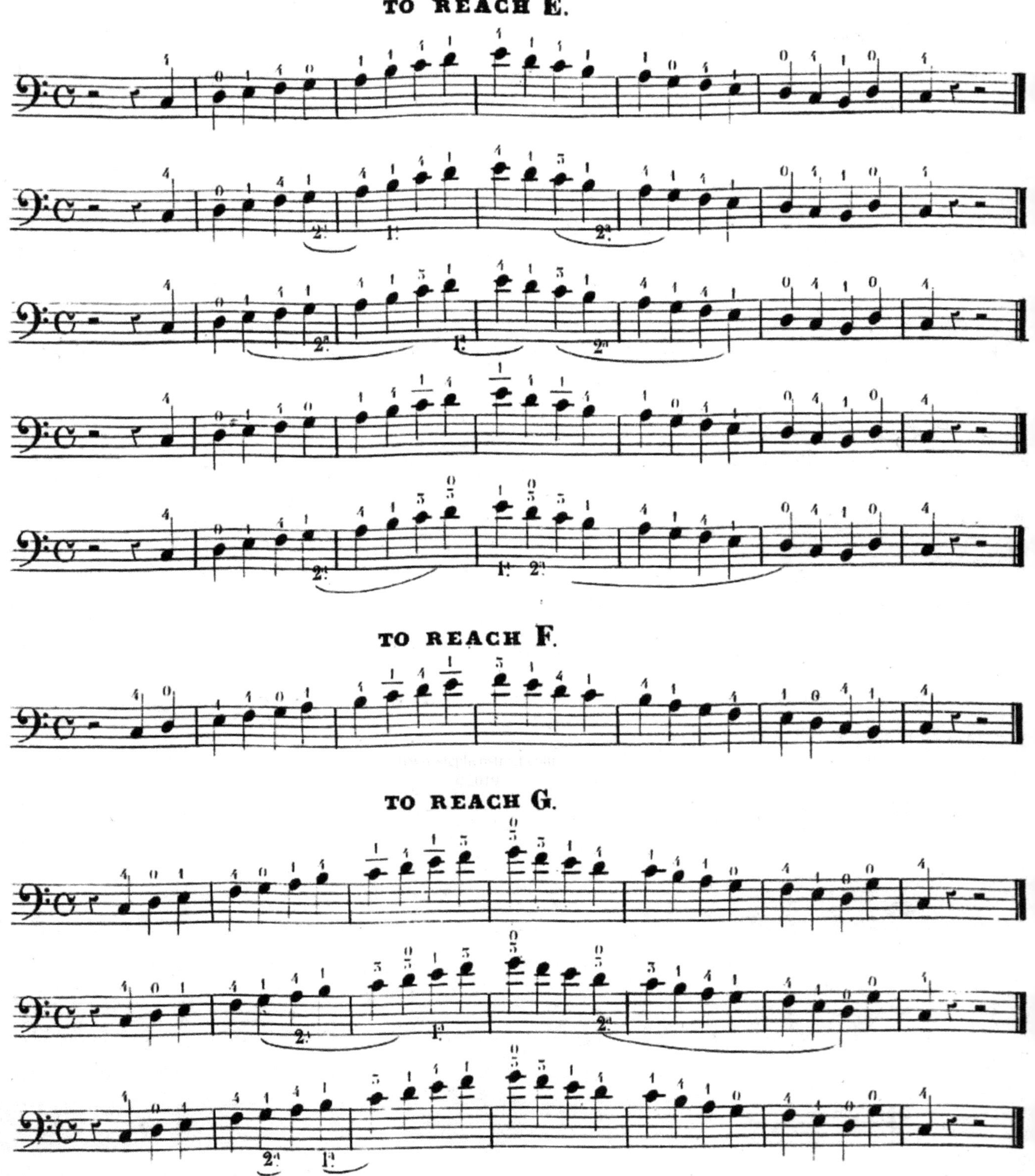


When the pupil is well practised in the scale of C, played in all the positions above indicated, the exercises which come after will appear to him much easier. We shall place after each scale a certain number of exercises, equally useful and agreeable. They will always be proportionate to the power of the pupil, they will progress imperceptibly from one difficulty to another and will smooth the way (sufficiently rough it must be admitted) leading to complete proficiency on the instrument.

And we must not be discouraged at the first difficulties: they are met with in the study of every other instrument. The first are necessarily the hardest to conquer. The pupil must have patience, courage and persistance.

N. B. The marks 1ª 2ª 3ª (prima, seconda, terza) denote the string on which the note is to be made.

EXERCICES. EXERCISES.

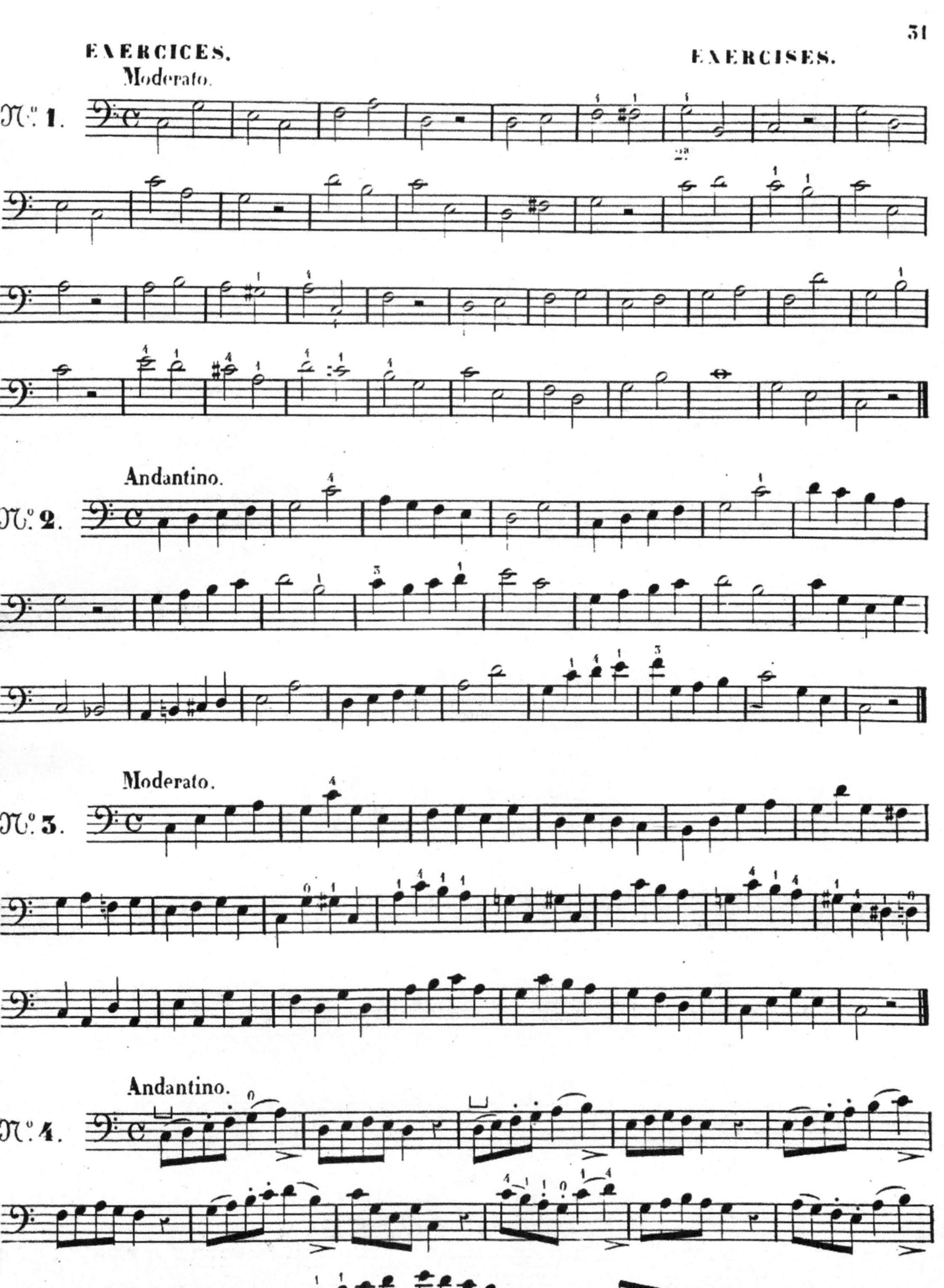

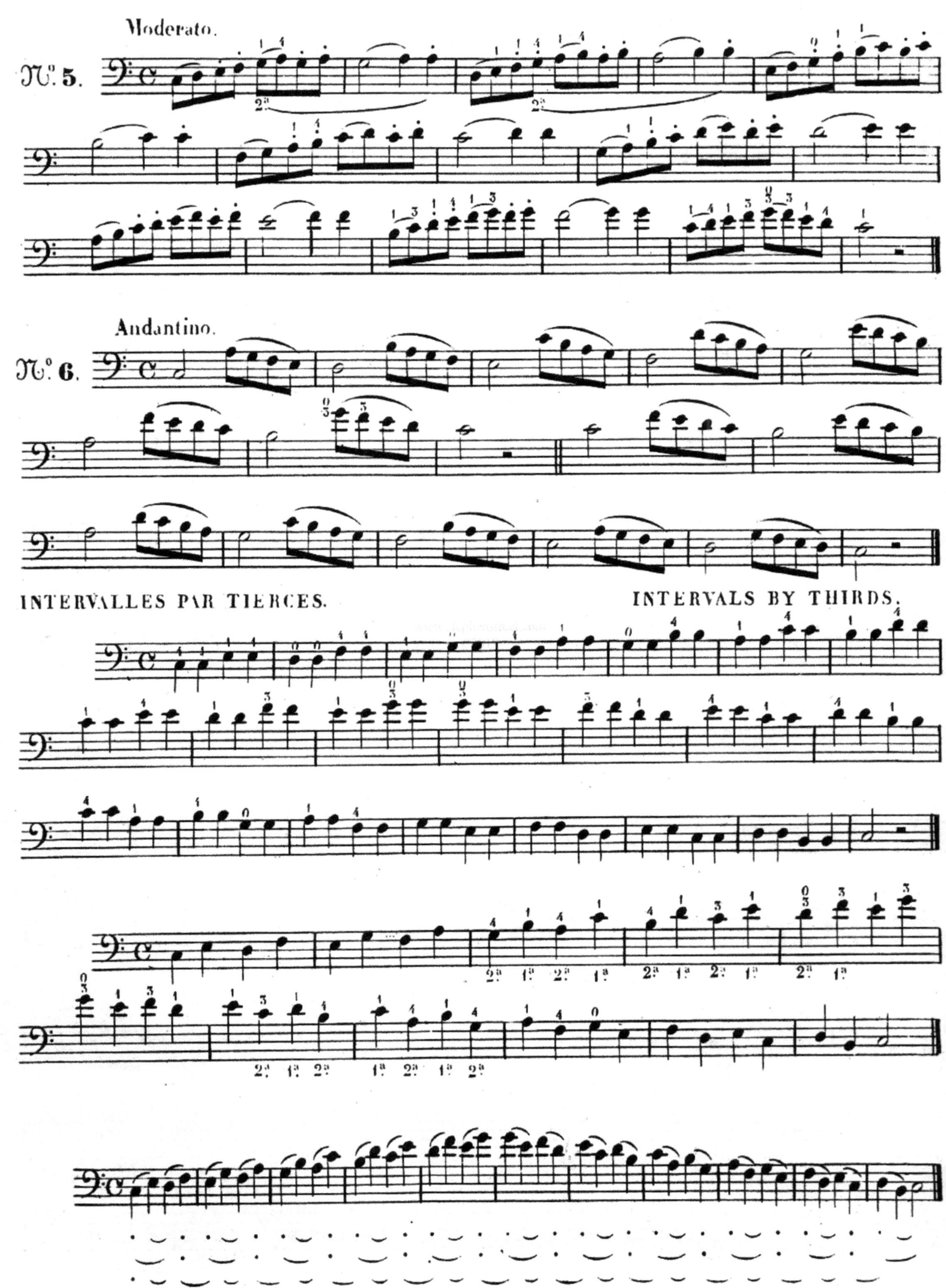
Moderato.
Nº 5.
Andantino.
Nº 6.
INTERVALLES PAR TIERCES.
INTERVALS BY THIRDS.

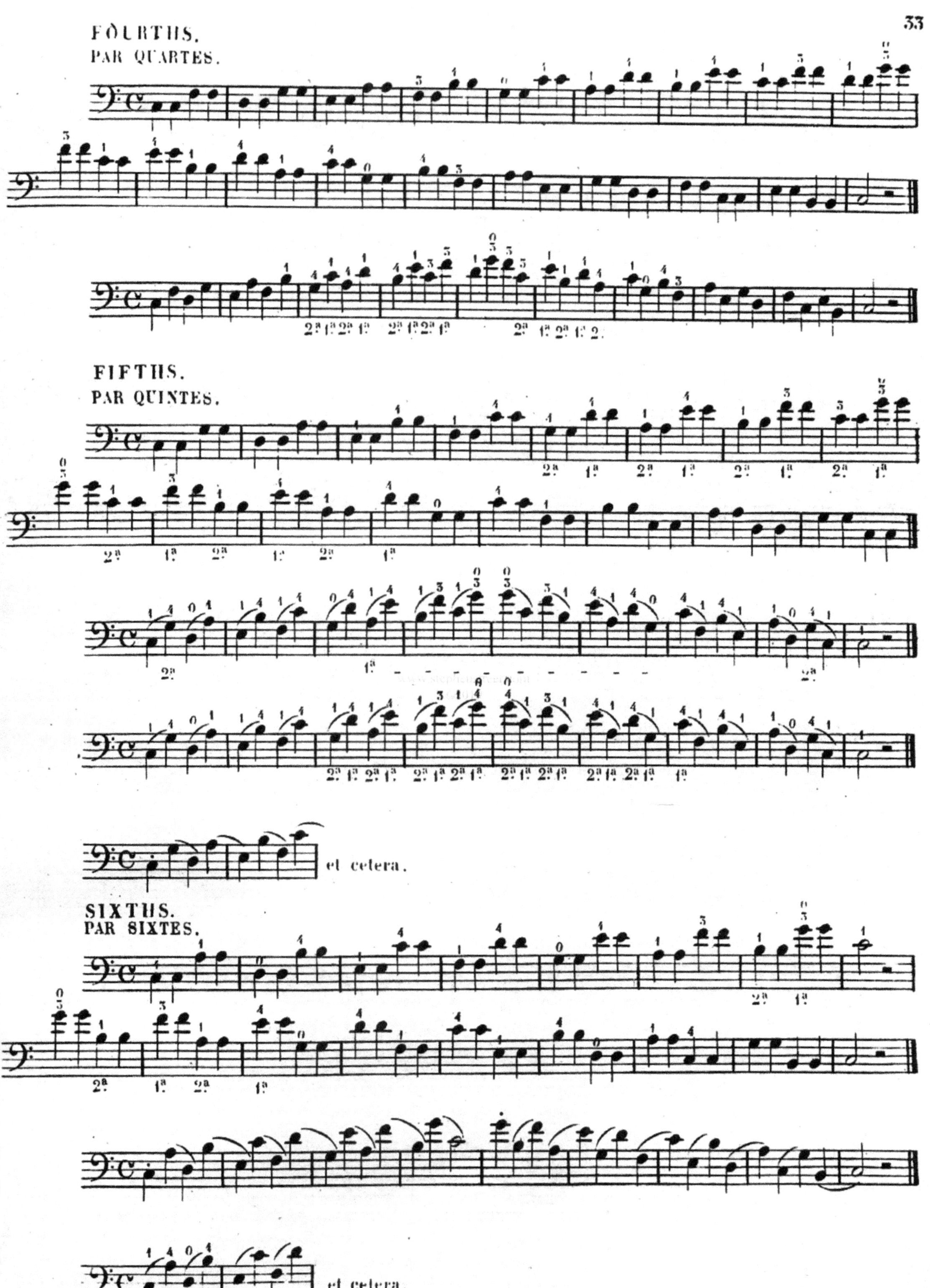
FOURTHS.
PAR QUARTES.
FIFTHS.
PAR QUINTES.
et cetera.
SIXTHS.
PAR SIXTES.
et cetera.

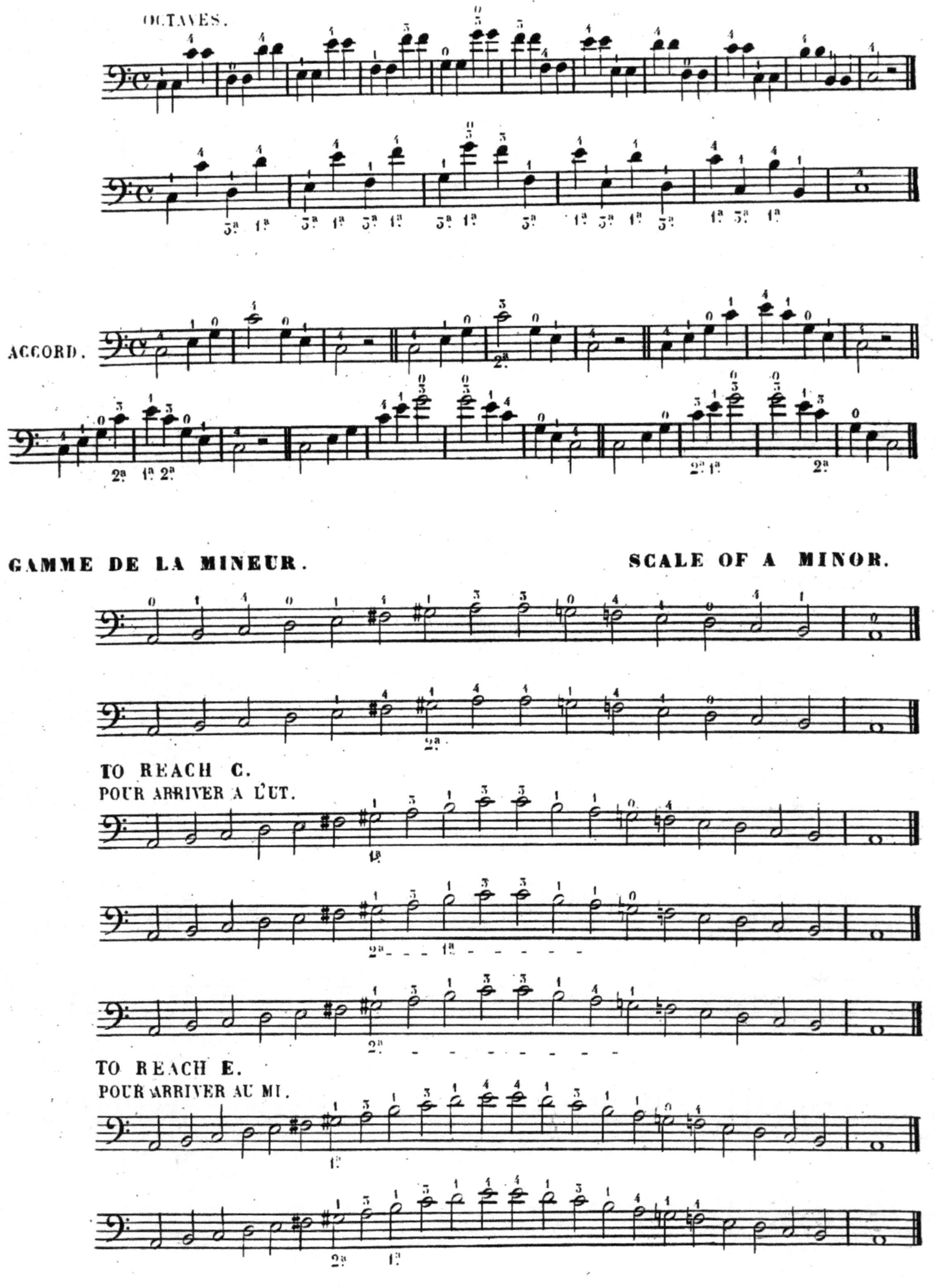
OCTAVES.
ACCORD.
GAMME DE LA MINEUR.
SCALE OF A MINOR.
TO REACH C.
POUR ARRIVER A L'UT.
TO REACH E.
POUR ARRIVER AU MI.

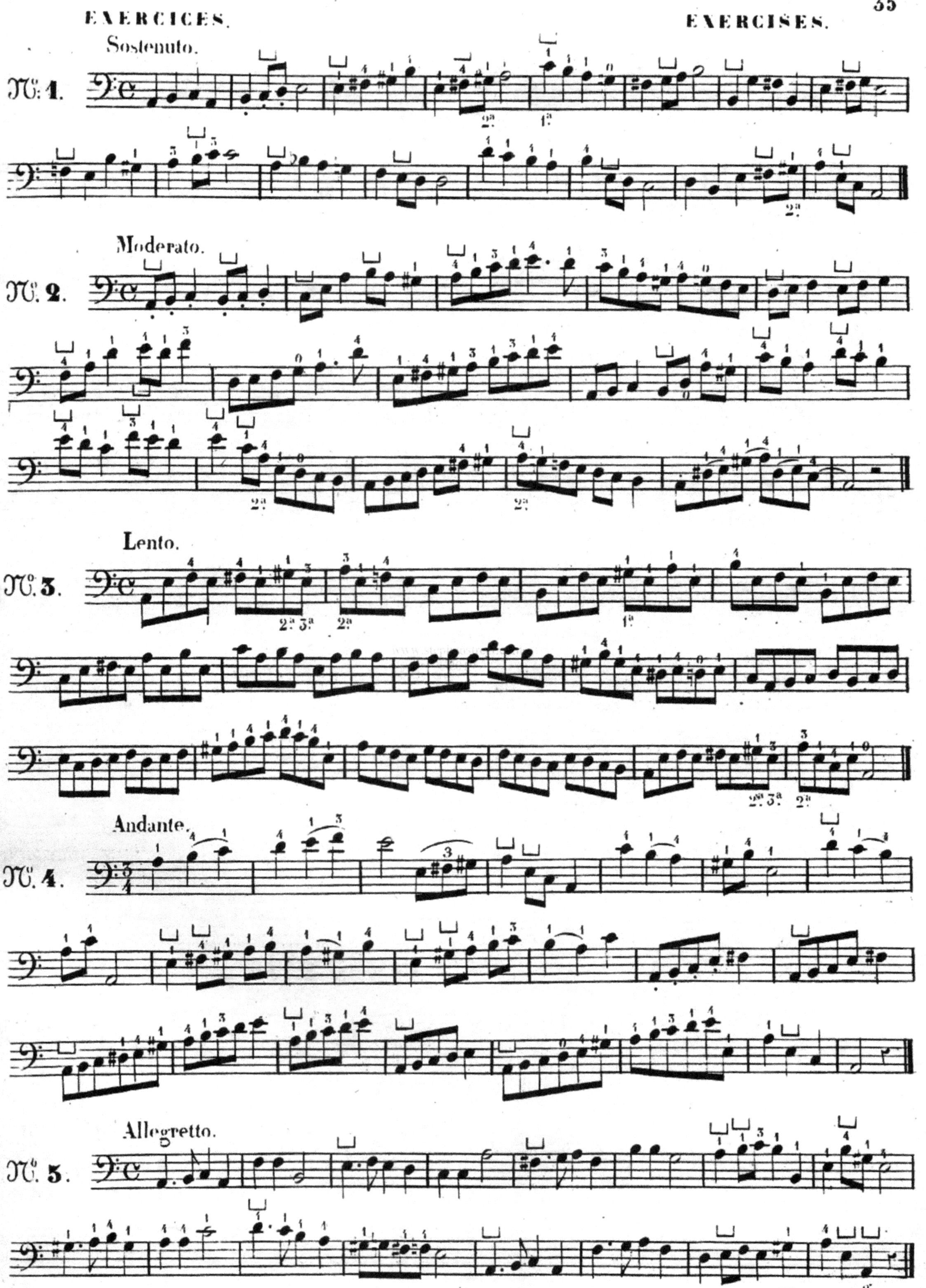
Sostenuto.
Nº 1.
Moderato.
Nº 2.
Lento.
Nº 3.
Andante.
Nº 4.
Allegretto.
Nº 5.

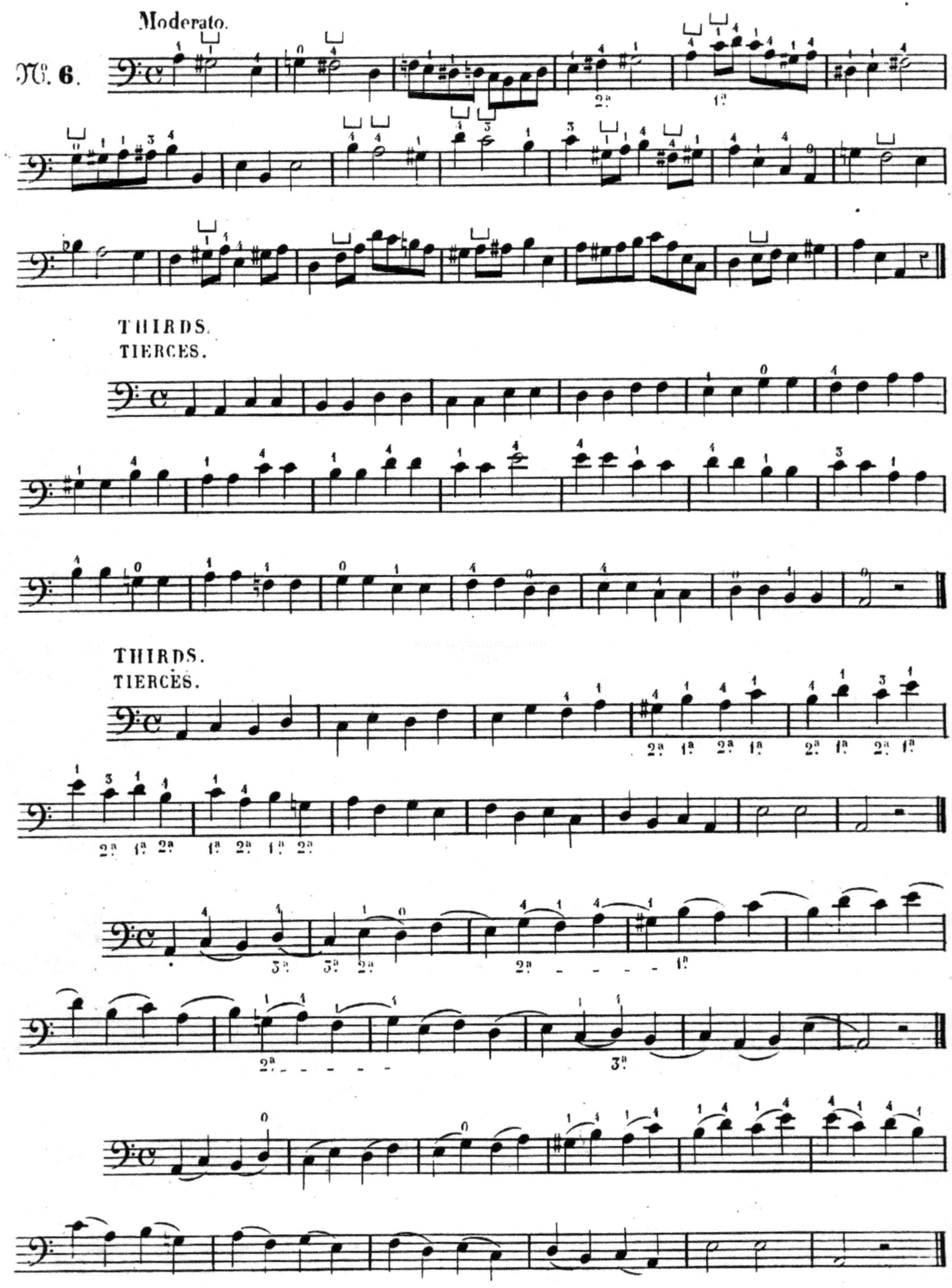
Moderato.
No. 6.
THIRDS.
TIERCES.
THIRDS.
TIERCES.

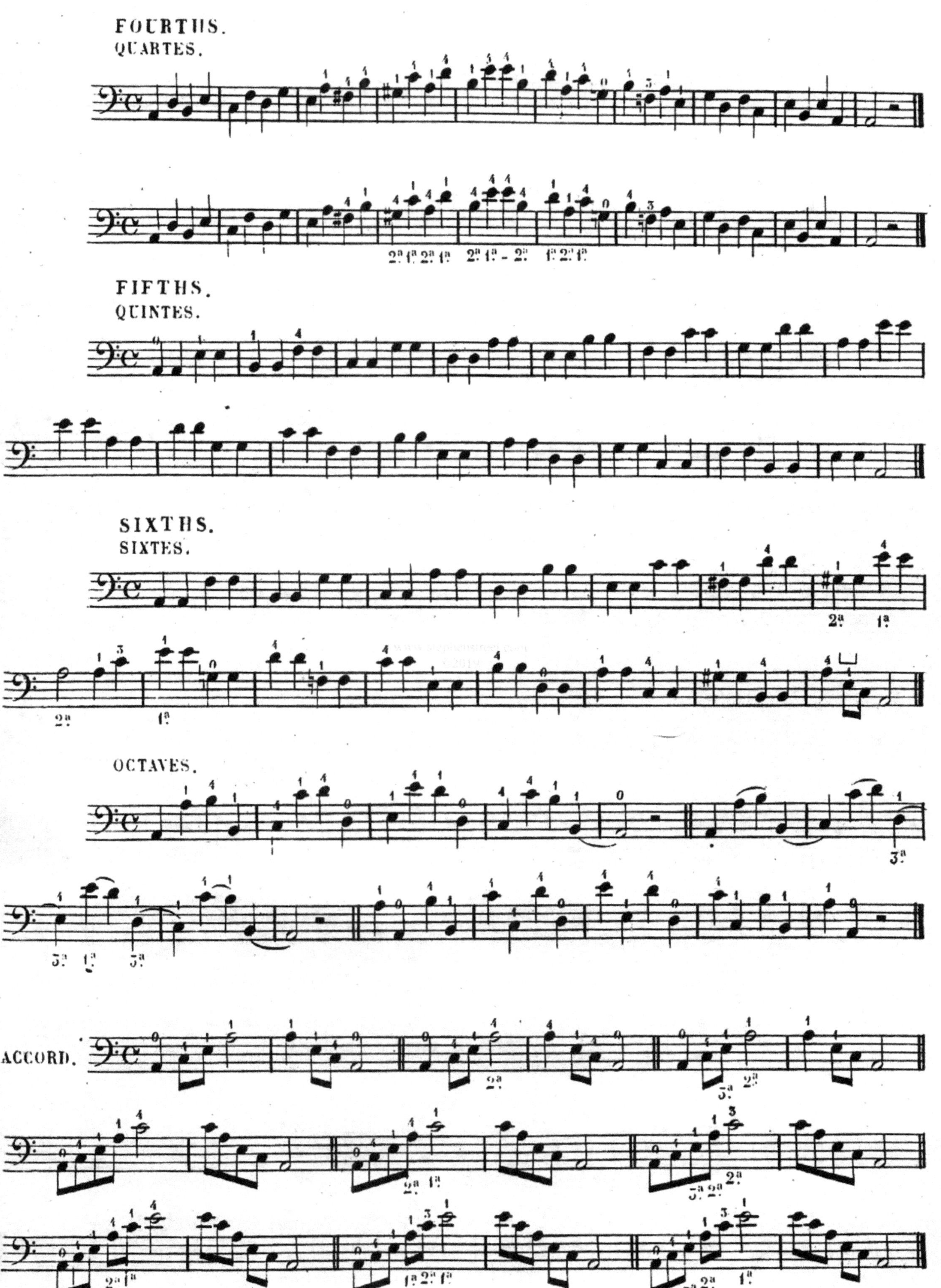
FOURTHS.
QUARTES.
FIFTHS.
QUINTES.
SIXTHS.
SIXTES.
OCTAVES.
ACCORD.

GAMME DE FA. SCALE OF F.

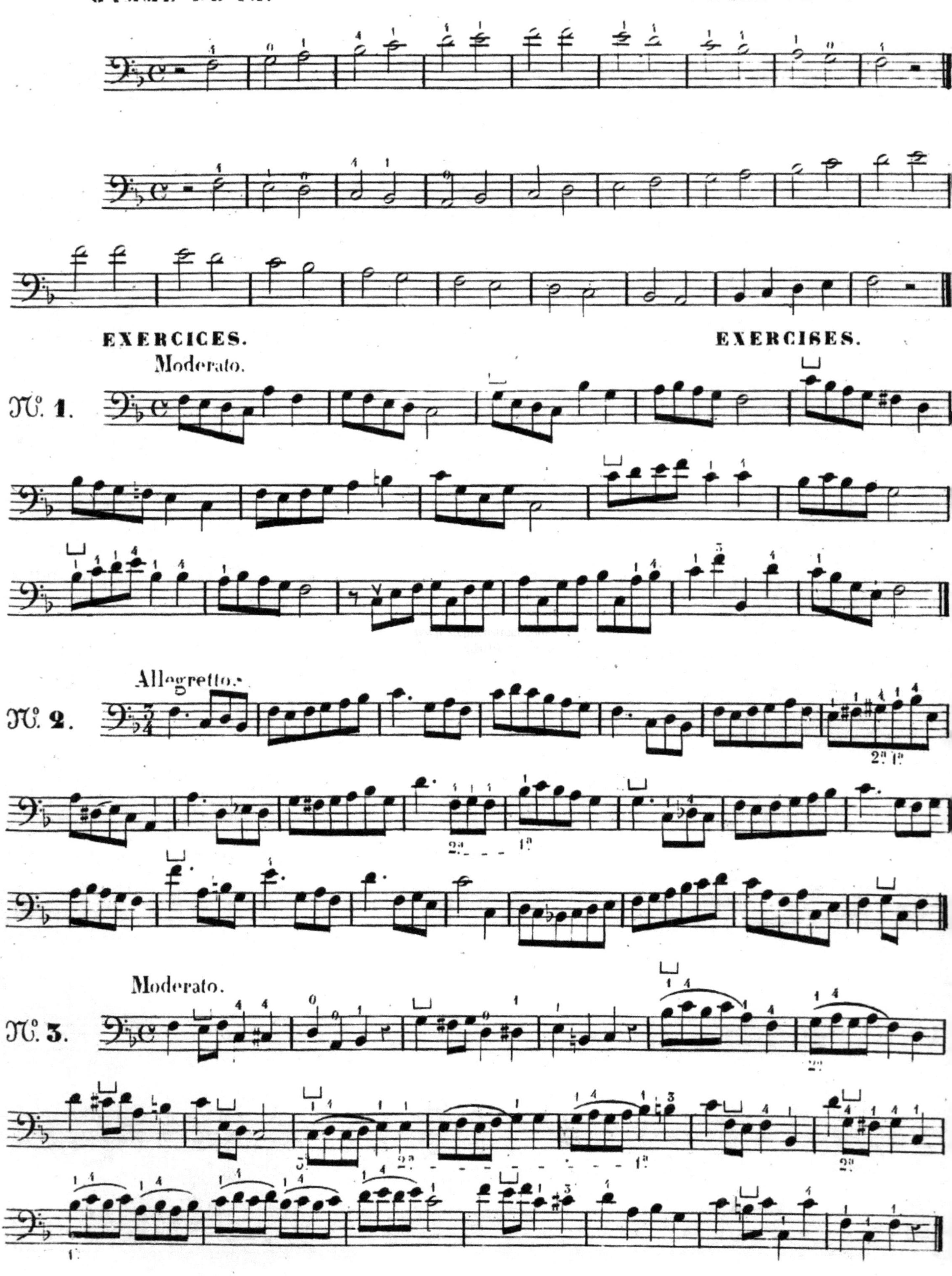

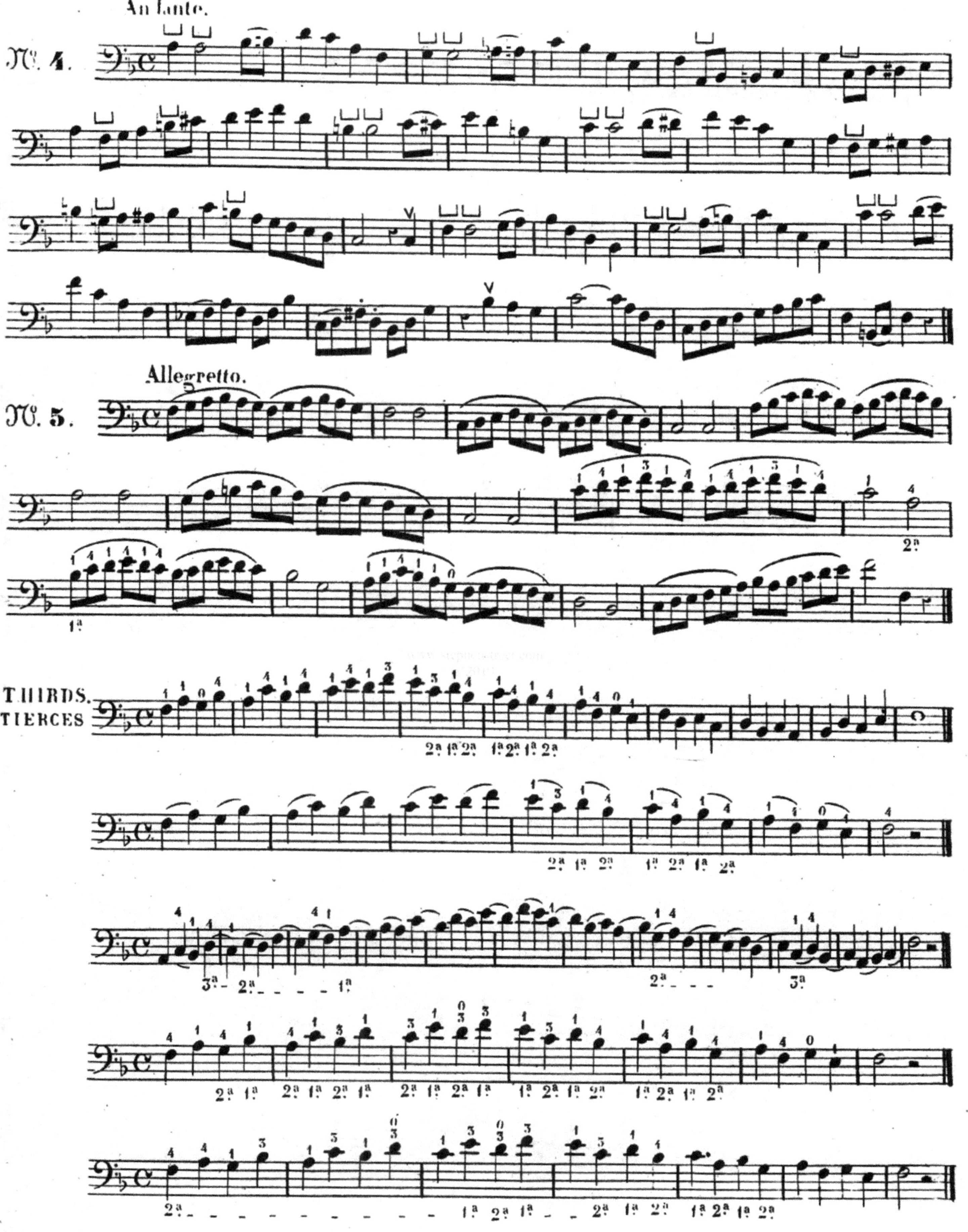
Andante.
Nº 4.
Allegretto.
Nº 5.
THIRDS.
TIERCES

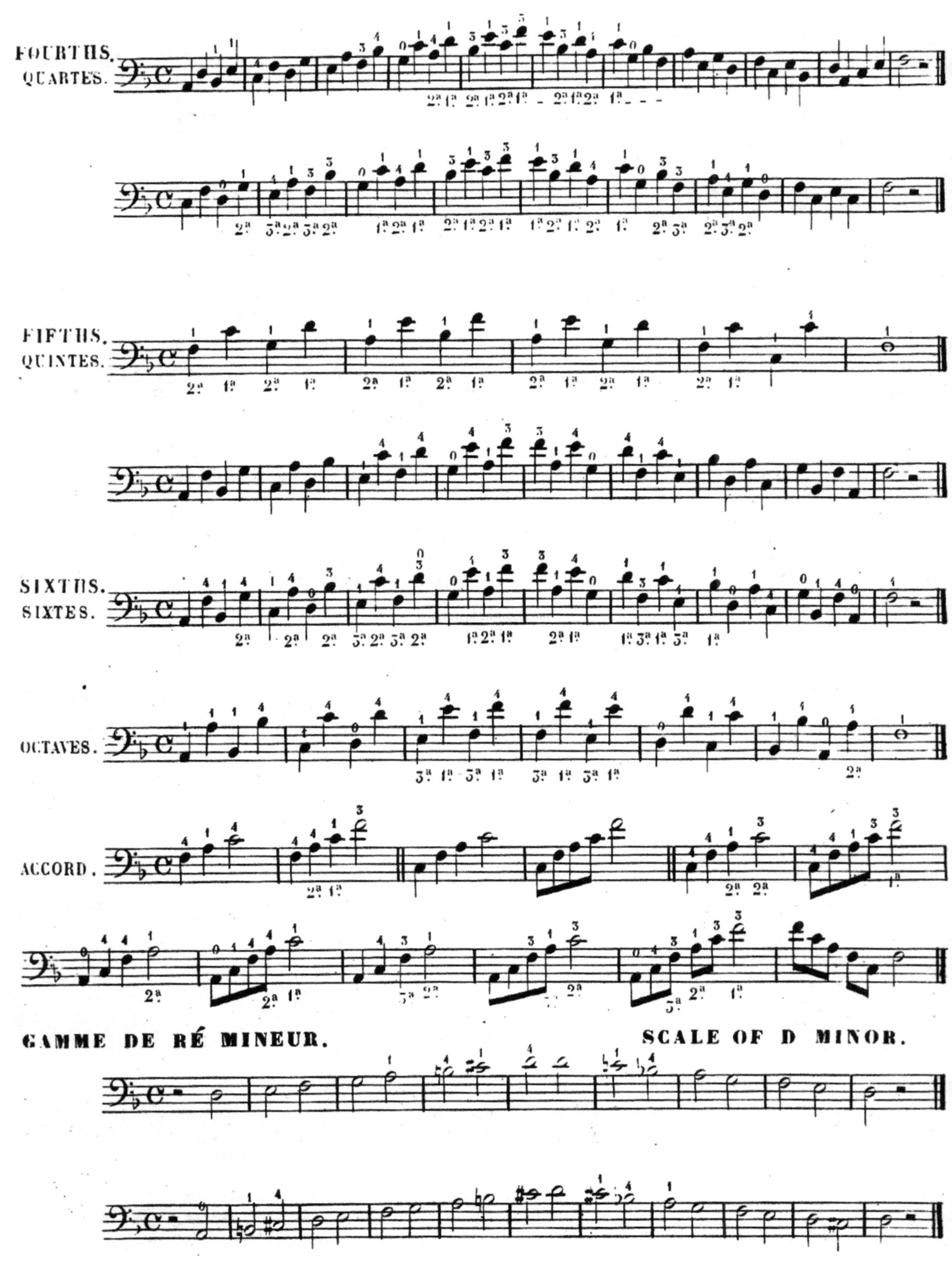
FOURTHS.
QUARTES.
FIFTHS.
QUINTES.
SIXTHS.
SIXTES.
OCTAVES.
ACCORD.
GAMME DE RÉ MINEUR.
SCALE OF D MINOR.

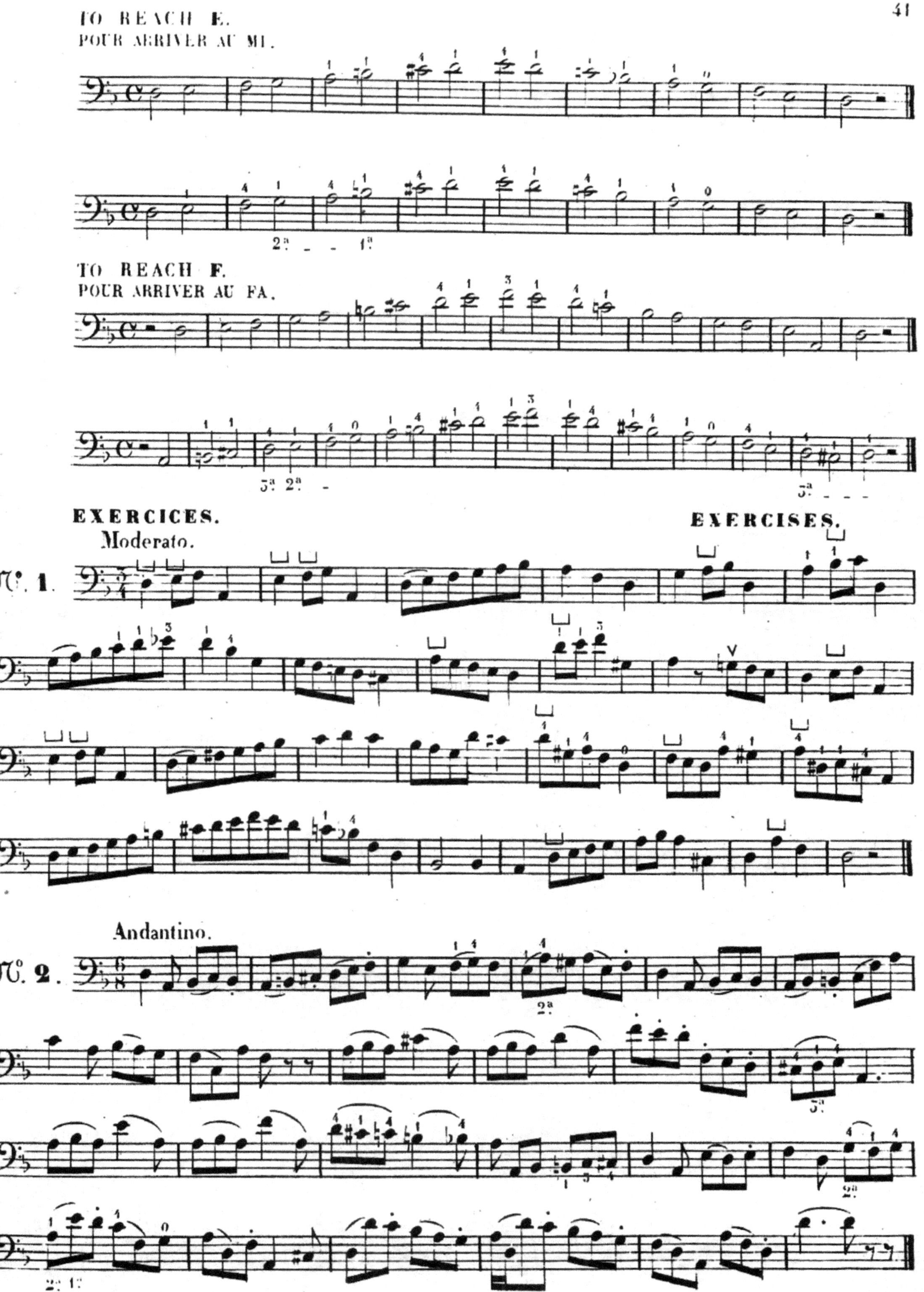
TO REACH E.
POUR ARRIVER AU MI.
TO REACH F.
POUR ARRIVER AU FA.
EXERCICES.
EXERCISES.
Moderato.
Nº. 1.
Andantino.
Nº. 2.

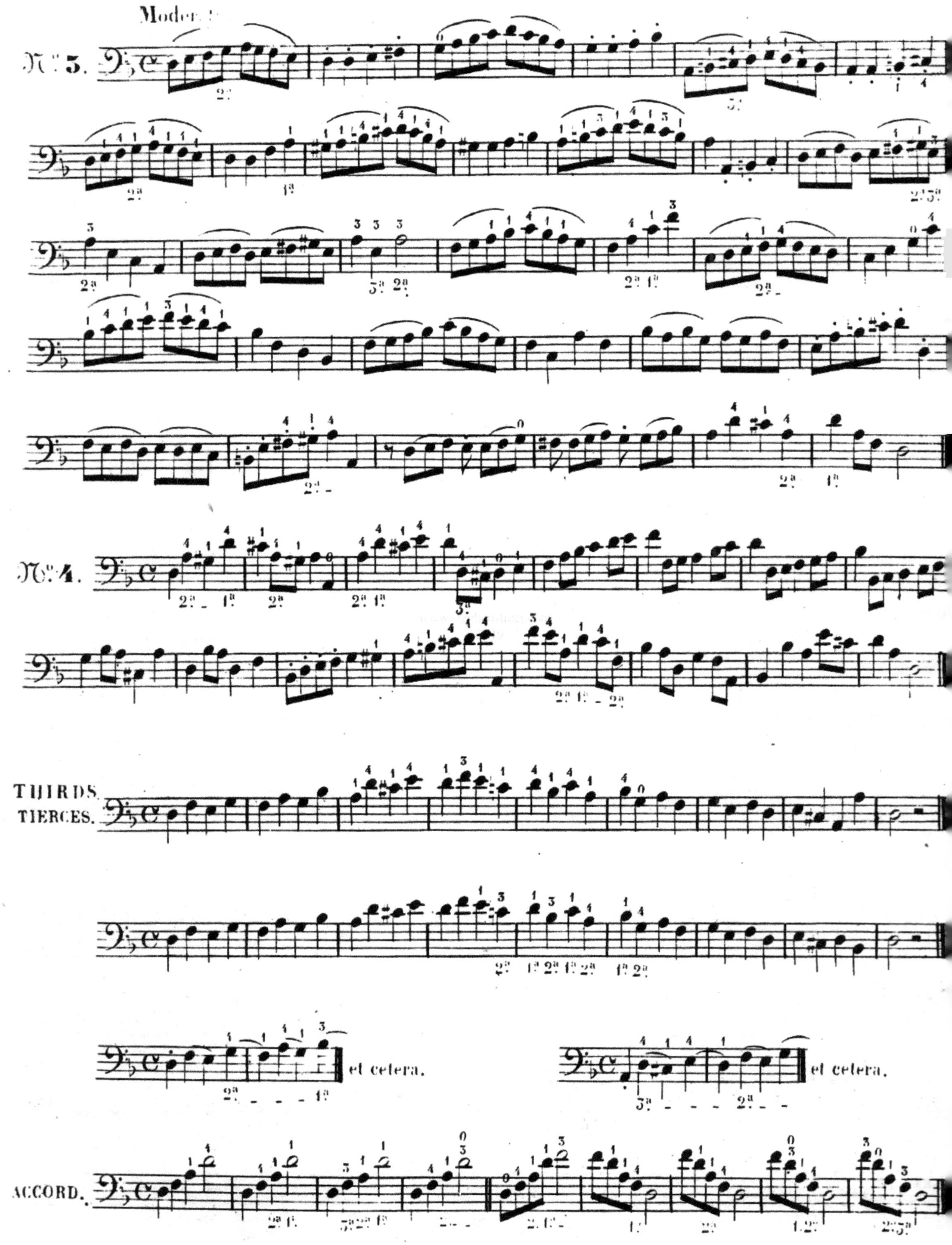
No 3.
No 4.
THIRDS
TIERCES.
et cetera.
et cetera.
ACCORD.

GAMME DE SOL. SCALE OF G.

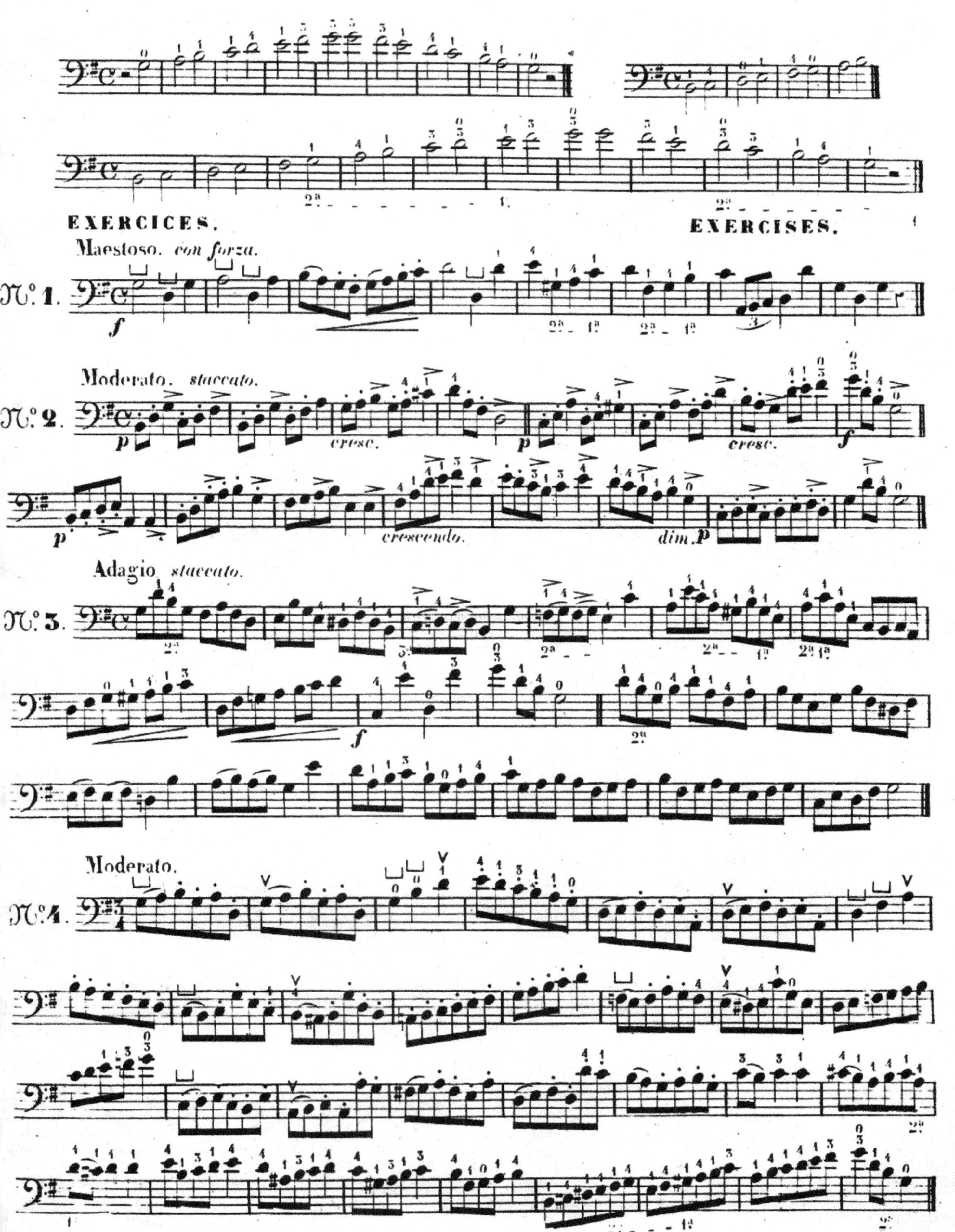

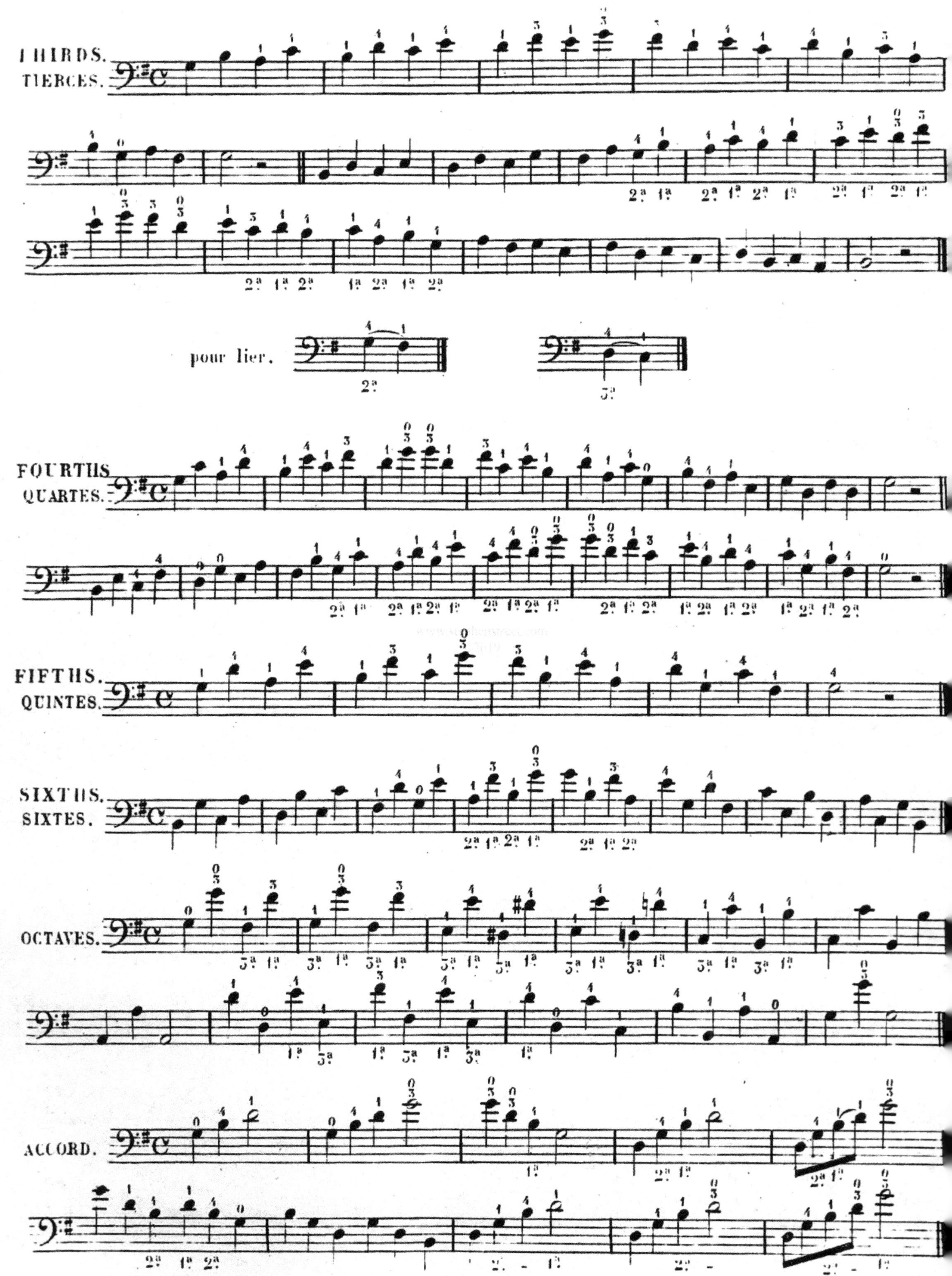
THIRDS.
TIERCES.
pour lier.
FOURTHS
QUARTES.
FIFTHS.
QUINTES.
SIXTHS.
SIXTES.
OCTAVES.
ACCORD.

GAMME DE MI MINEUR. SCALE OF E MINOR.

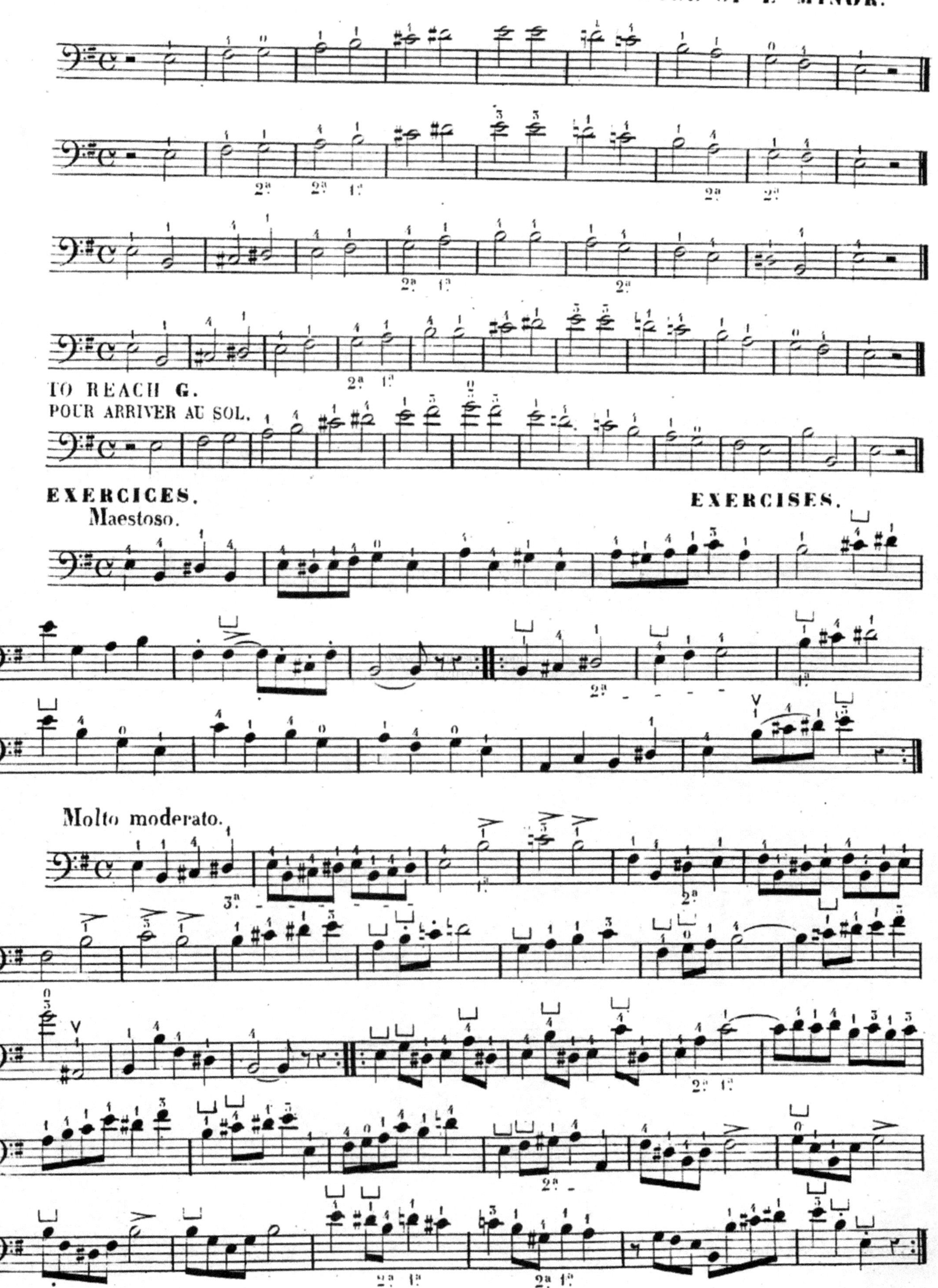

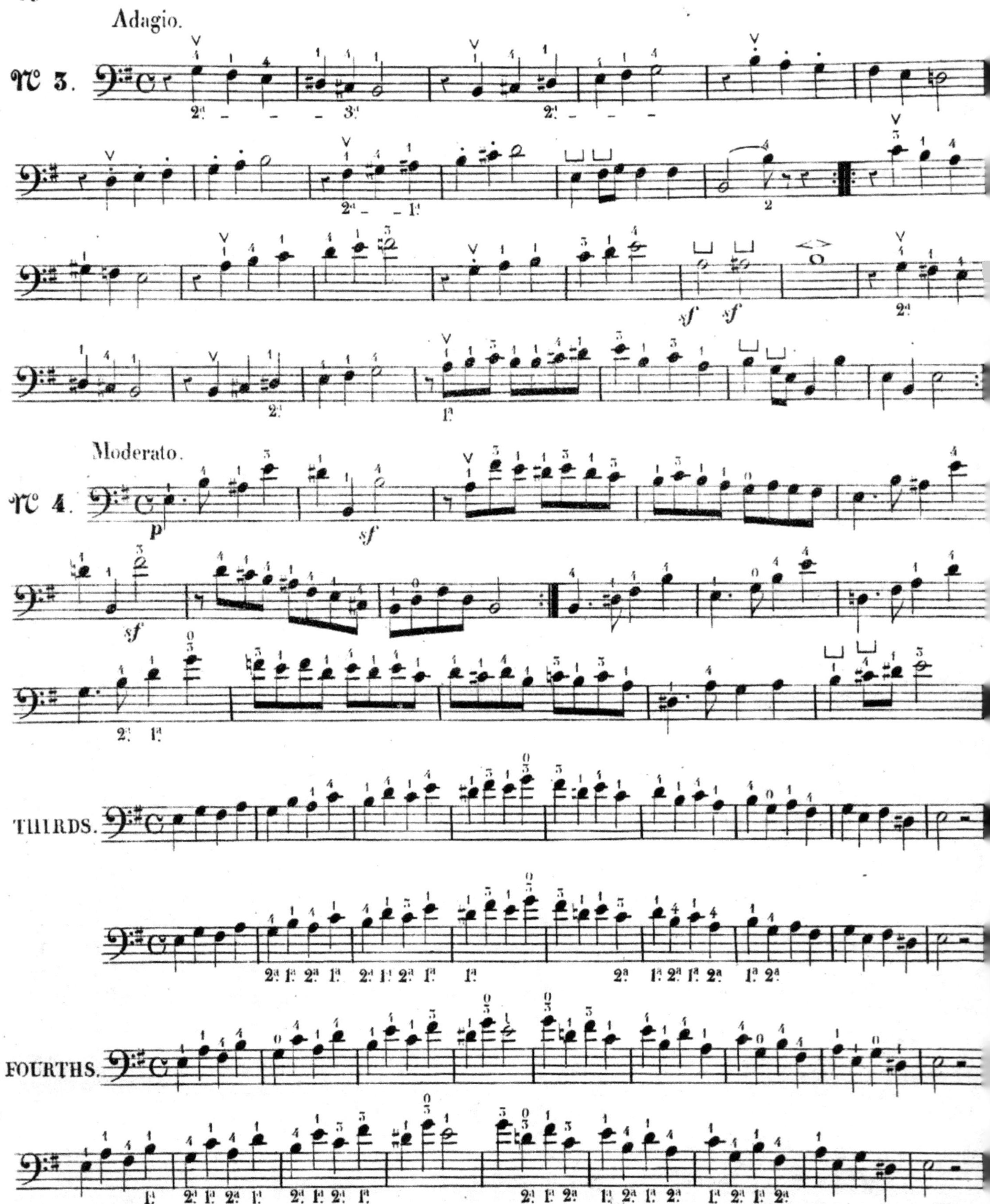


The Intervals of Fifths, same as in the preceding scales.

For octaves we must use the fingering of the scale of G, except C♯ and D♯ the sixth and seventh augmented.

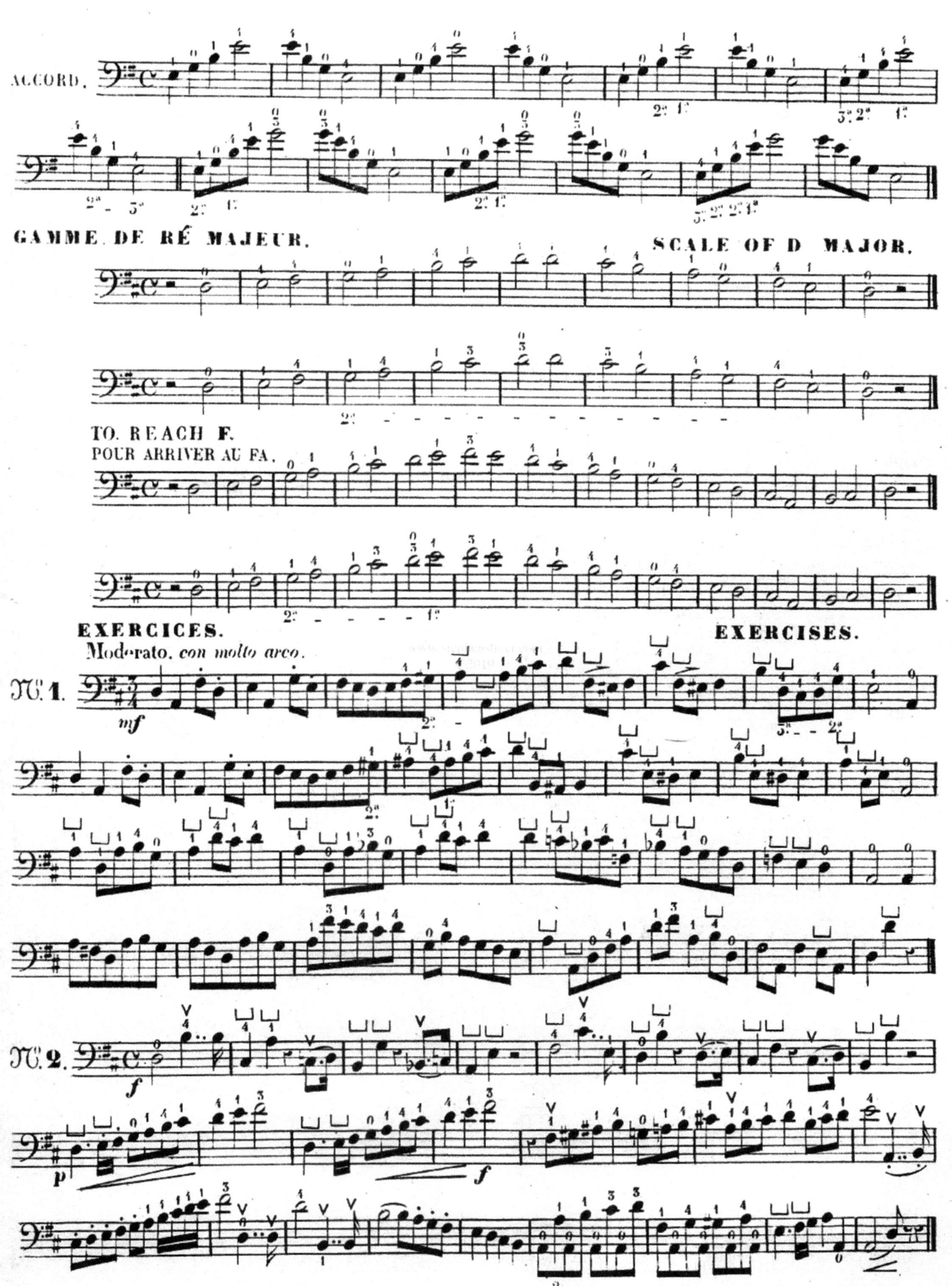
ACCORD.
GAMME DE RÉ MAJEUR.
SCALE OF D MAJOR.
TO. REACH F.
POUR ARRIVER AU FA.
EXERCICES.
EXERCISES.
Moderato. con molto arco.
Nº 1.
mf
Nº 2.
f
p

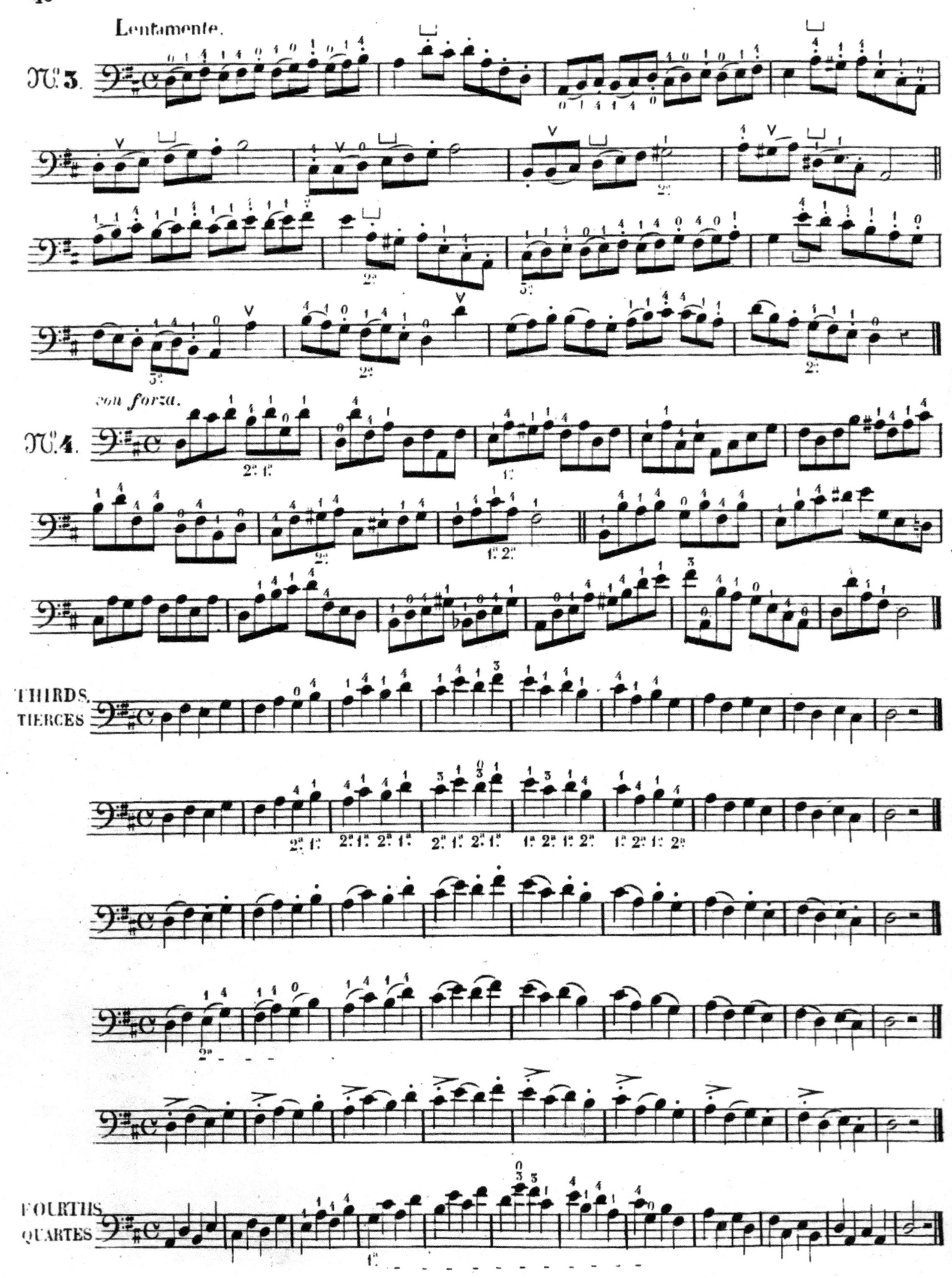
Lentamente.
N.o 3.
con forza.
N.o 4.
THIRDS.
TIERCES
FOURTHS
QUARTES

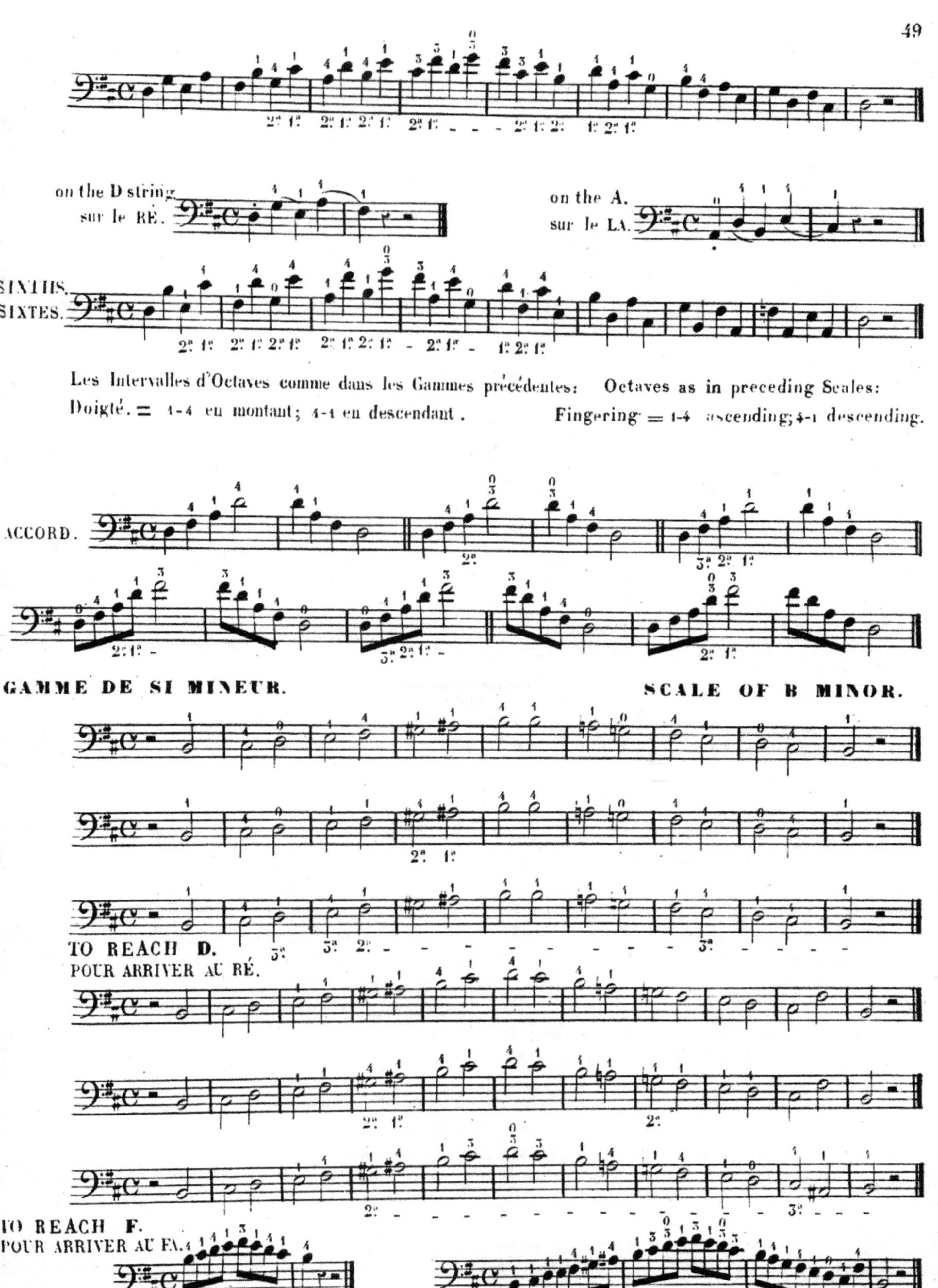
on the D string.
sur le RÉ.
on the A.
sur le LA.
SIXTHS.
SIXTES.
Les Intervalles d'Octaves comme dans les Gammes précédentes:
Doigté. = 1-4 en montant; 4-1 en descendant.
Octaves as in preceding Scales:
Fingering = 1-4 ascending; 4-1 descending.
ACCORD.
GAMME DE SI MINEUR.
SCALE OF B MINOR.
TO REACH D.
POUR ARRIVER AU RÉ.
TO REACH F.
POUR ARRIVER AU FA.

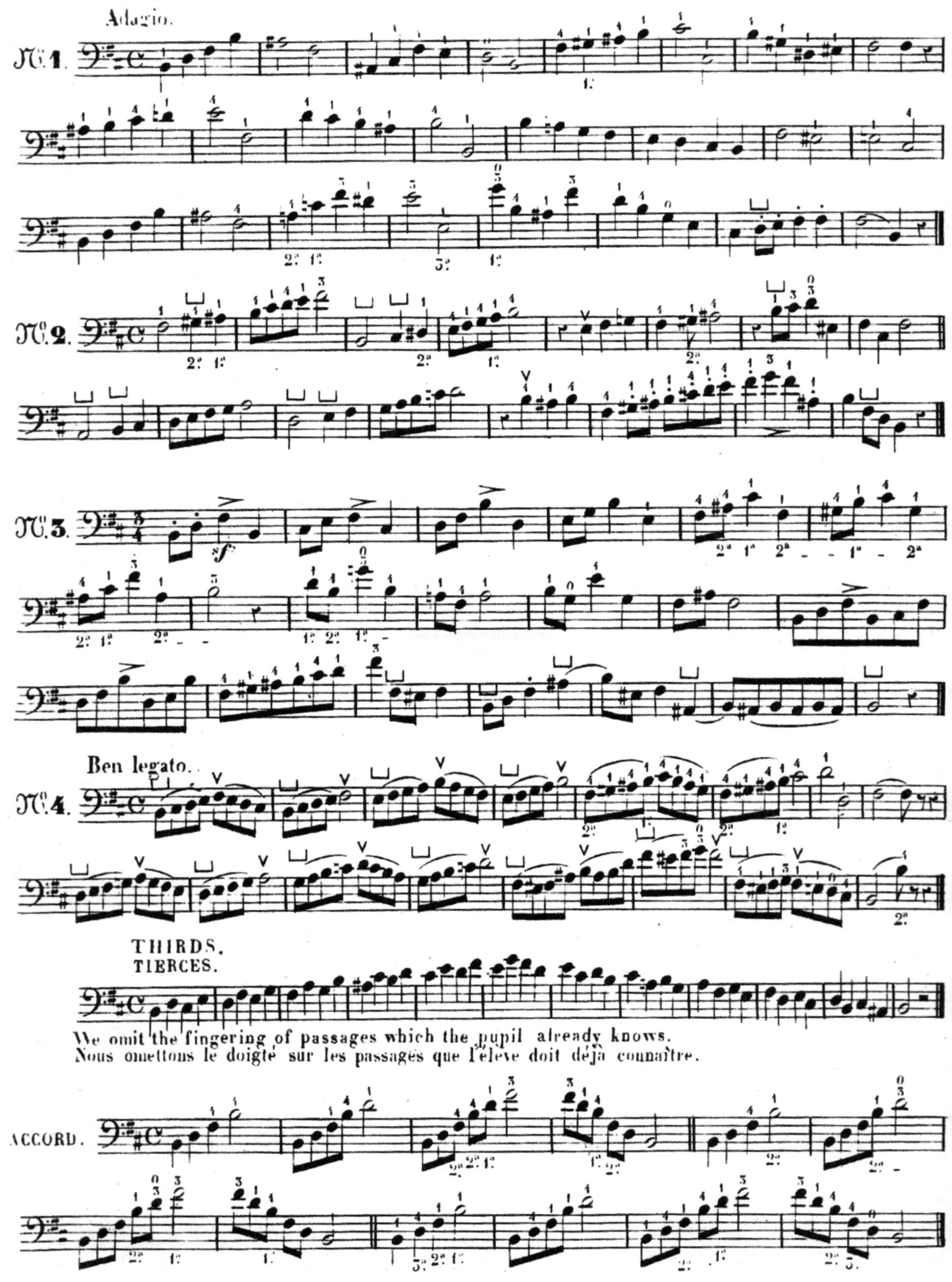
EXERCICES.
EXERCISES.
Adagio.
Nº 1.
Nº 2.
Nº 3.
Ben legato.
Nº 4.
THIRDS.
TIERCES.
We omit the fingering of passages which the pupil already knows.
Nous omettons le doigté sur les passages que l'élève doit déjà connaître.
ACCORD.

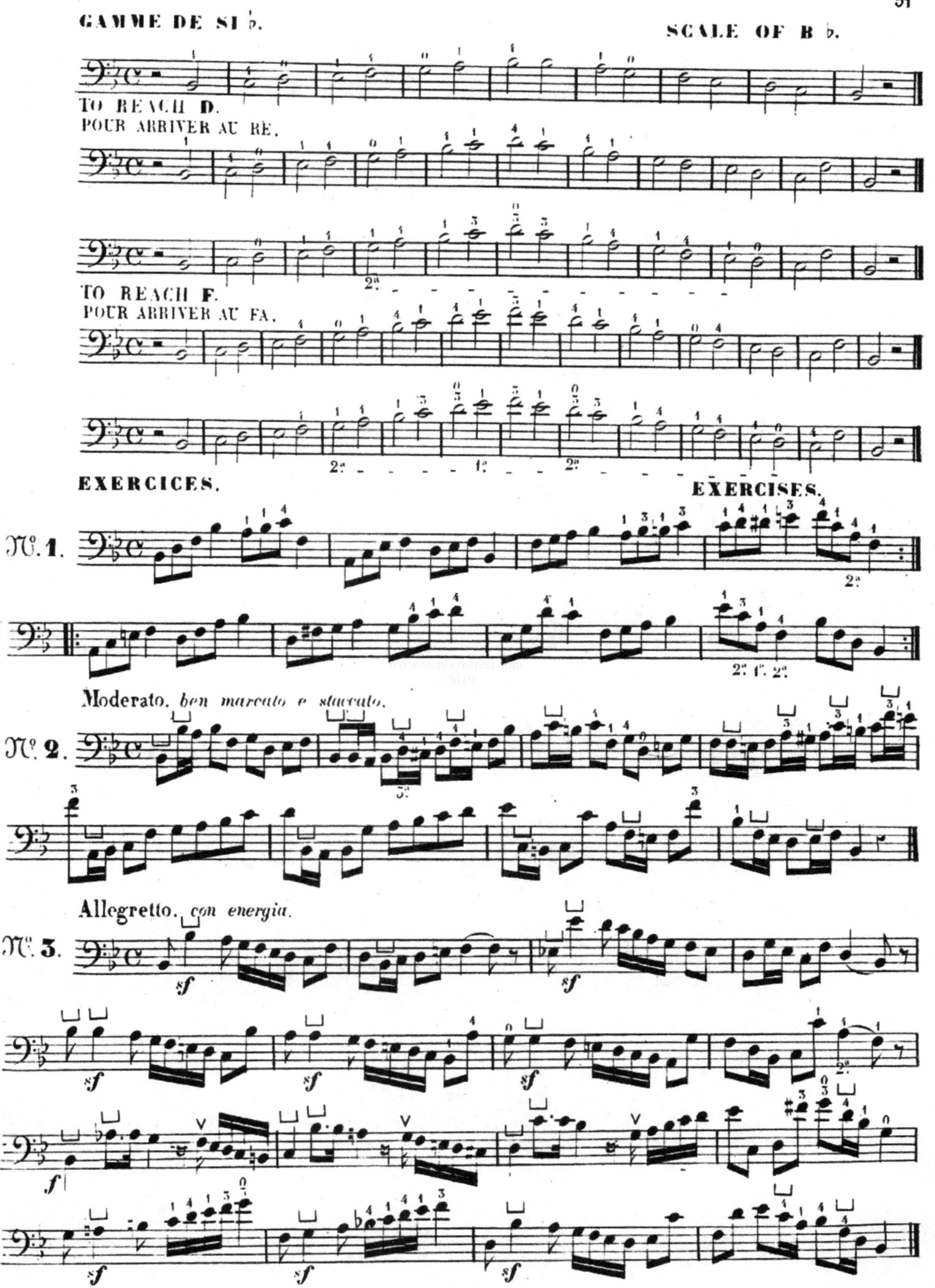
GAMME DE SI ♭.
SCALE OF B ♭.
TO REACH D.
POUR ARRIVER AU RE.
TO REACH F.
POUR ARRIVER AU FA.
EXERCICES.
EXERCISES.
Nº 1.
Moderato. ben marcato e staccato.
Nº 2.
Allegretto. con energia.
Nº 3.
sf
f

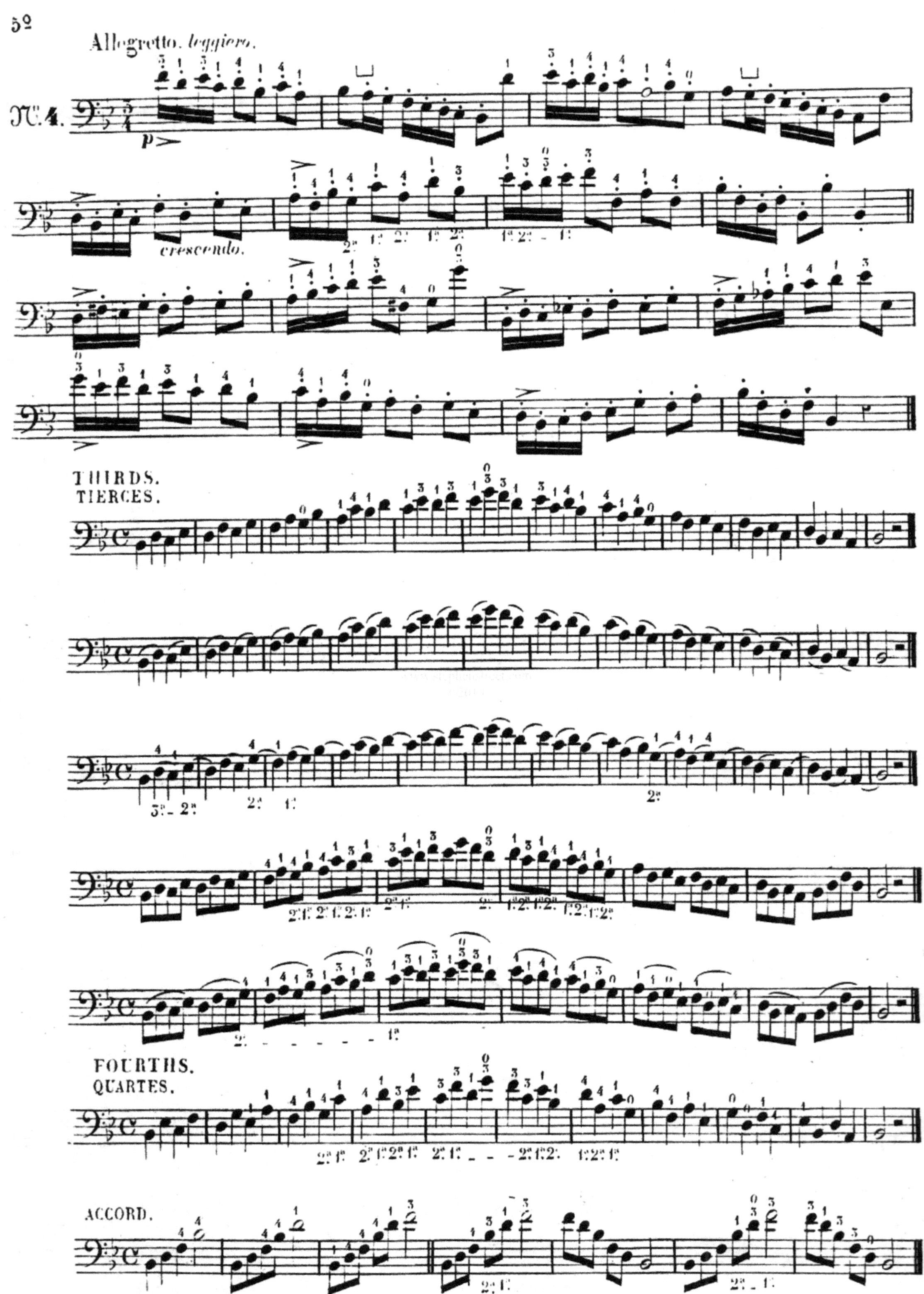
Allegretto. leggiero.
Nº. 4.
p
crescendo.
THIRDS.
TIERCES.
FOURTHS.
QUARTES.
ACCORD.

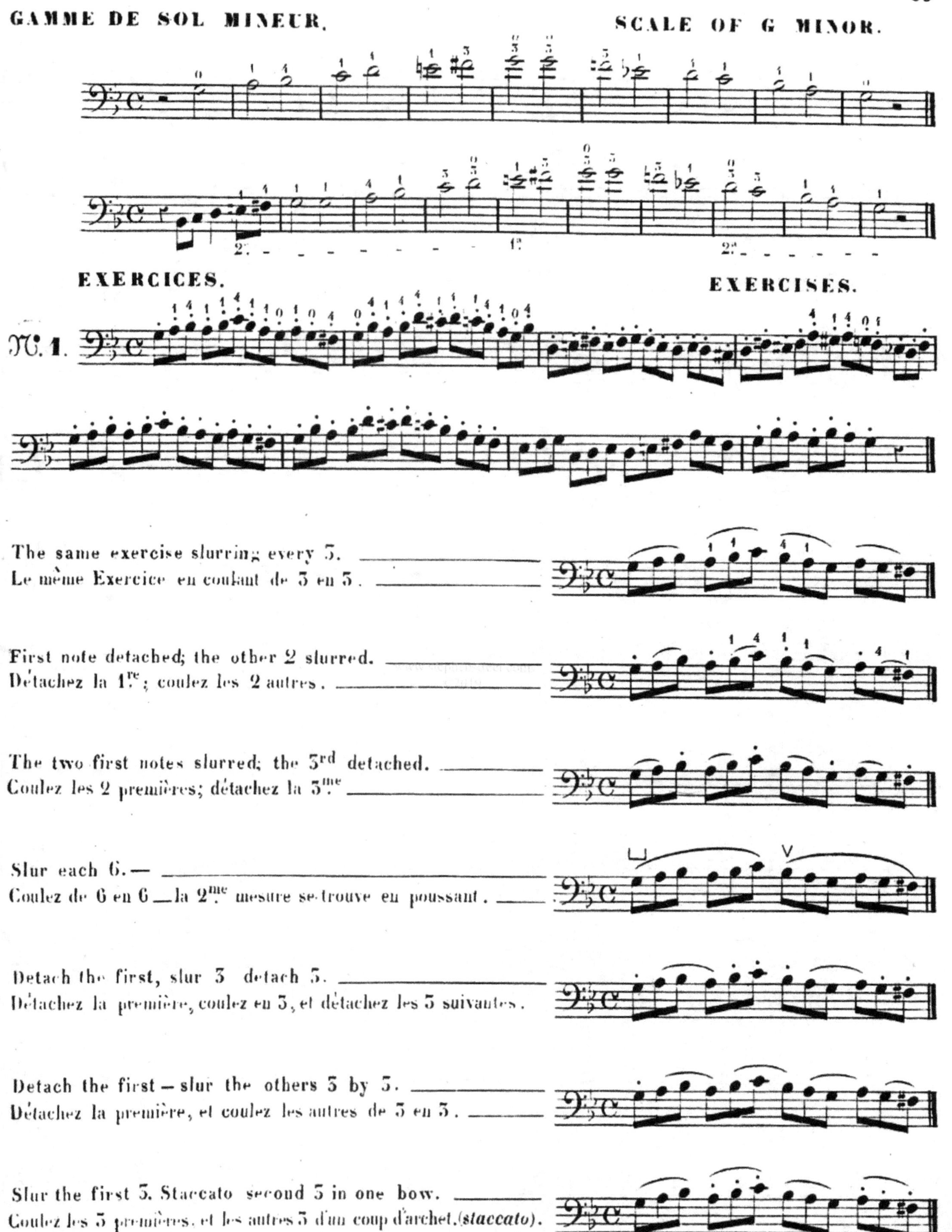
GAMME DE SOL MINEUR.
SCALE OF G MINOR.
EXERCICES.
EXERCISES.
Nº 1.
The same exercise slurring every 3.
Le même Exercice en coulant de 3 en 3.
First note detached; the other 2 slurred.
Détachez la 1.re; coulez les 2 autres.
The two first notes slurred; the 3rd detached.
Coulez les 2 premières; détachez la 3.me
Slur each 6.—
Coulez de 6 en 6 — la 2.me mesure se trouve en poussant.
Detach the first, slur 3 detach 3.
Détachez la première, coulez en 3, et détachez les 3 suivantes.
Detach the first — slur the others 3 by 3.
Détachez la première, et coulez les autres de 3 en 3.
Slur the first 3. Staccato second 3 in one bow.
Coulez les 3 premières, et les autres 3 d'un coup d'archet. (staccato).
We recommend this Exercise to the pupil.
Nous recommandons cet Exercice à l'Elève.

Emphasise the first note of each triplet.
Appuyez sur la premiere note de chaque Triolet.

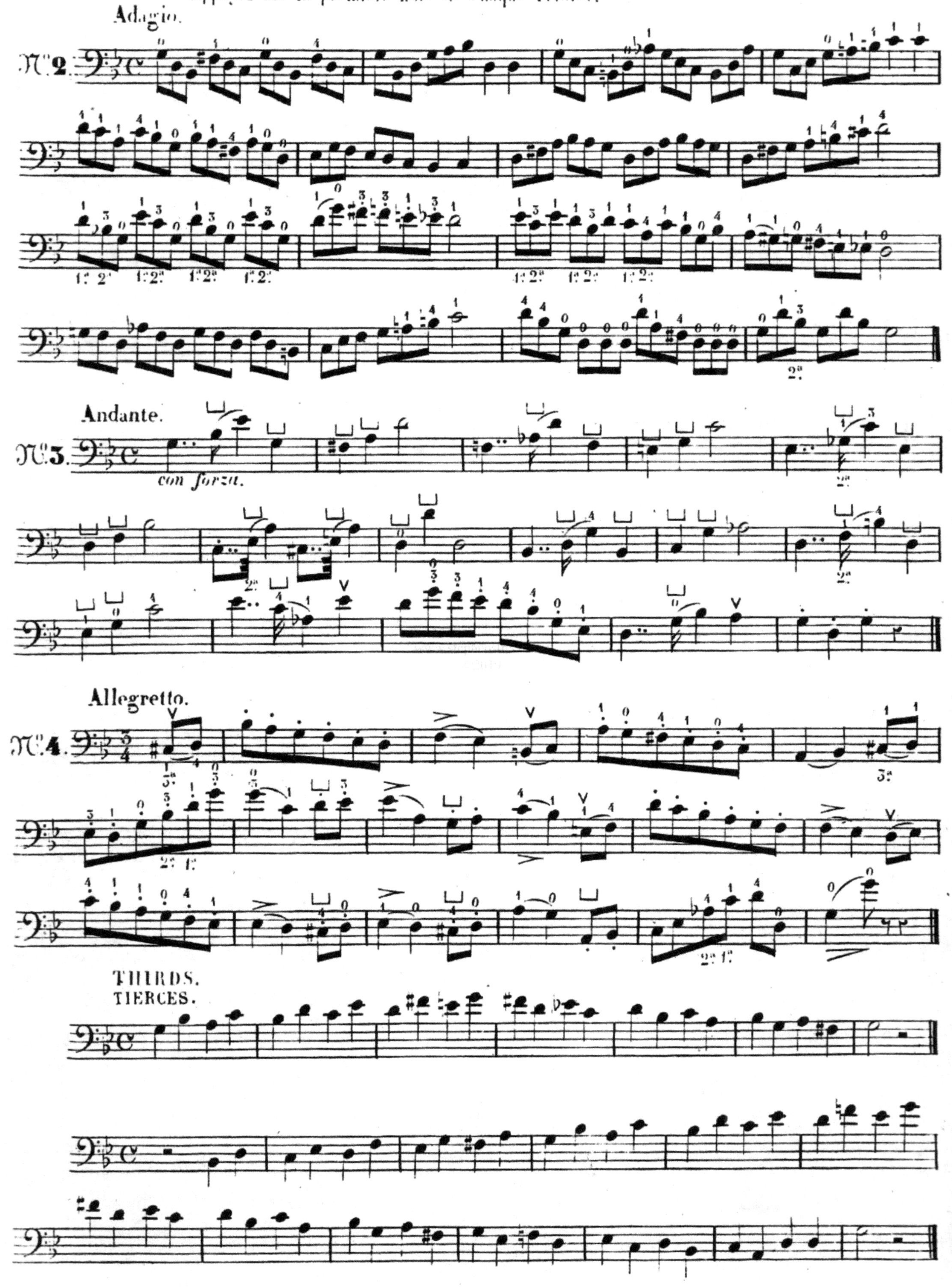

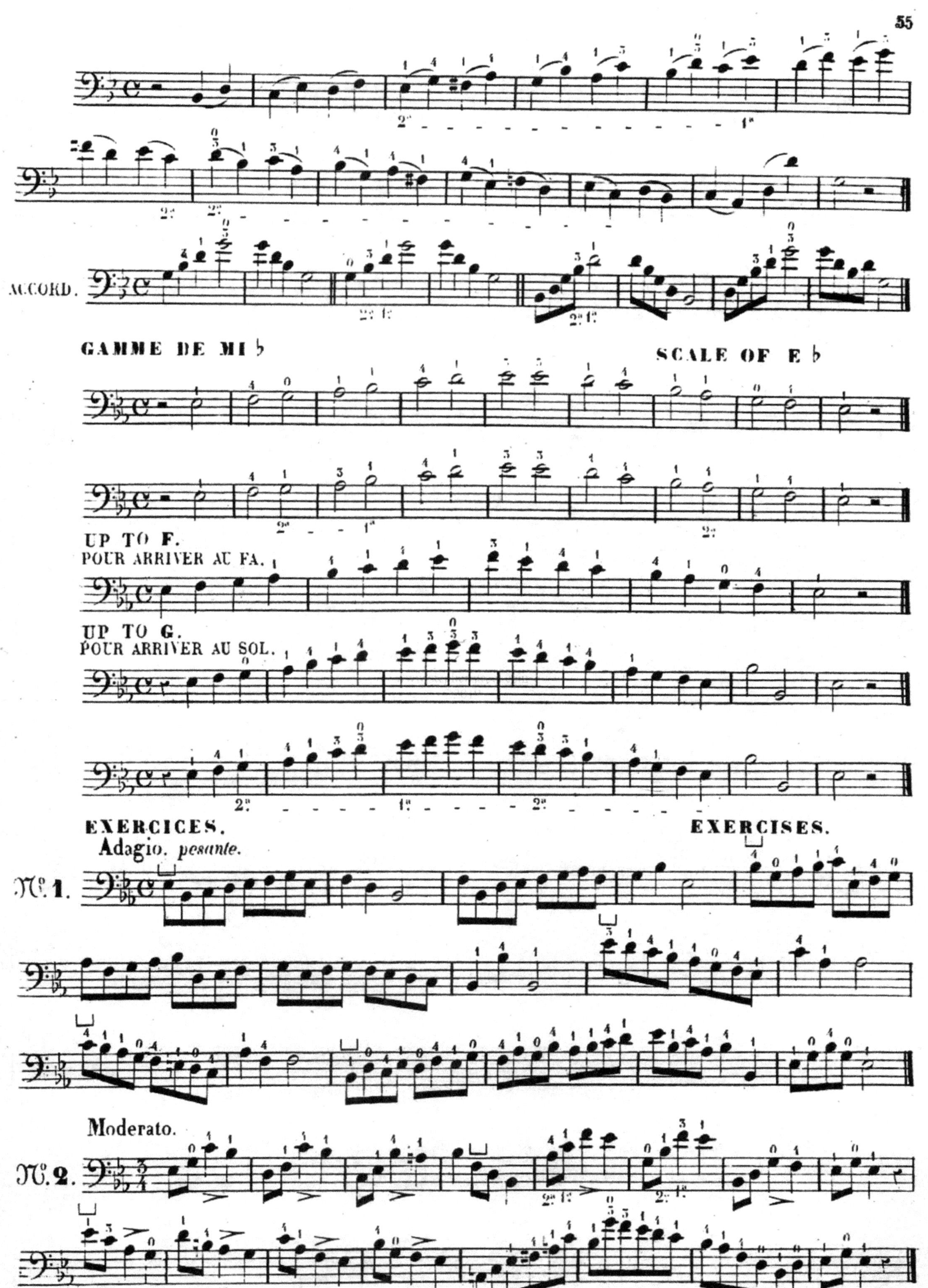
ACCORD.
GAMME DE MI ♭
SCALE OF E ♭
UP TO F.
POUR ARRIVER AU FA.
UP TO G.
POUR ARRIVER AU SOL.
EXERCICES.
EXERCISES.
Adagio. pesante.
Nº 1.
Moderato.
Nº 2.

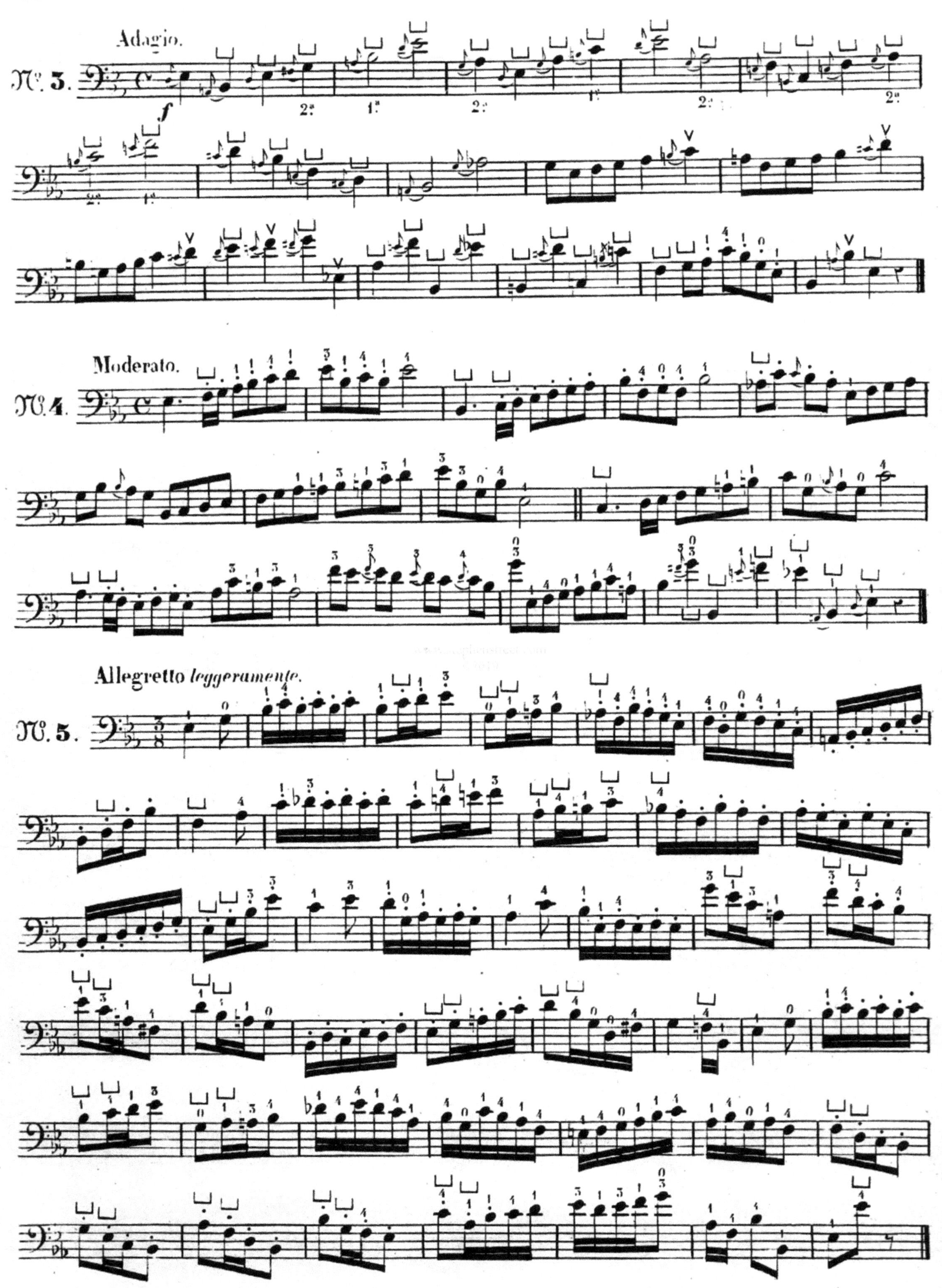
Adagio.
Nº 3.
Moderato.
Nº 4.
Allegretto leggeramente.
Nº 5.

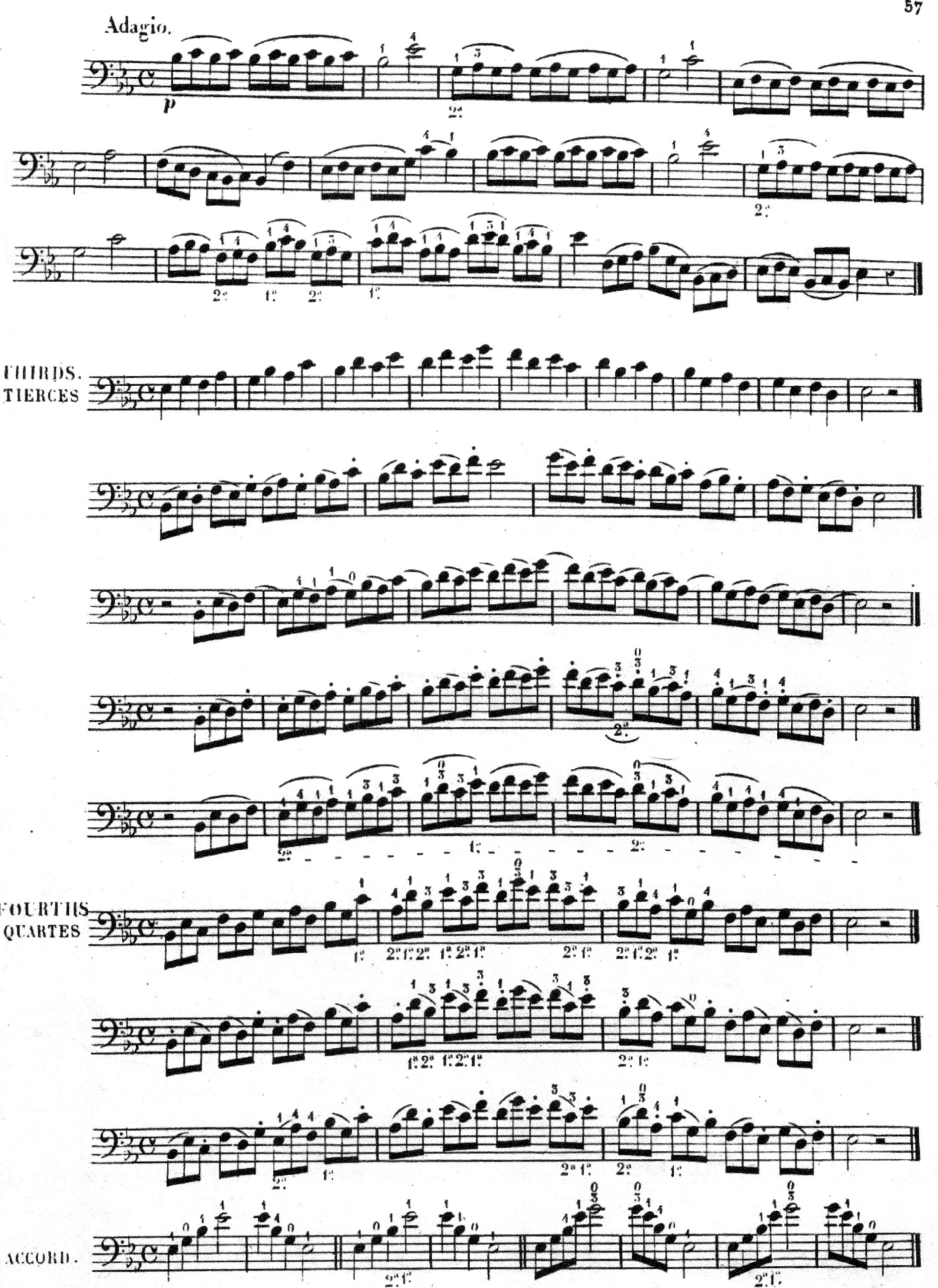
Adagio.
p
THIRDS.
TIERCES
FOURTHS
QUARTES
ACCORD.

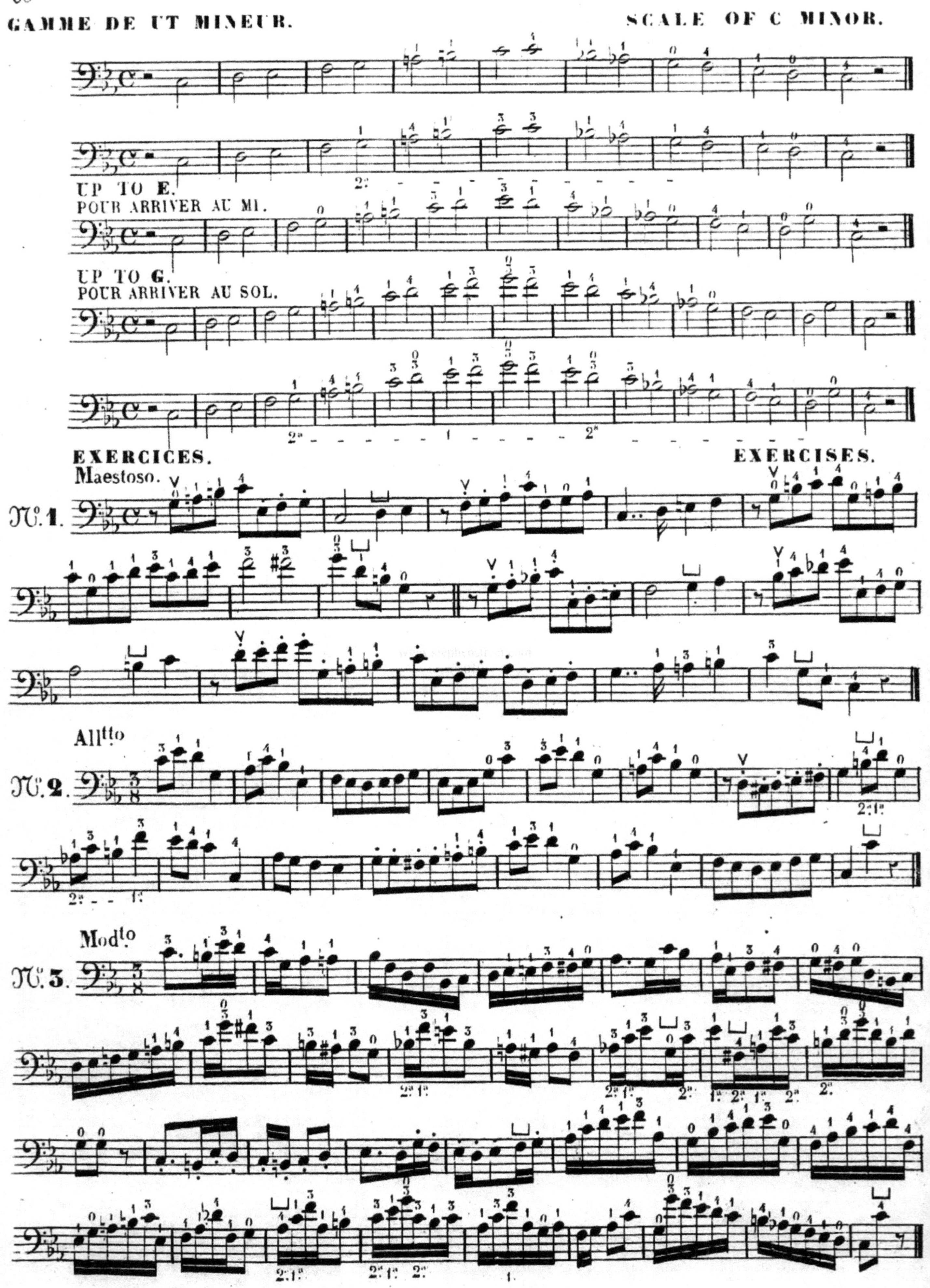
GAMME DE UT MINEUR.
SCALE OF C MINOR.
UP TO E.
POUR ARRIVER AU MI.
UP TO G.
POUR ARRIVER AU SOL.
EXERCICES.
EXERCISES.
Maestoso.
Nº 1.
Alltto
Nº 2.
Modto
Nº 3.

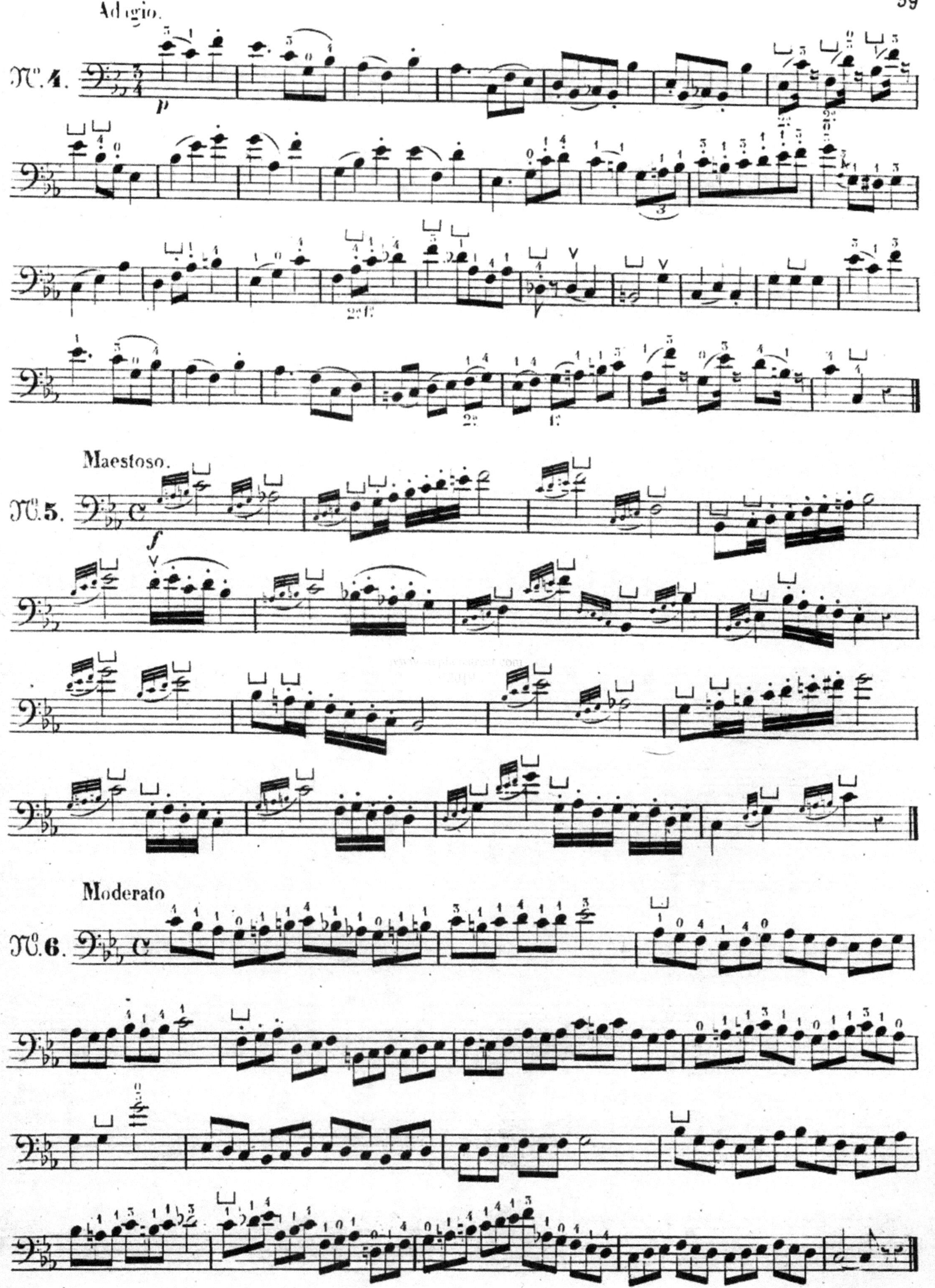
Adagio.
Nº. 4.
Maestoso.
Nº. 5.
Moderato
Nº. 6.

THIRDS.
TIERCES.

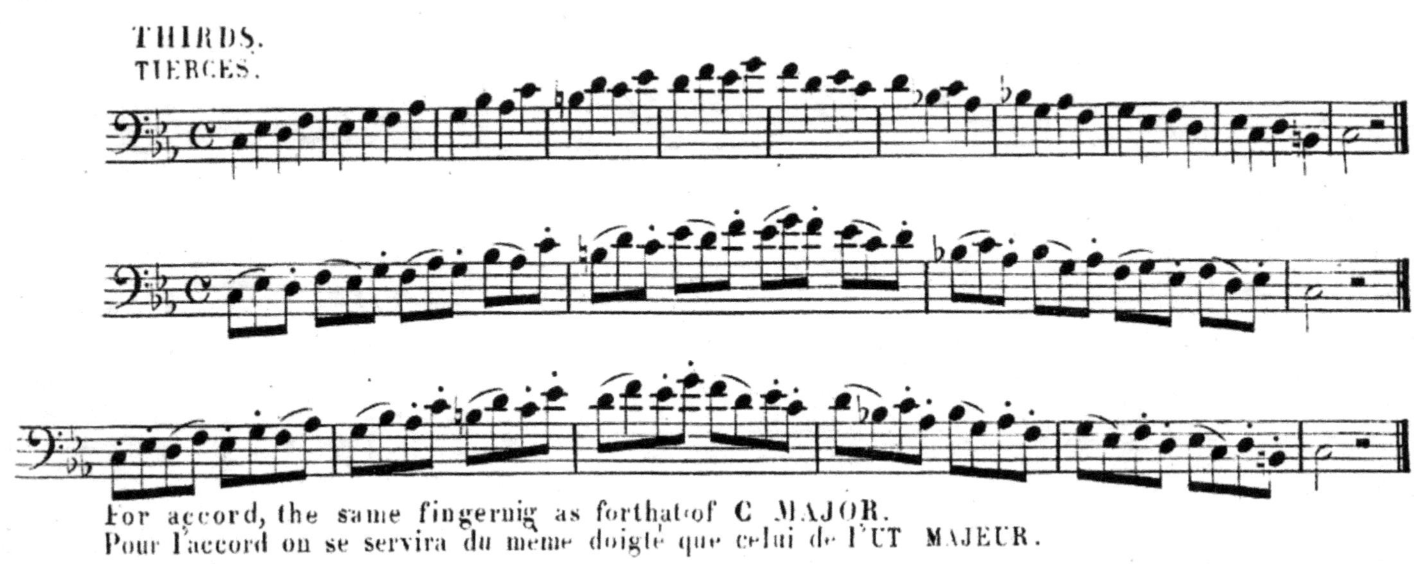

For accord, the same fingernig as forthat of C MAJOR.
Pour l'accord on se servira du même doigté que celui de l'UT MAJEUR.

## GAMME DE LA MAJEUR. / SCALE OF A MAJOR.

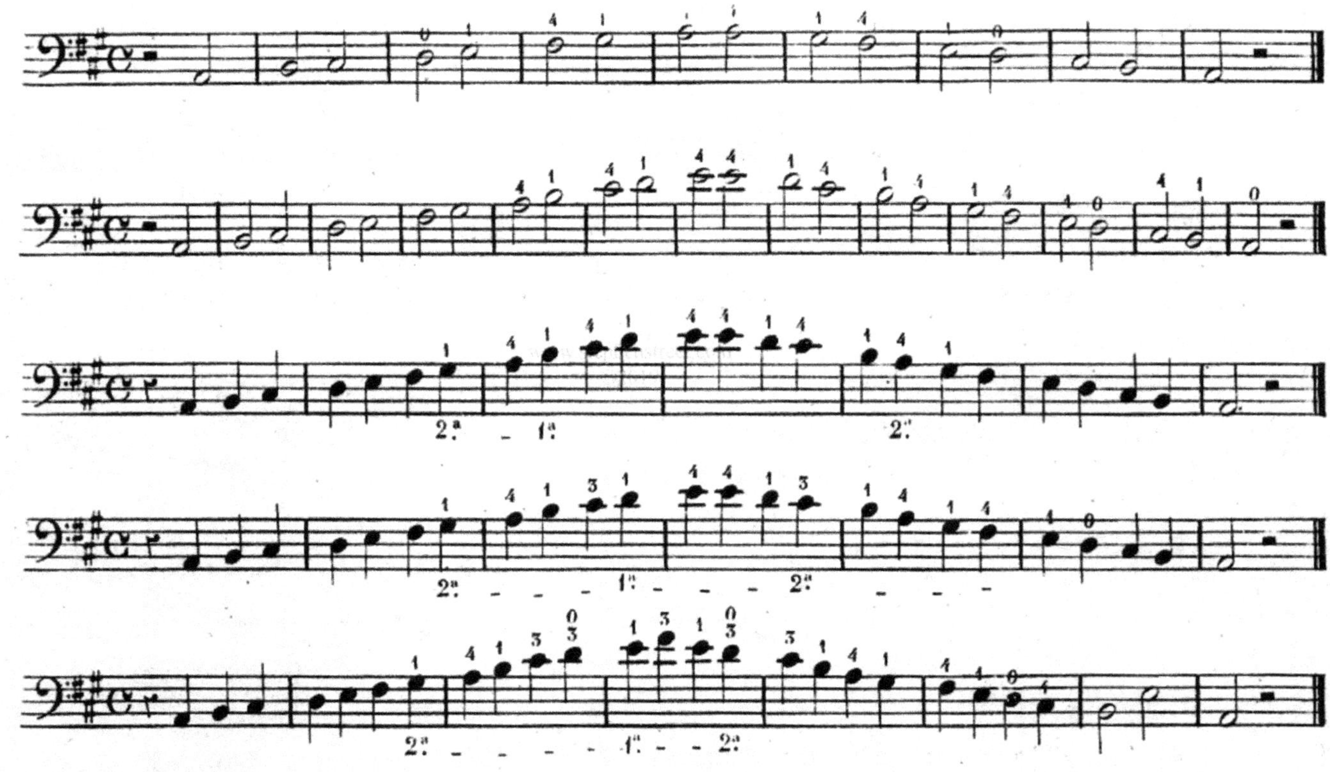

## EXERCICES. / EXERCISES.

Allegro energia.

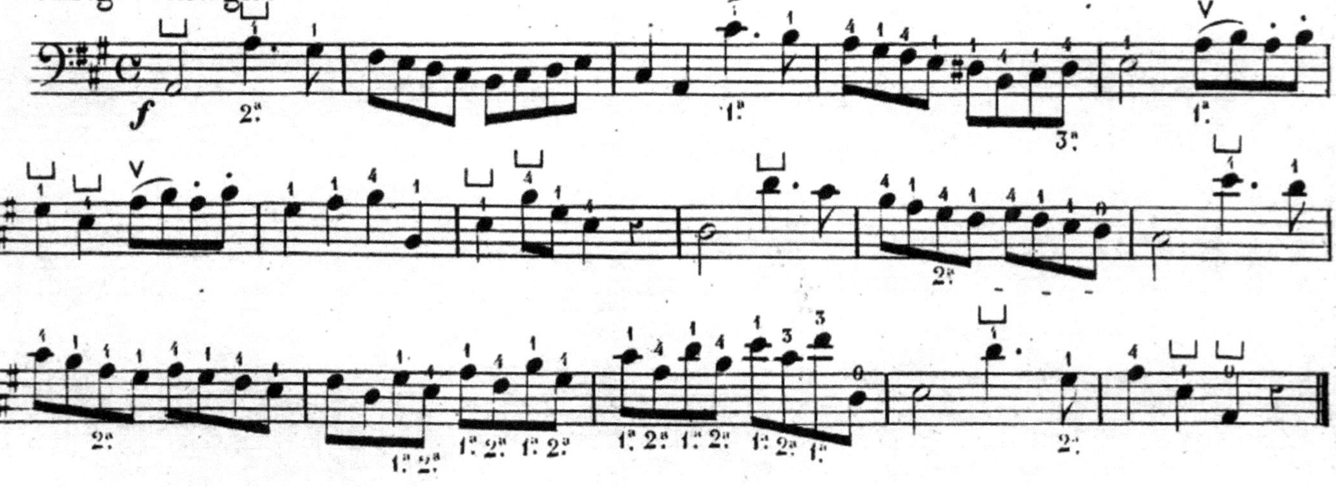

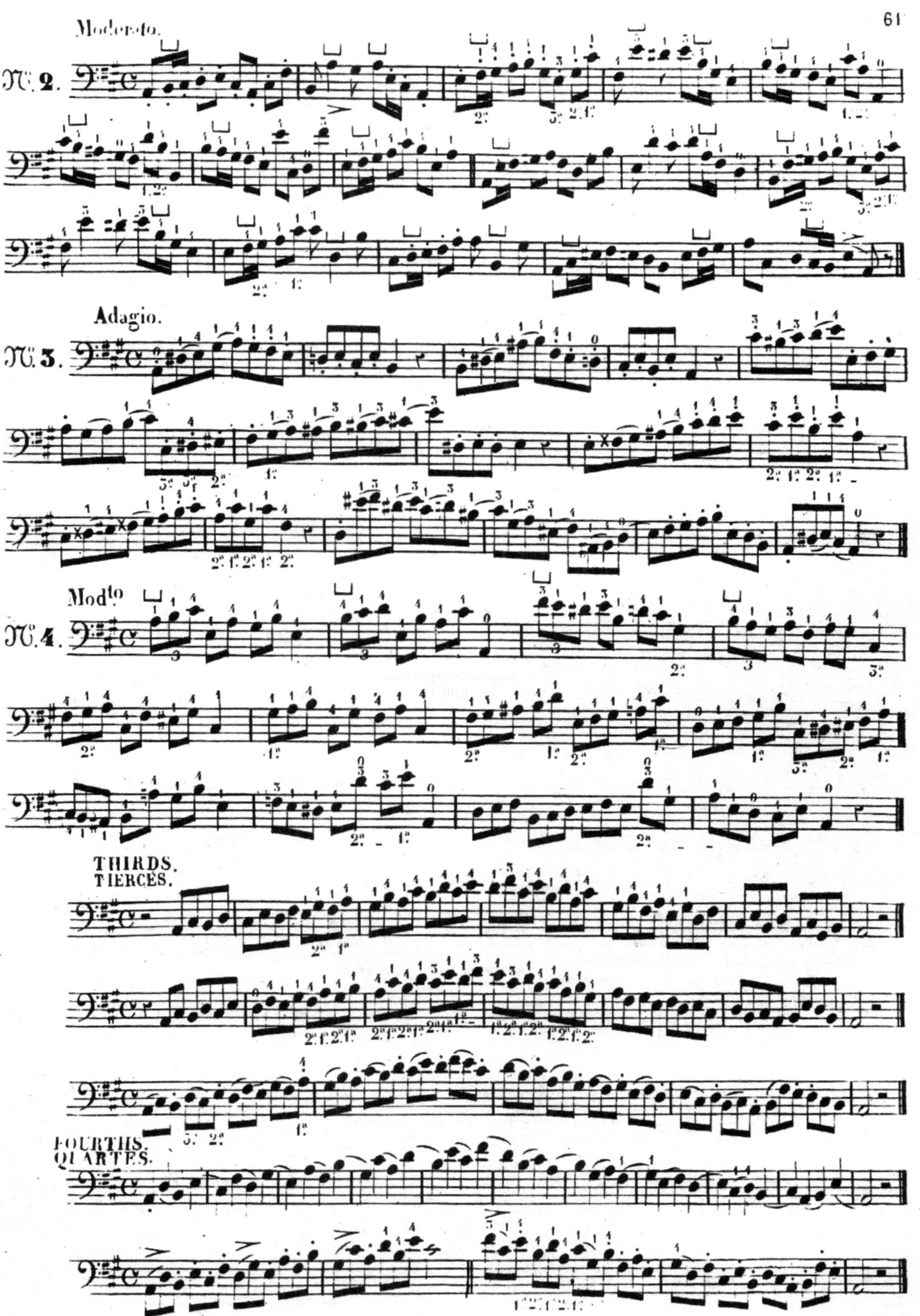
Moderato.
No. 2.
Adagio.
No. 3.
Modto
No. 4.
THIRDS.
TIERCES.
FOURTHS.
QUARTES.

GAMME DE FA♯ MINEUR. SCALE OF F♯ MINOR.

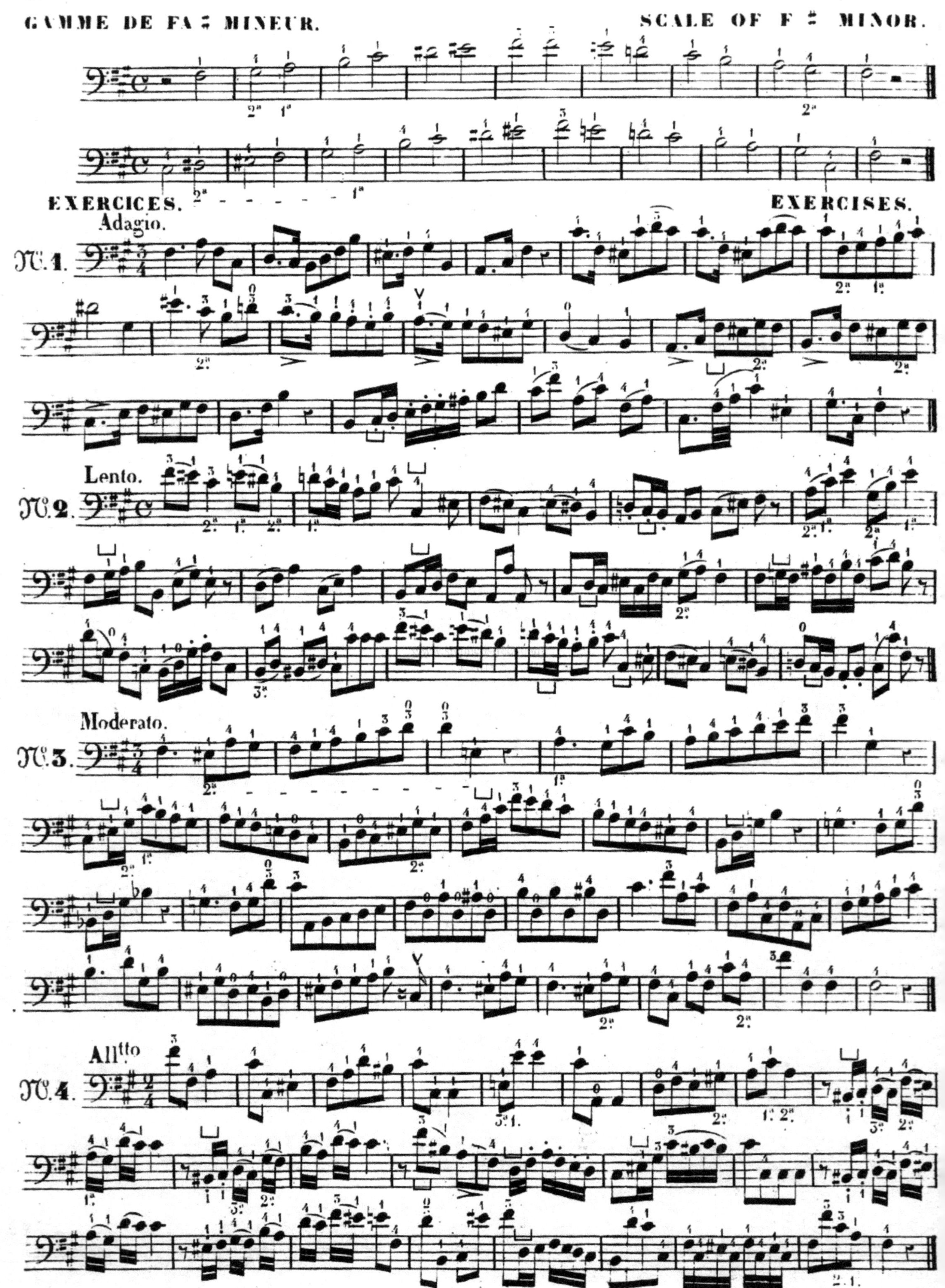

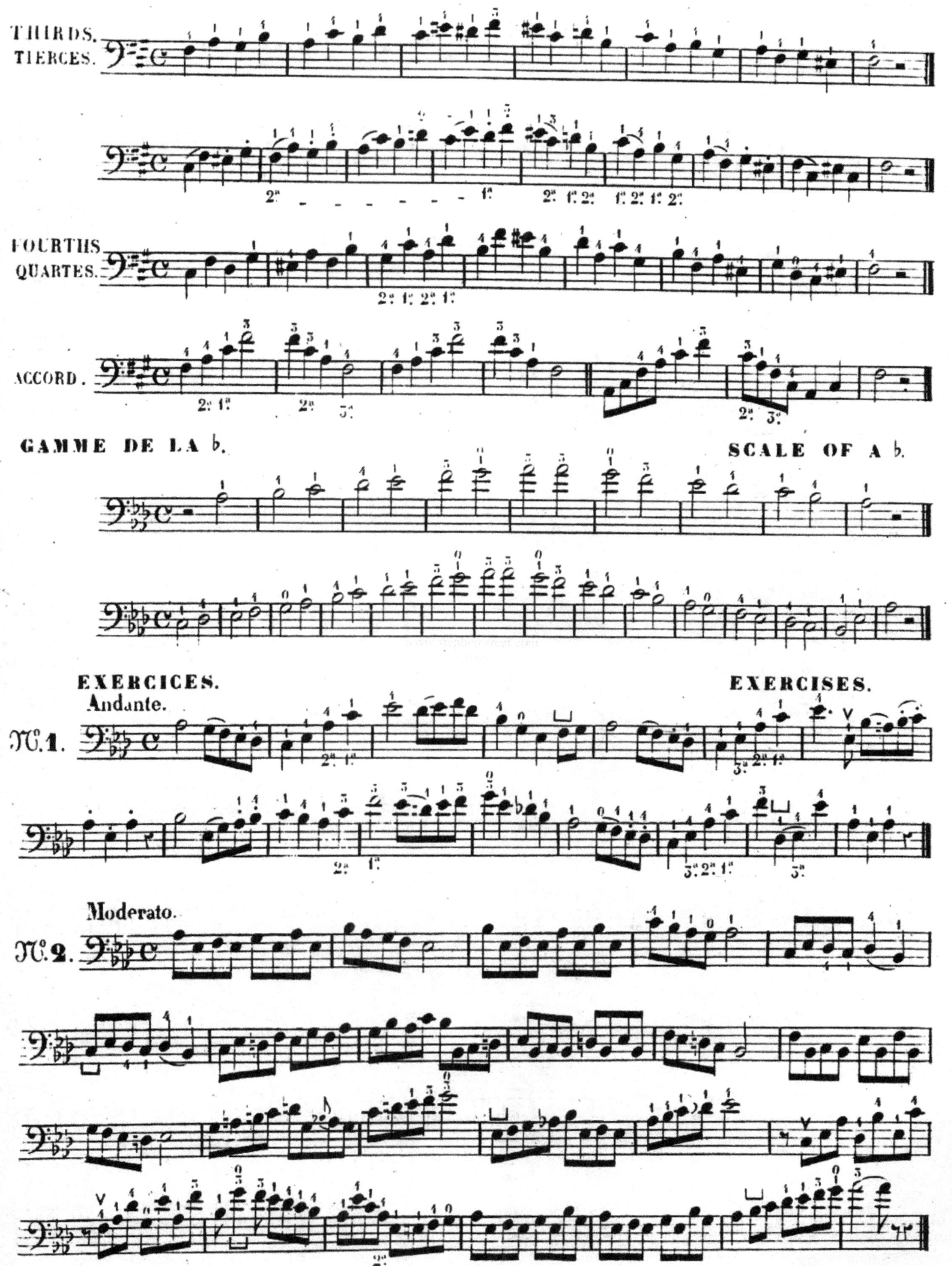
THIRDS.
TIERCES.
FOURTHS
QUARTES.
ACCORD.
GAMME DE LA ♭.
SCALE OF A ♭.
EXERCICES.
EXERCISES.
Andante.
Nº 1.
Moderato.
Nº 2.

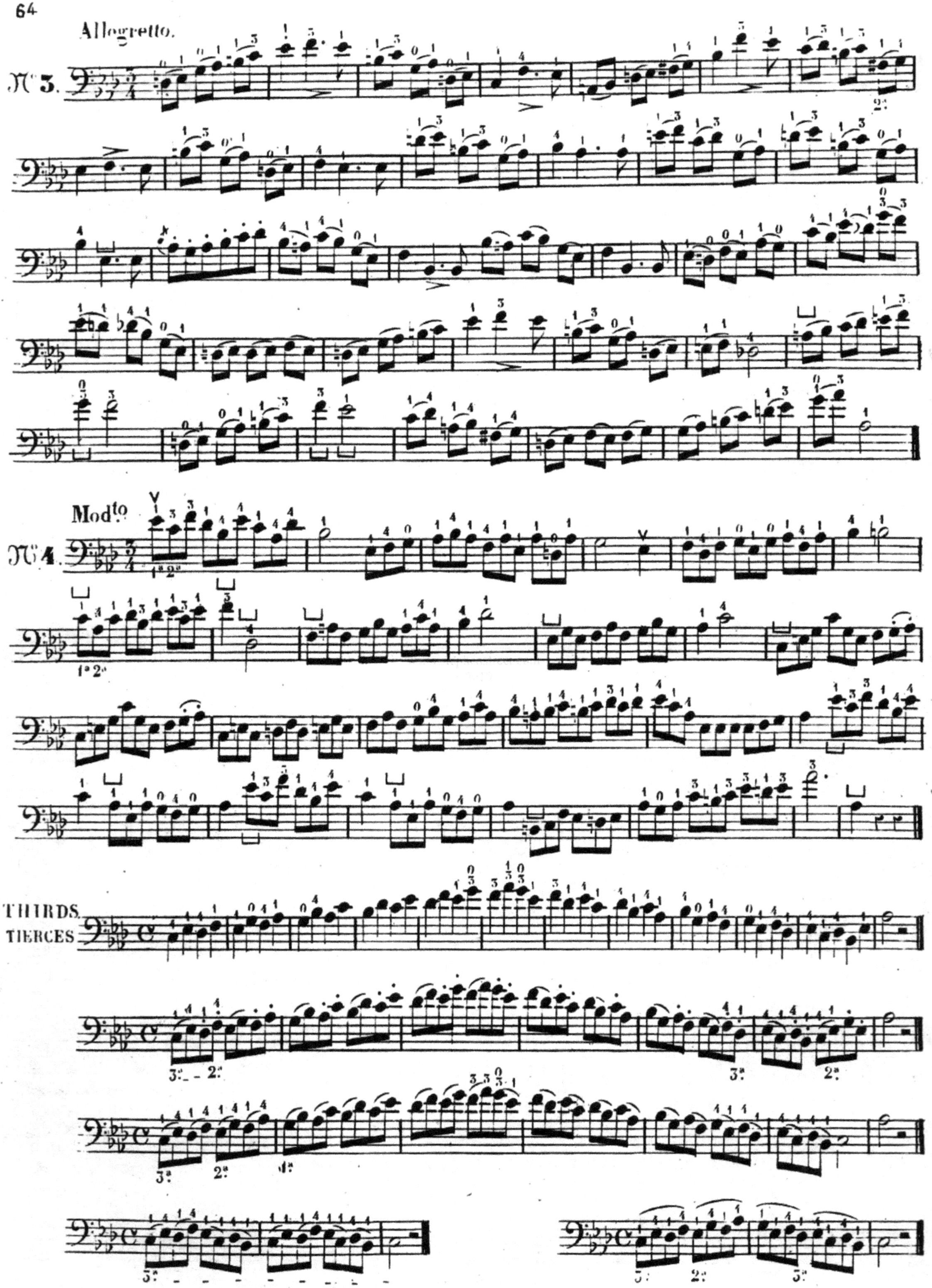
Allegretto.
N° 3.
Mod^to
N° 4.
THIRDS
TIERCES

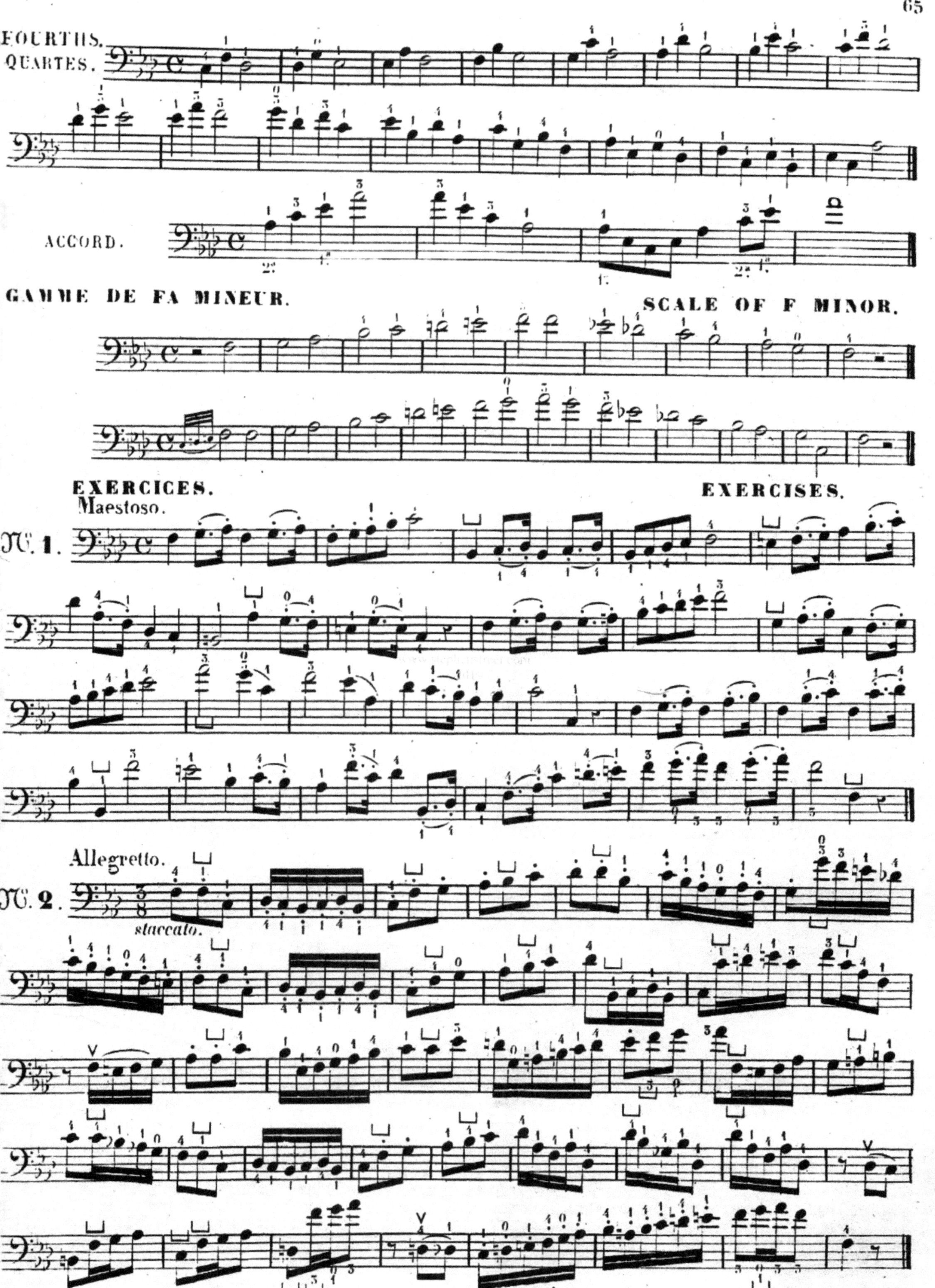
FOURTHS.
QUARTES.
ACCORD.
GAMME DE FA MINEUR.
SCALE OF F MINOR.
EXERCICES.
EXERCISES.
Maestoso.
Nº 1.
Allegretto.
Nº 2.
staccato.

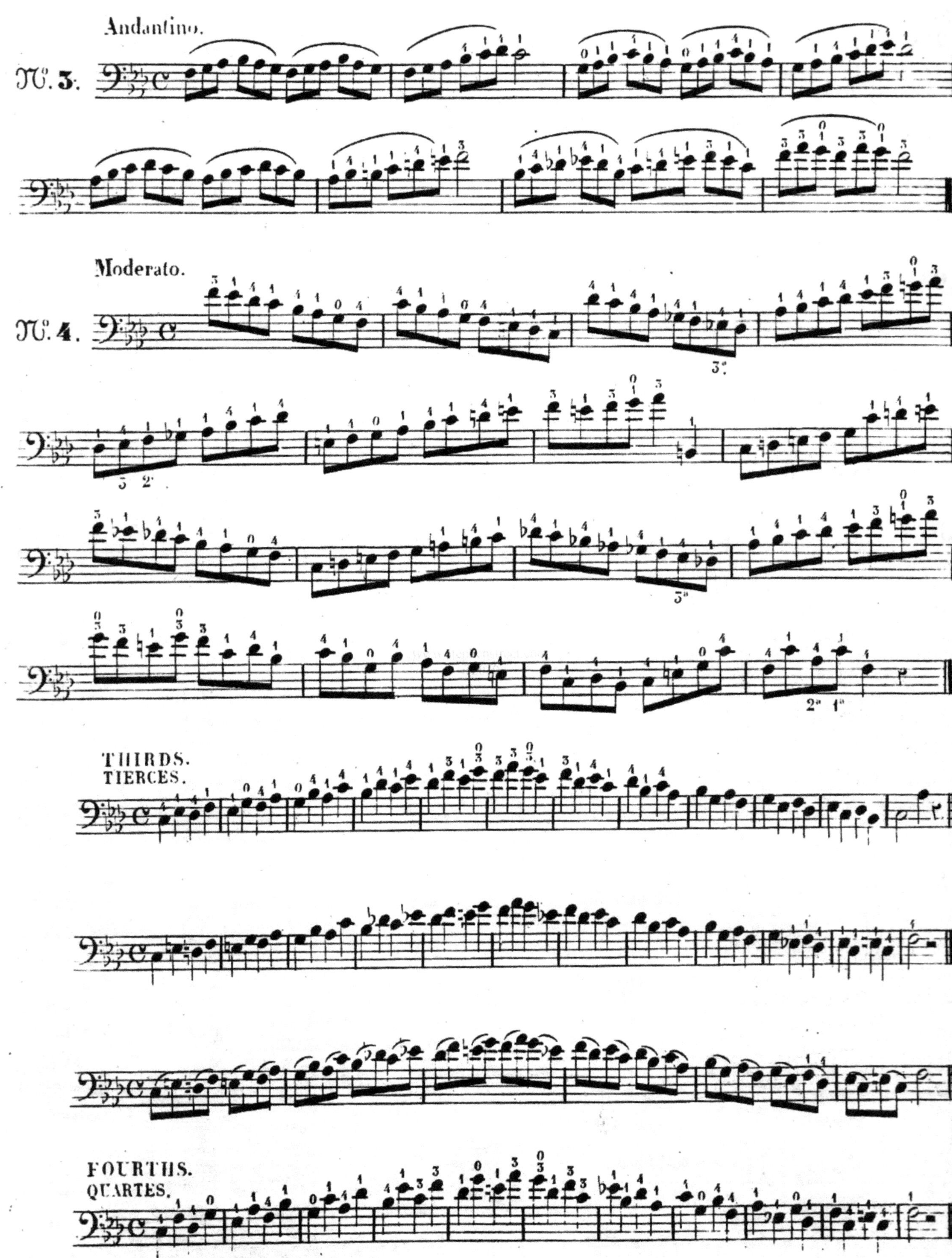
Andantino.
No. 3.
Moderato.
No. 4.
THIRDS.
TIERCES.
FOURTHS.
QUARTES.

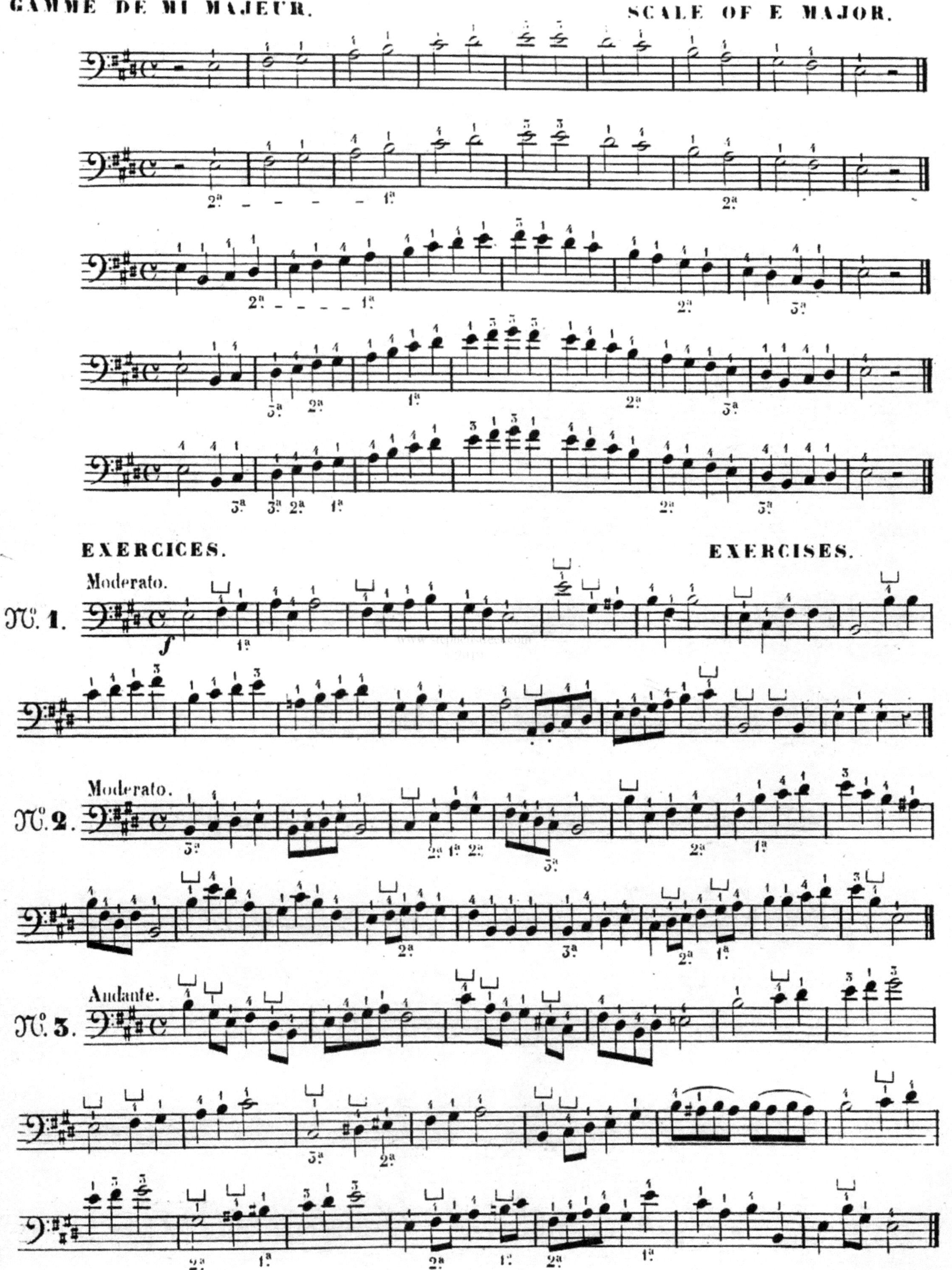
GAMME DE MI MAJEUR.
SCALE OF E MAJOR.
EXERCICES.
EXERCISES.
Moderato.
No. 1.
Moderato.
No. 2.
Andante.
No. 3.

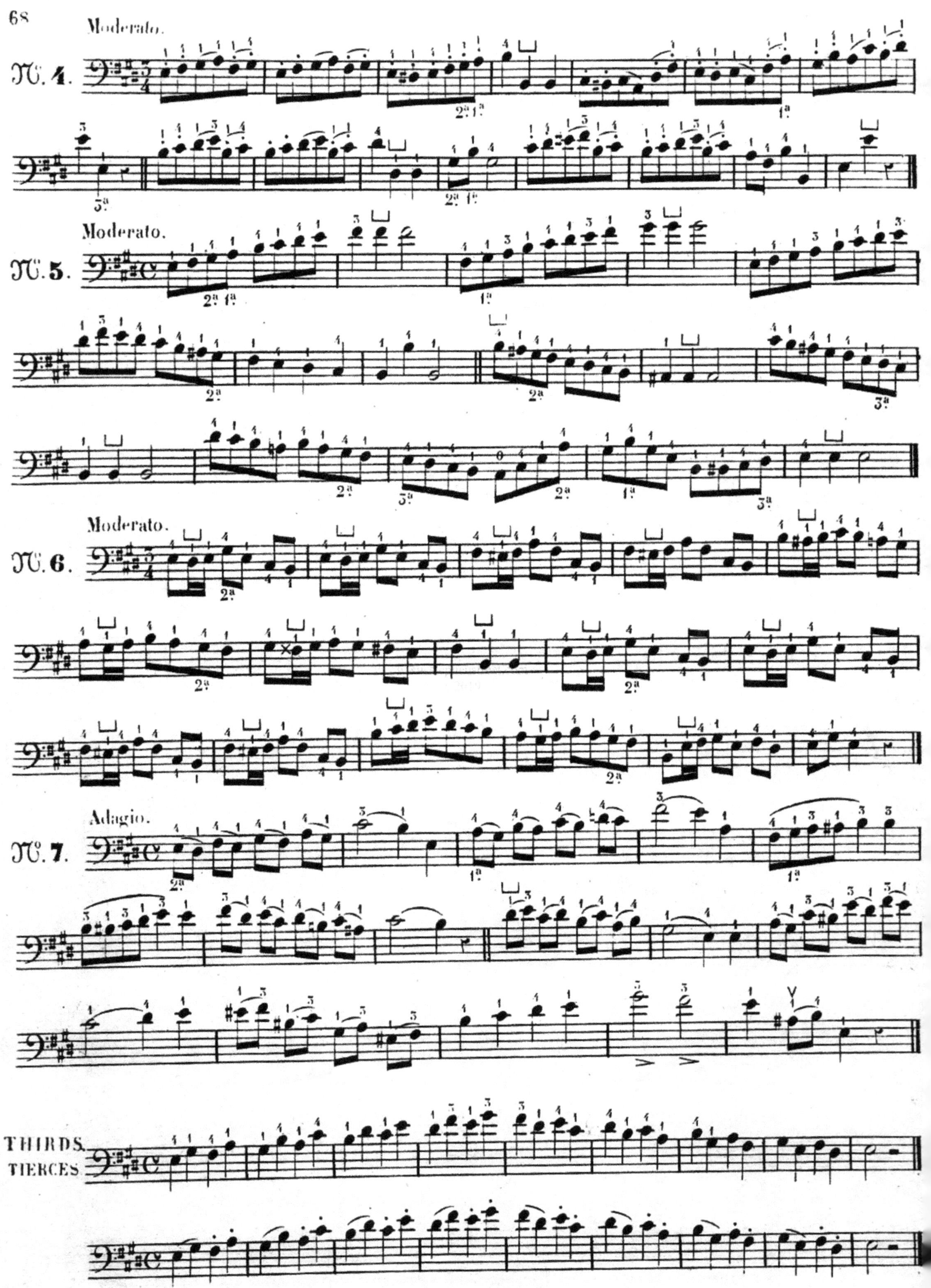
Moderato.
N.º 4.
Moderato.
N.º 5.
Moderato.
N.º 6.
Adagio.
N.º 7.
THIRDS.
TIERCES

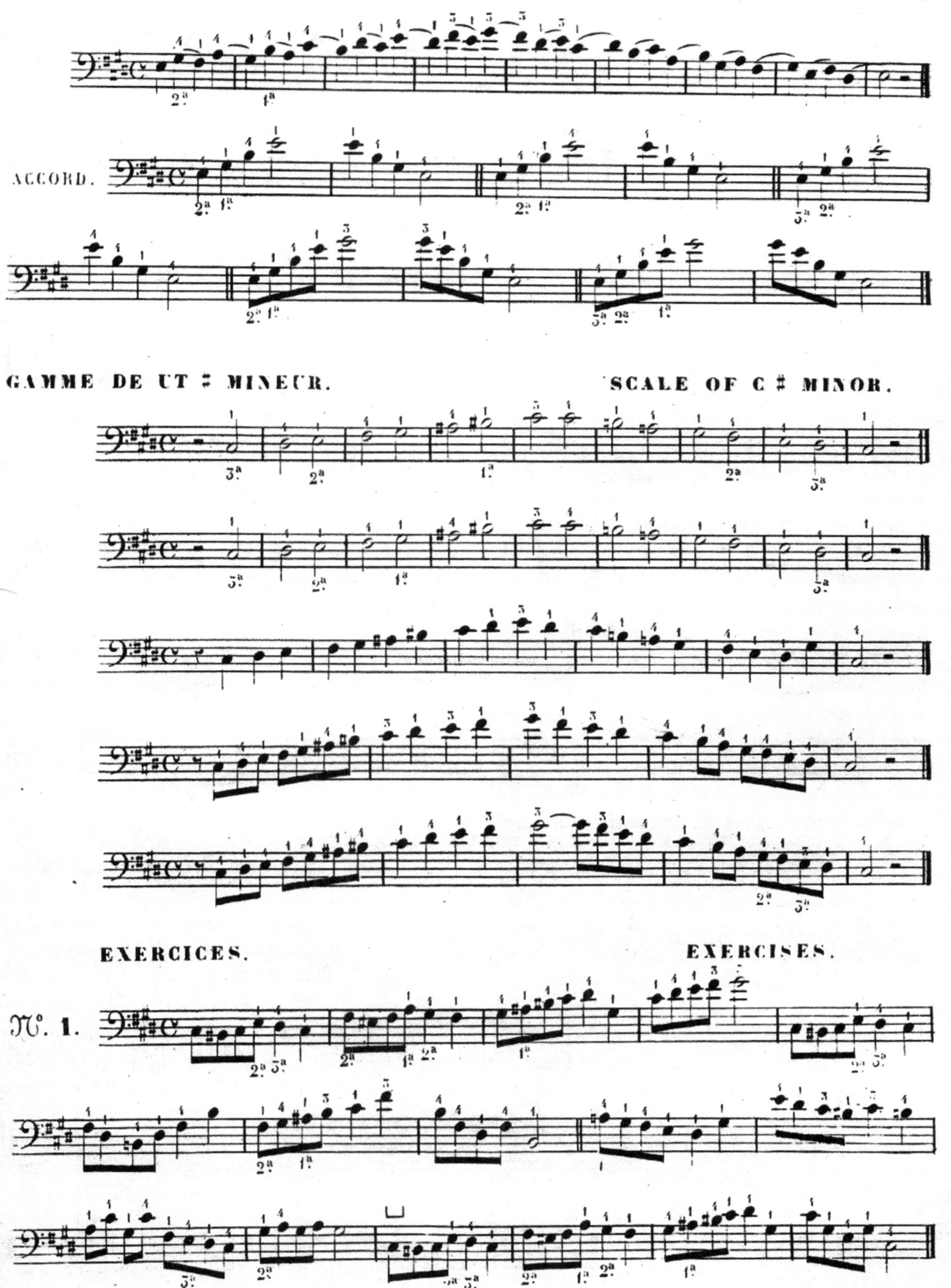
ACCORD.
GAMME DE UT ♯ MINEUR.
SCALE OF C ♯ MINOR.
EXERCICES.
EXERCISES.
N°. 1.

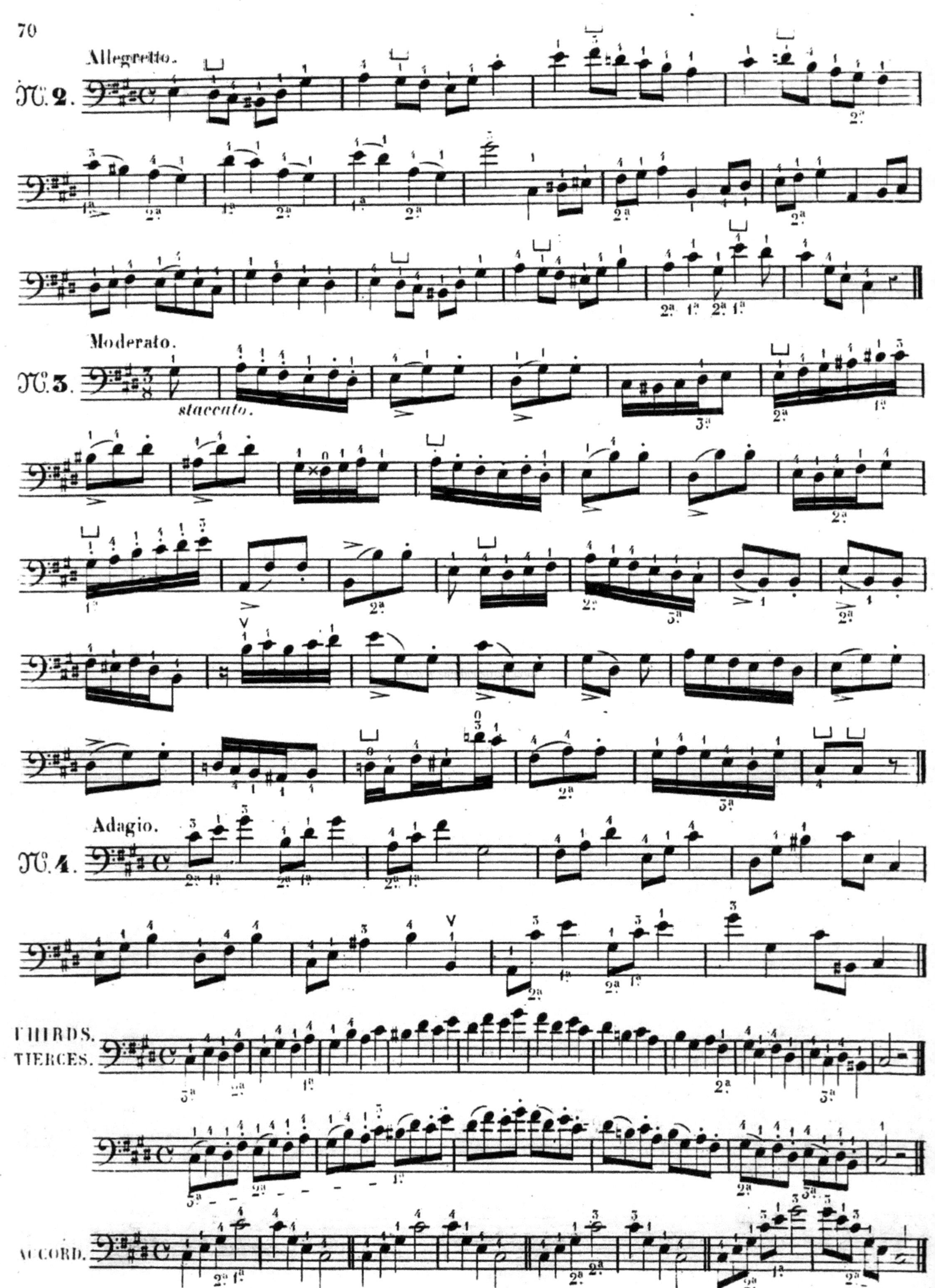
Allegretto.
N.º 2.
Moderato.
N.º 3.
staccato.
Adagio.
N.º 4.
THIRDS.
TIERCES.
ACCORD.

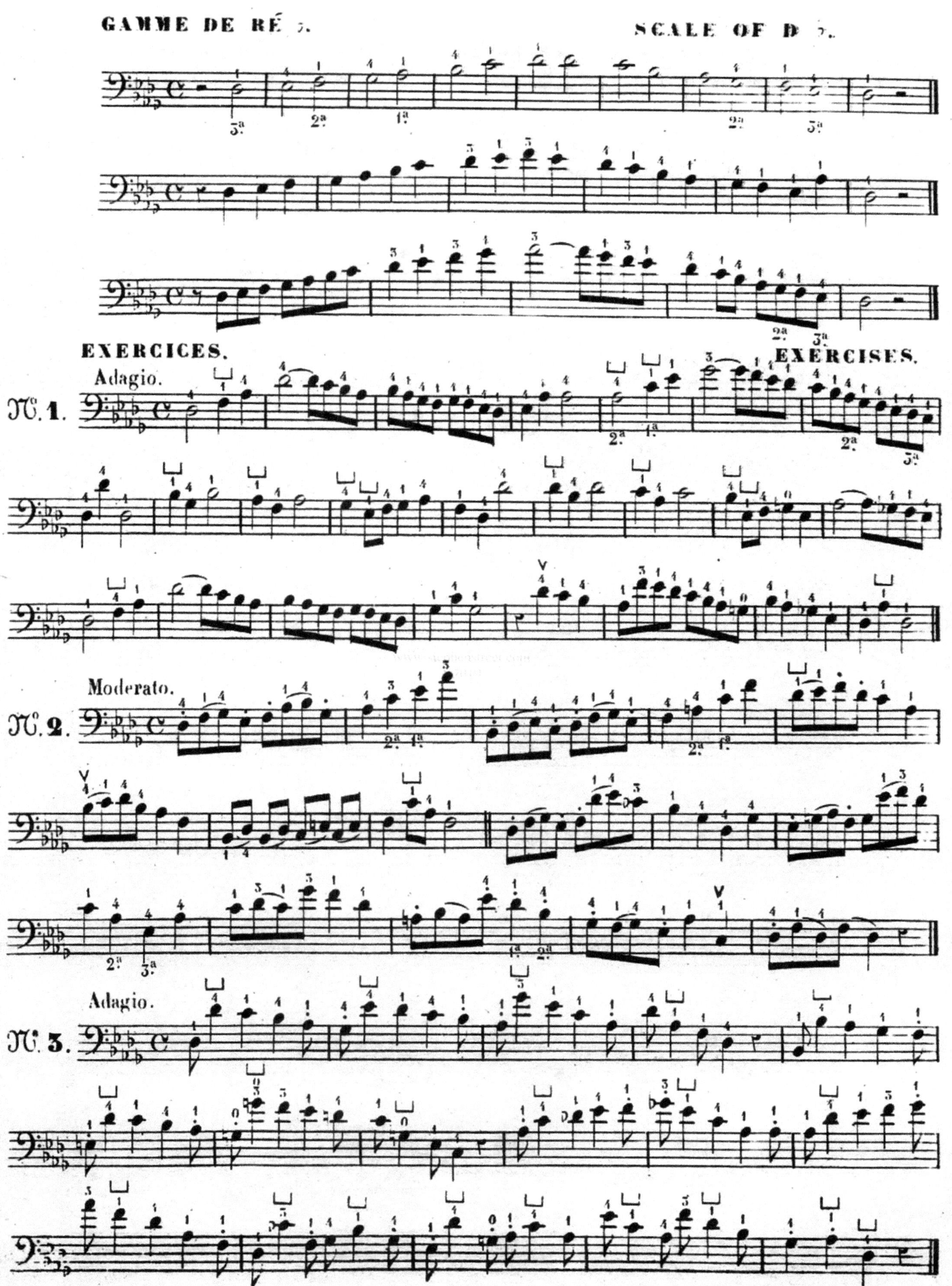
GAMME DE RÉ ♭.
SCALE OF D ♭.
EXERCICES.
EXERCISES.
Adagio.
Nº 1.
Moderato.
Nº 2.
Adagio.
Nº 3.

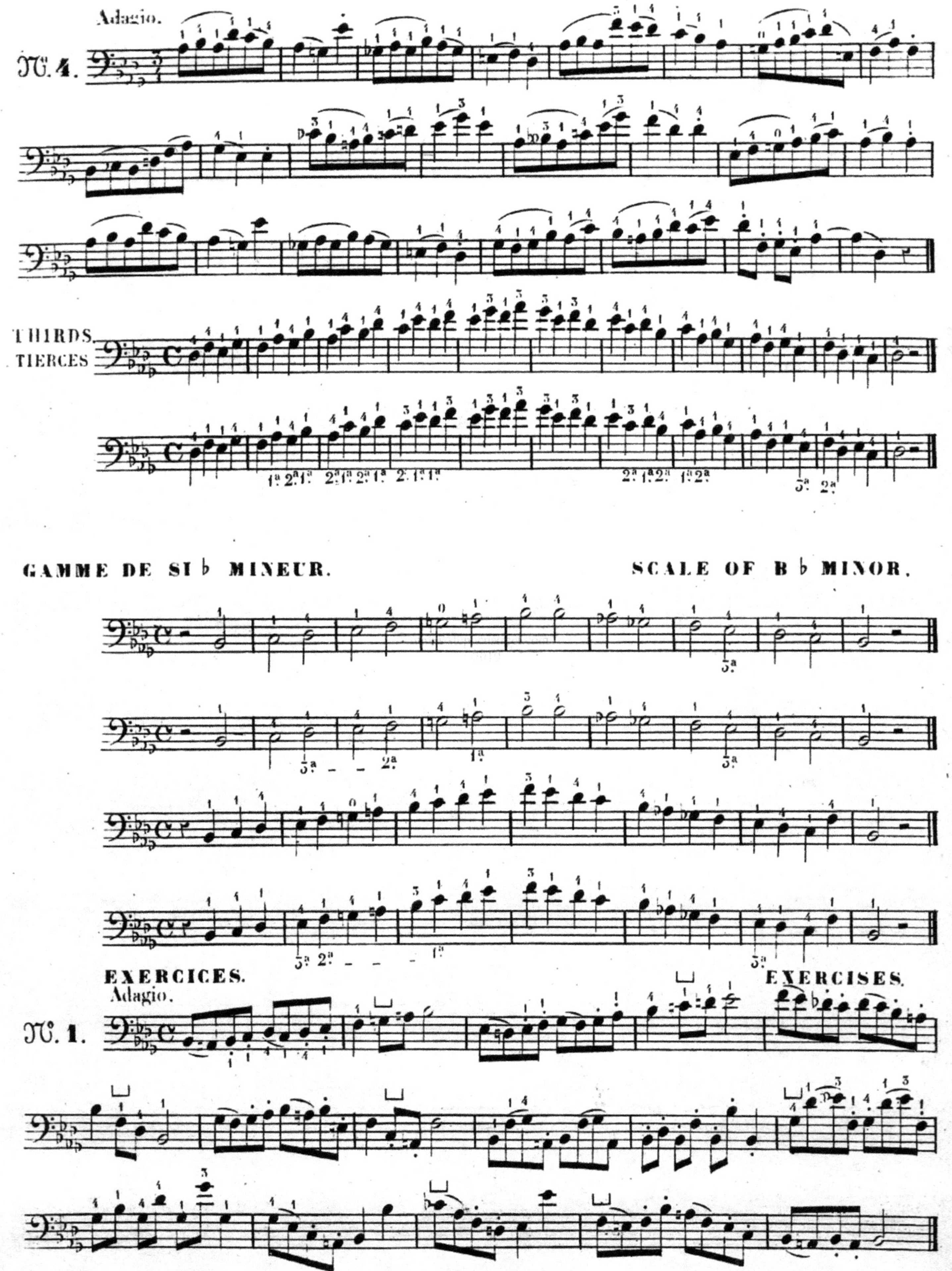
Adagio.
Nº. 4.
THIRDS.
TIERCES
GAMME DE SI ♭ MINEUR.
SCALE OF B ♭ MINOR.
EXERCICES.
EXERCISES.
Adagio.
Nº. 1.

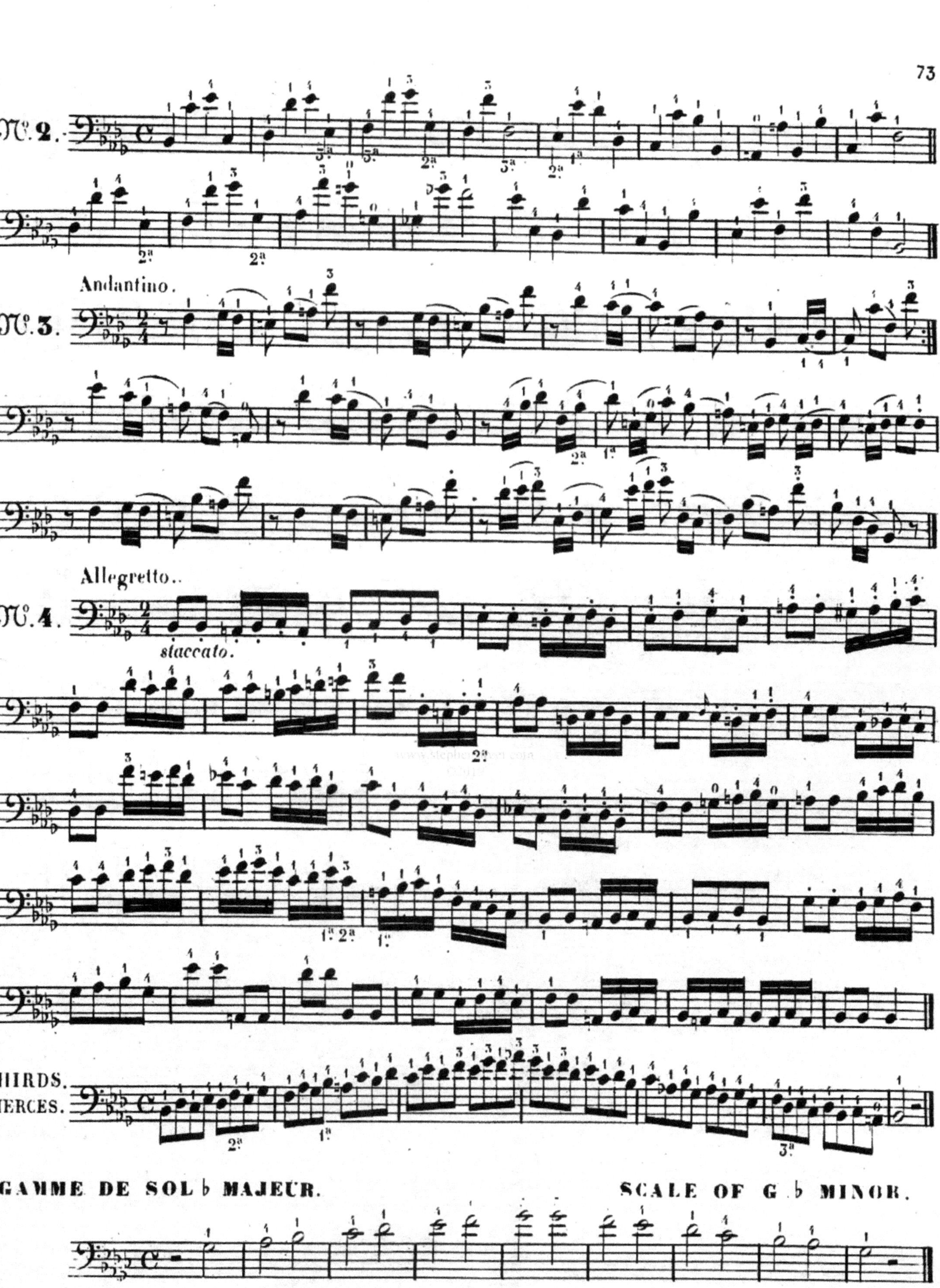
Nº 2.
Andantino.
Nº 3.
Allegretto..
Nº 4.
staccato.
THIRDS.
TIERCES.
GAMME DE SOL ♭ MAJEUR.
SCALE OF G ♭ MINOR.

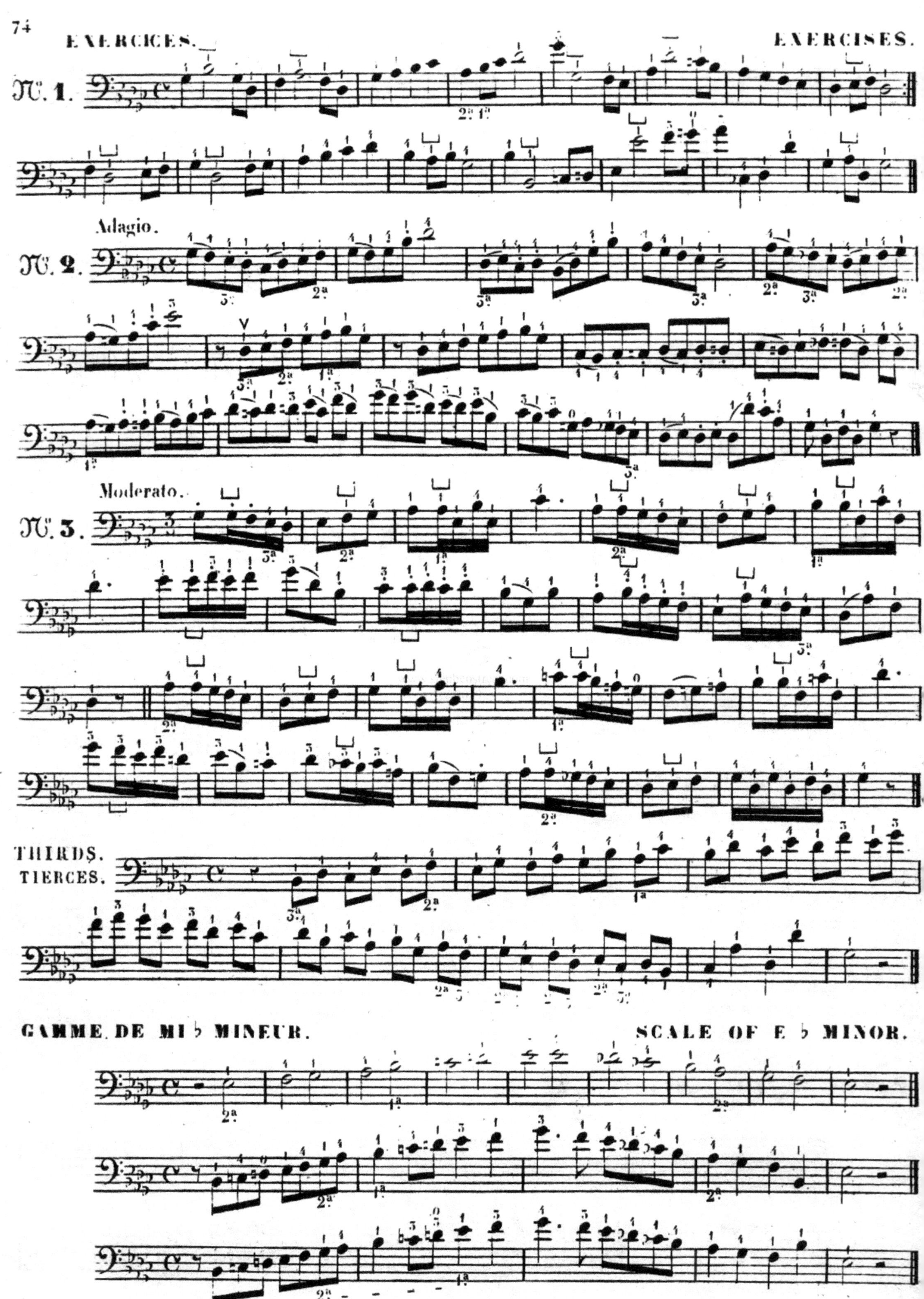
EXERCICES.
EXERCISES.
Nº. 1.
Adagio.
Nº. 2.
Moderato.
Nº. 3.
THIRDS.
TIERCES.
GAMME DE MI ♭ MINEUR.
SCALE OF E ♭ MINOR.

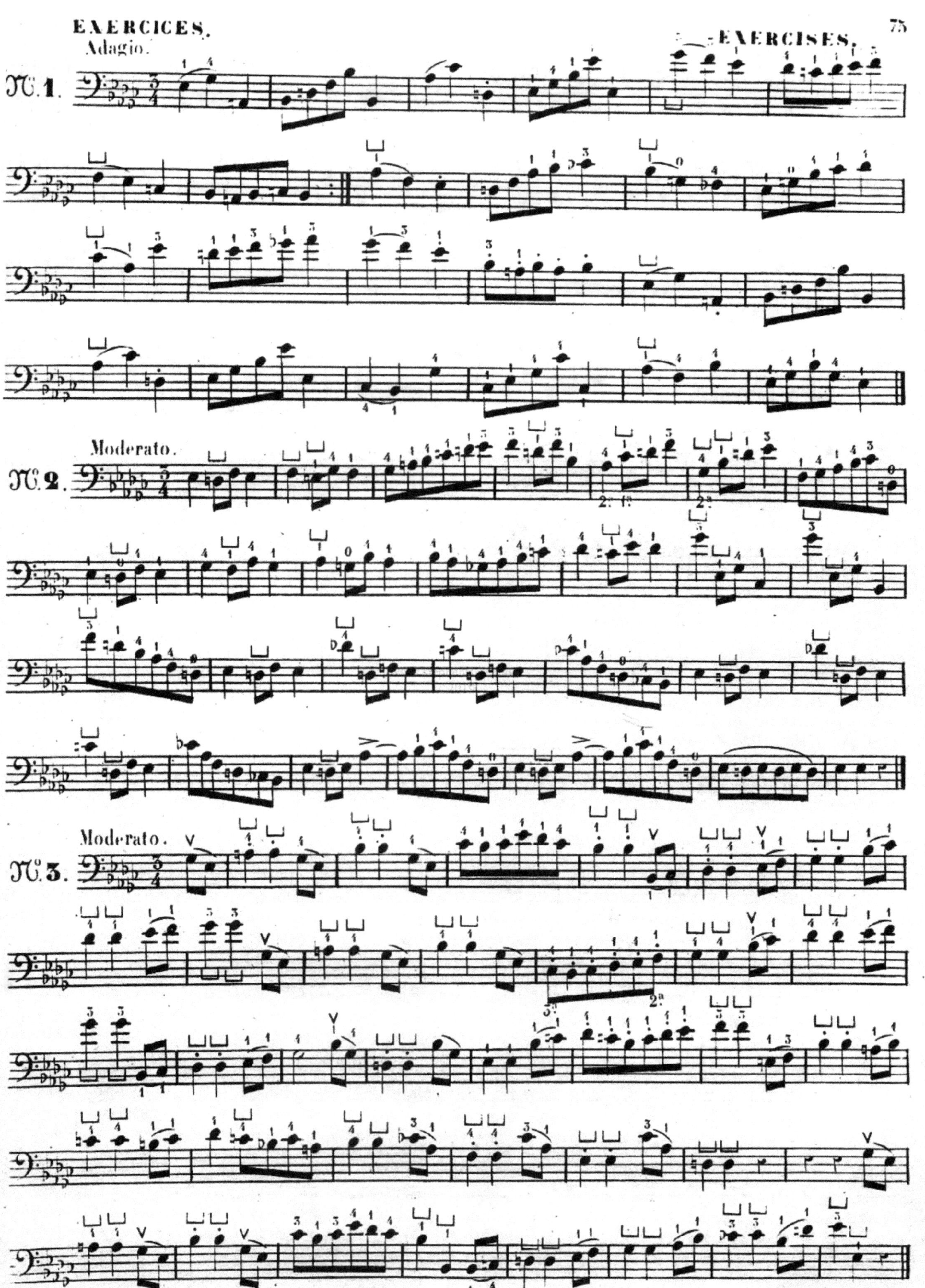
Adagio.
Nº 1.
Moderato.
Nº 2.
Moderato.
Nº 3.

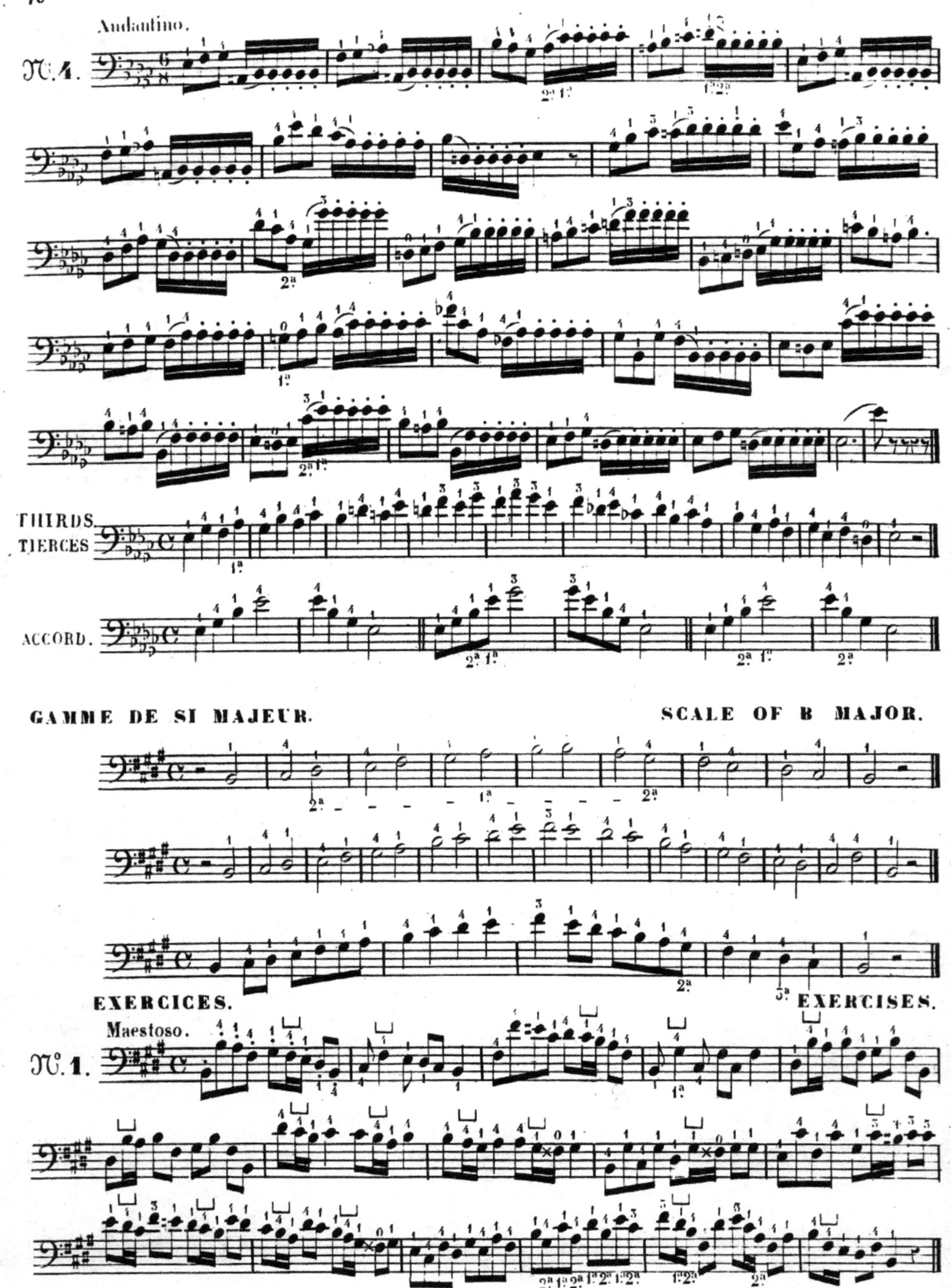
Andantino.
No. 4.
THIRDS.
TIERCES
ACCORD.
GAMME DE SI MAJEUR.
SCALE OF B MAJOR.
EXERCICES.
EXERCISES.
Maestoso.
No. 1.

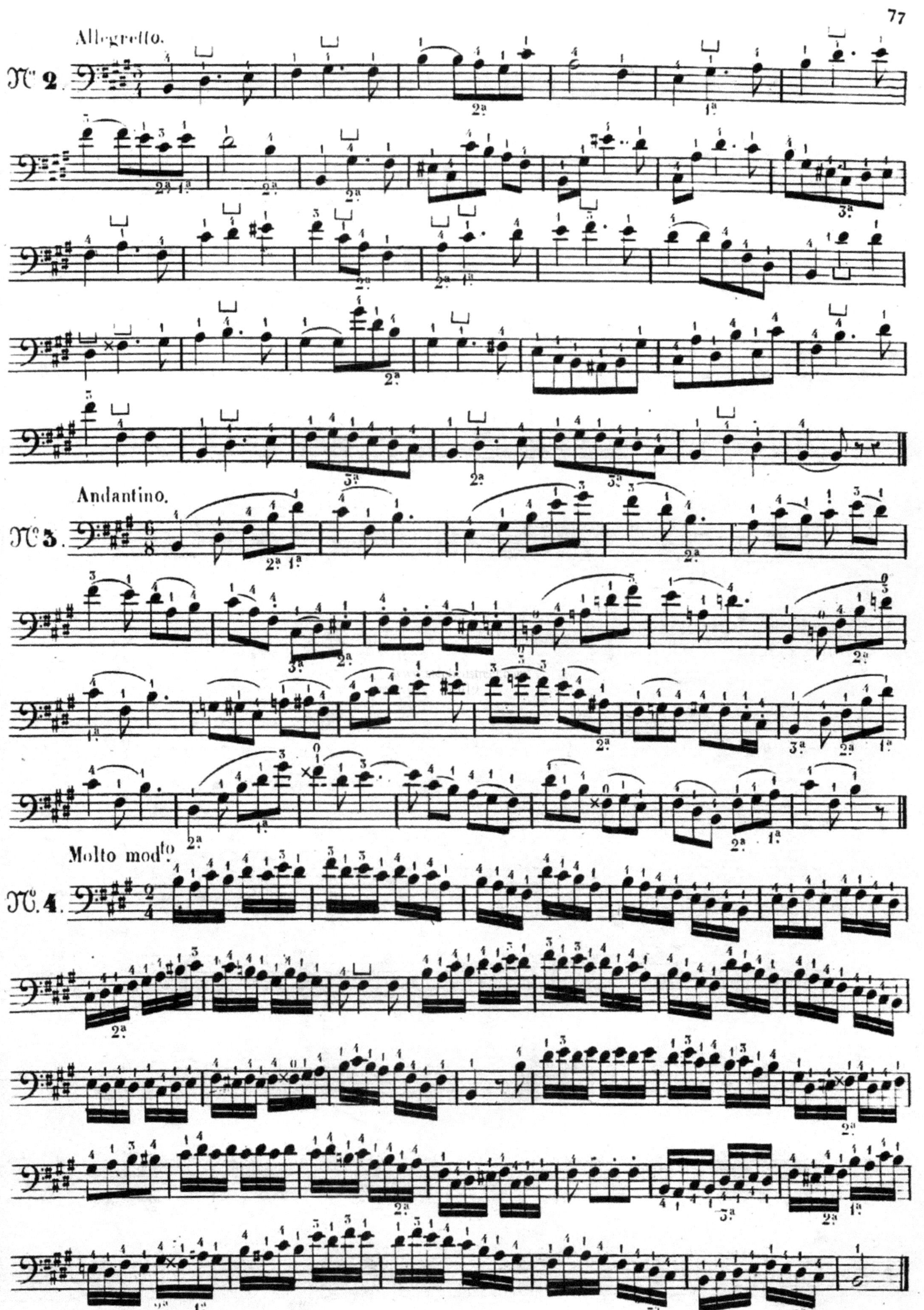
Allegretto.
Nº 2.
Andantino.
Nº 3.
Molto modto.
Nº 4.

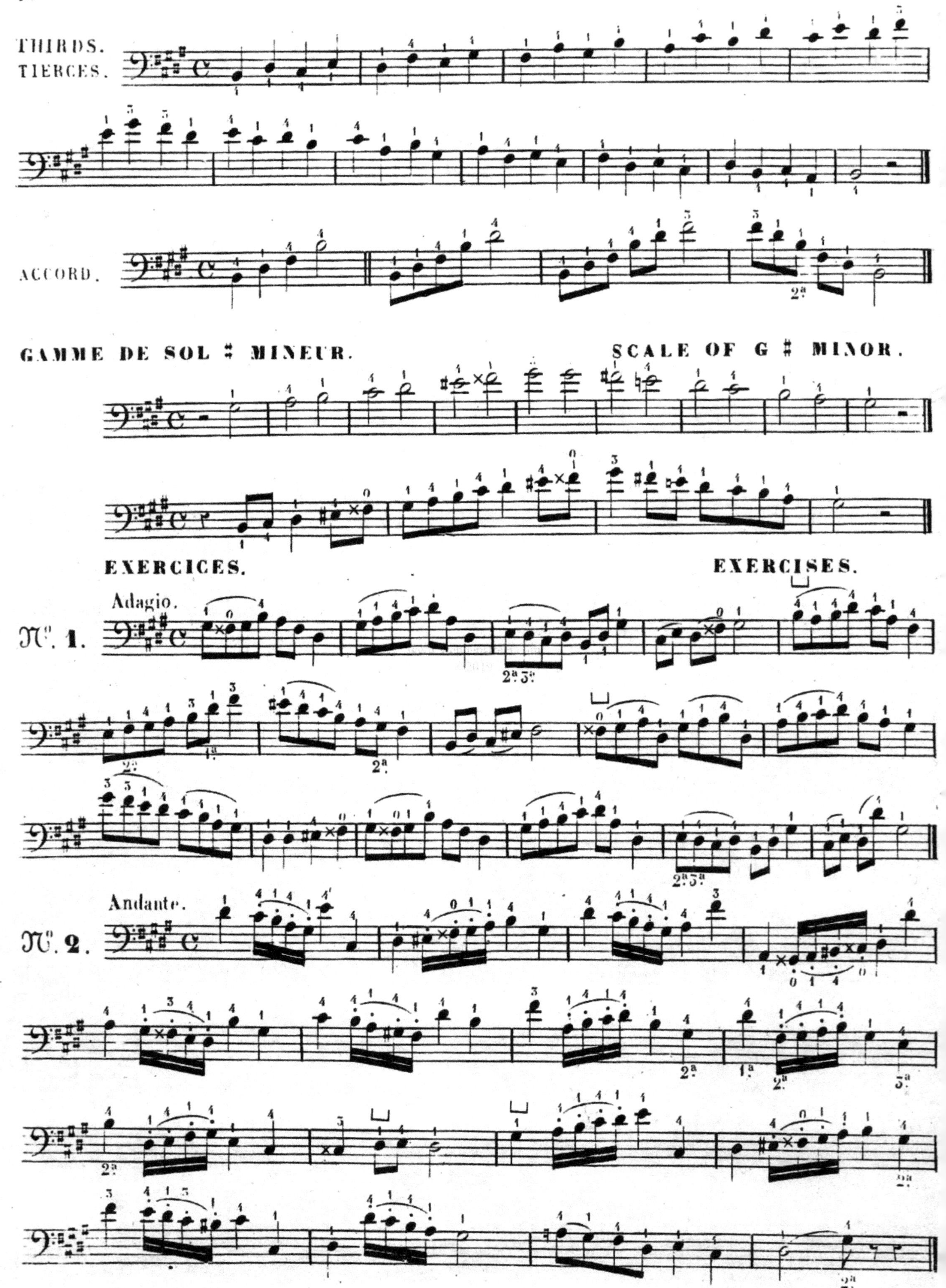
THIRDS.
TIERCES.
ACCORD.
GAMME DE SOL ♯ MINEUR.
SCALE OF G ♯ MINOR.
EXERCICES.
EXERCISES.
Adagio.
Nº. 1.
Andante.
Nº. 2.

# EMBELLISHMENTS OF MELODY.

## THE SHAKE (OR TRILLE), THE APPOGIATURA, THE MORDANT, THE TURN.

The caprice of the artist has so increased the number of styles for embellishing melody that it is no longer easy to enumerate them. We will limit ourselves to the following, which are those most in use.

The appogiatura is used when instead of immediately sounding the principal note we take the one above or below it, passing to the principal. There are two sorts.

1st The simple appogiatura, consisting of a single note.

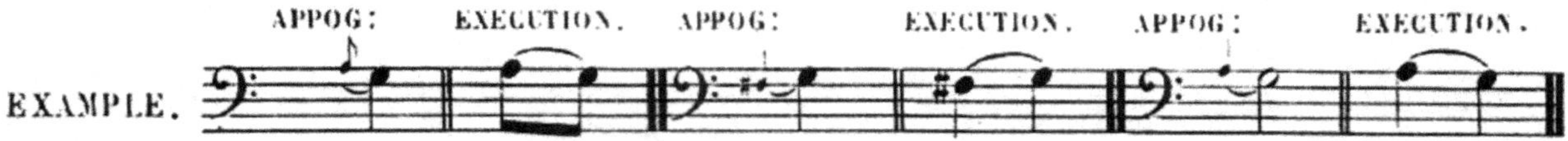


It divides, as is seen, the value of the note into two equal parts; the following, on the contrary, take no value from the notes they press on, and for that reason they are represented by quavers semiquavers or demisemiquavers.

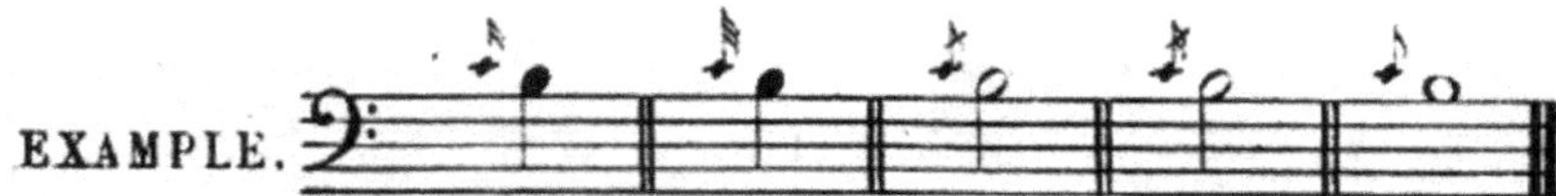


2nd The Double appogiatura when two successive notes are taken.

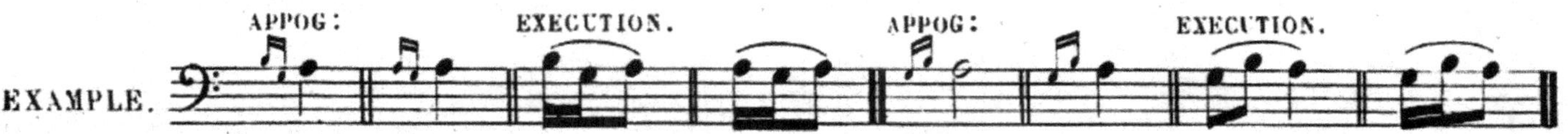


3rd The Triple appogiatura, when three notes are taken. This is also called the Grupetto or turn when between the 1st and 3rd note we play the principal note.

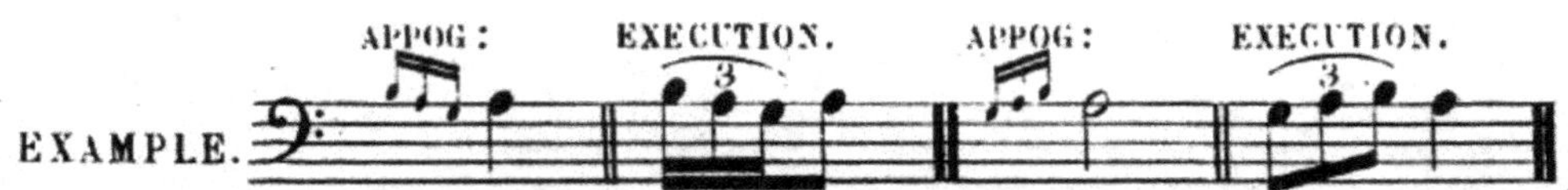


The appogiatura is written with small notes placed before the note upon which we stay. These notes are divided in groups of two or three, which invariably correspond with half the value of the following note, from which they draw precisely their value. At all times when the note is not divisible the appogiatura is only worth the moiety of that note.

The Trille (or shake) is a rapid alternation of the note of the melody with a small note written above or below. It is also called *Cadence* because in former times it was employed in *harmonic cadences*, but it is no longer used in that way.

The plain trille must only be commenced after having dwelt upon an upper note, and must be finished by adding a small note a semitone above the principal note. The trille is indicated by these two letters ***tr*** being placed above the note on which it is to be made.

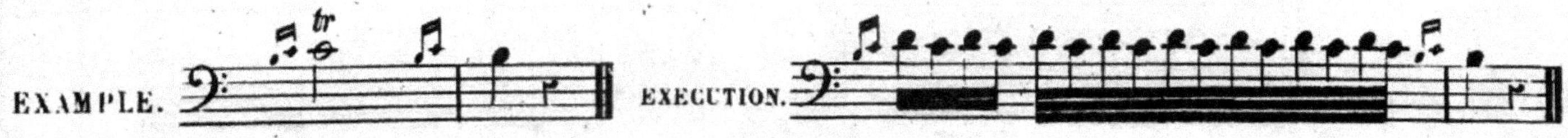

2nd The demitrille (half shake) takes place upon a note of less value, and is denoted by the sign ~

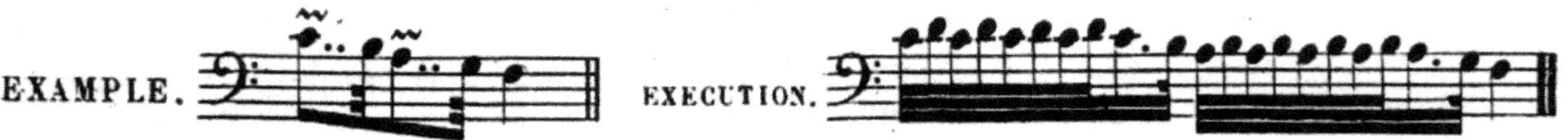


The mordant is a species of ornament made by pressing almost imperceptibly a note on the minor second so as to give a greater emphasis to the first.

The mordant occurs generally in progressions ascending by semitones. It is indicated by the sign Y over the note.

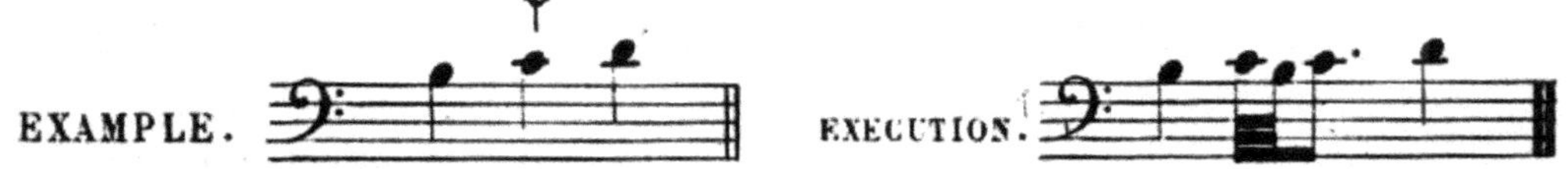


The Grupetto or turn consists of three notes which return upon the principal note. It is indicated by the sign ∾.

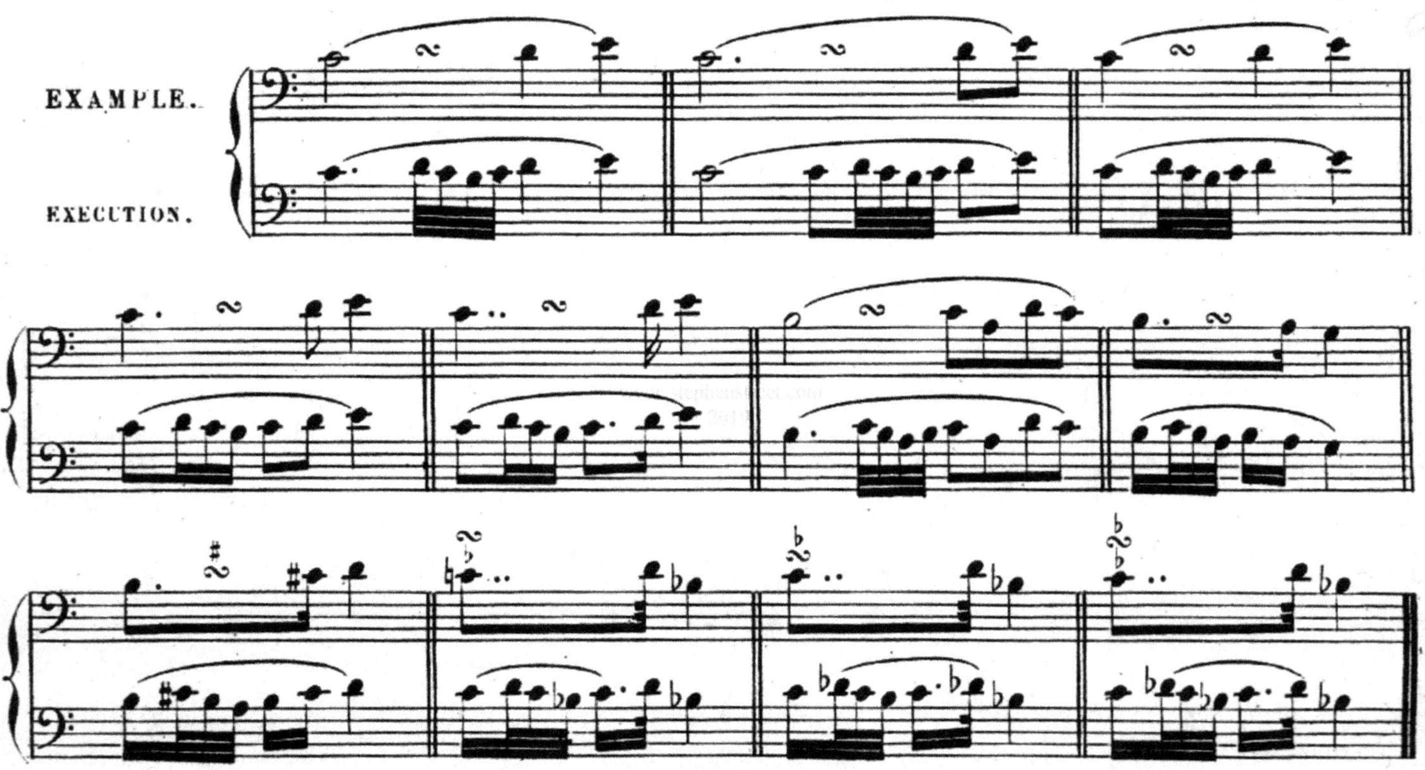


The Trille must be commenced slowly, so that the accelerated progression may be more perceptible. The finger must fall exactly on the same place and precisely upon the first major or minor. The trille. is always bad when it embraces more than a whole tone.

Although on other instruments the trille is a display of agility rather than of power, on the Contre Basse it must have both those qualities. It requiresgreat practice.

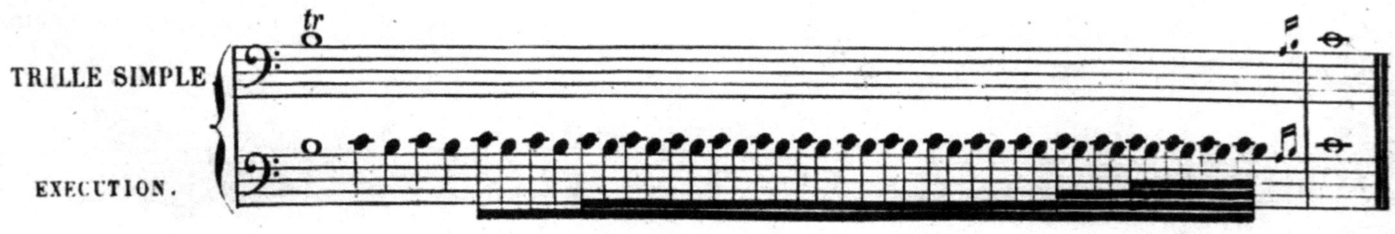


A note more or less does not spoil the shake. It must, above all, be accelerated by degrees and as quick as possible.

## OF THE "PORTAMENTO."

By this term is understood the passage (carrying) of one note tied to another whatever may be the interval, by "carrying" the sound without removing the hand from the string. This passing must be made with a certain rapidity, in order to avoid falling into a dragging style or exaggerated sliding which would be always in bad taste.

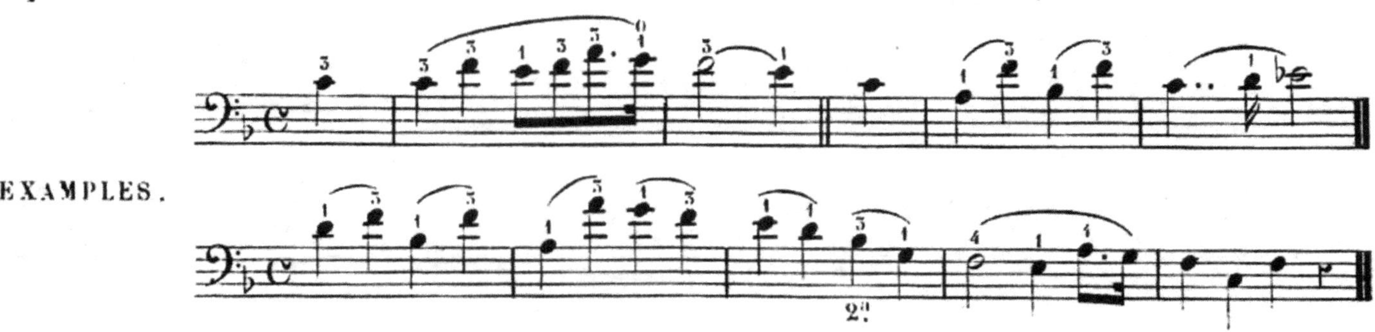


## OF THE PIZZICATO.

"Pizzicato," is to make the string vibrate by touching it with the fingers in the manner of the harp. The string must be pulled obliquely by the first finger of the right hand so as to cause a strong vibration. The thumb placed against the finger board serves as a fulcrum or prop to the finger. The other three fingers will hold the bow in such a manner that it does not touch the string.

Before passing to the second part of this Method, namely that of the Soloist we give some exercises; varied, and in the keys most suitable to the Contre Basse.

C MAJOR.

No. 1.

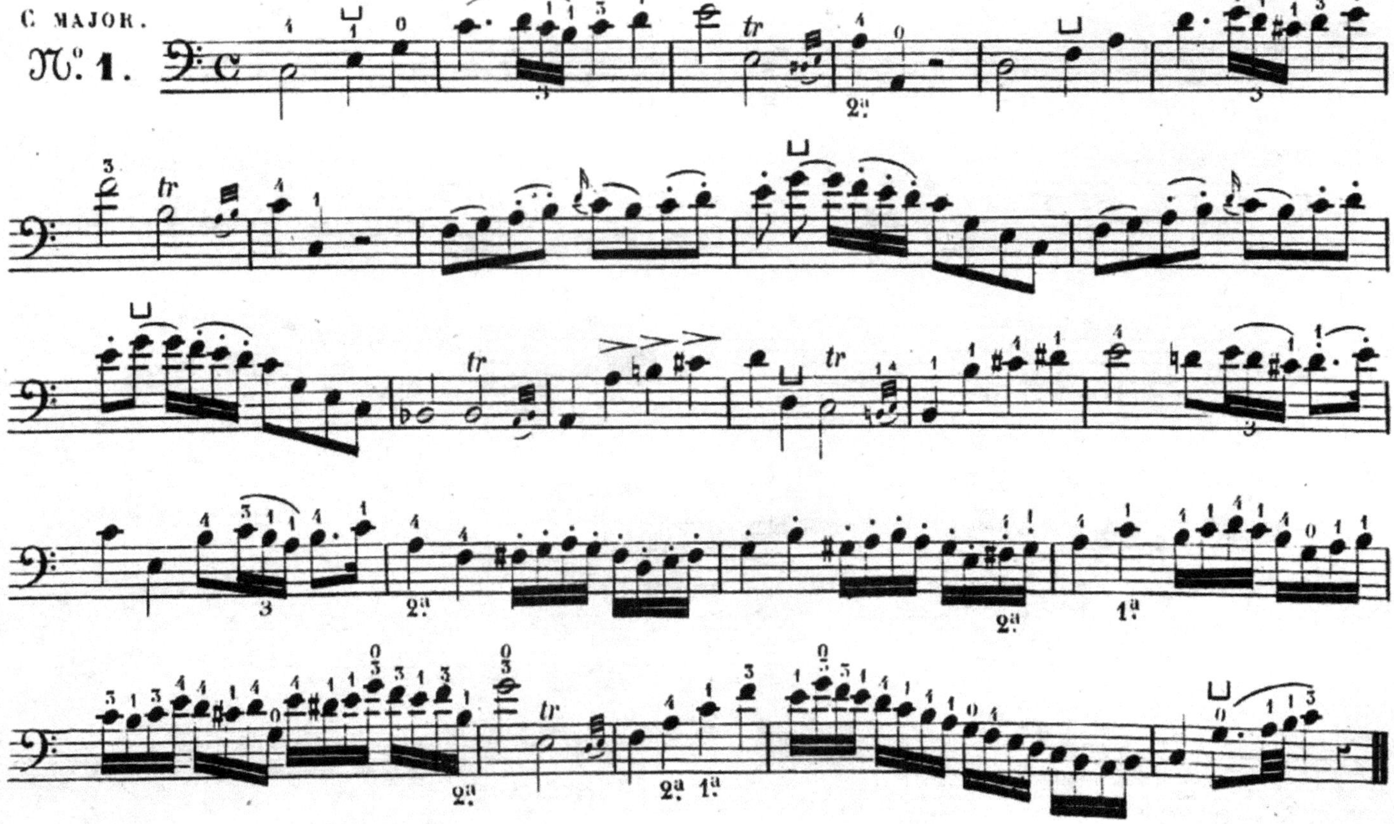

Andante.

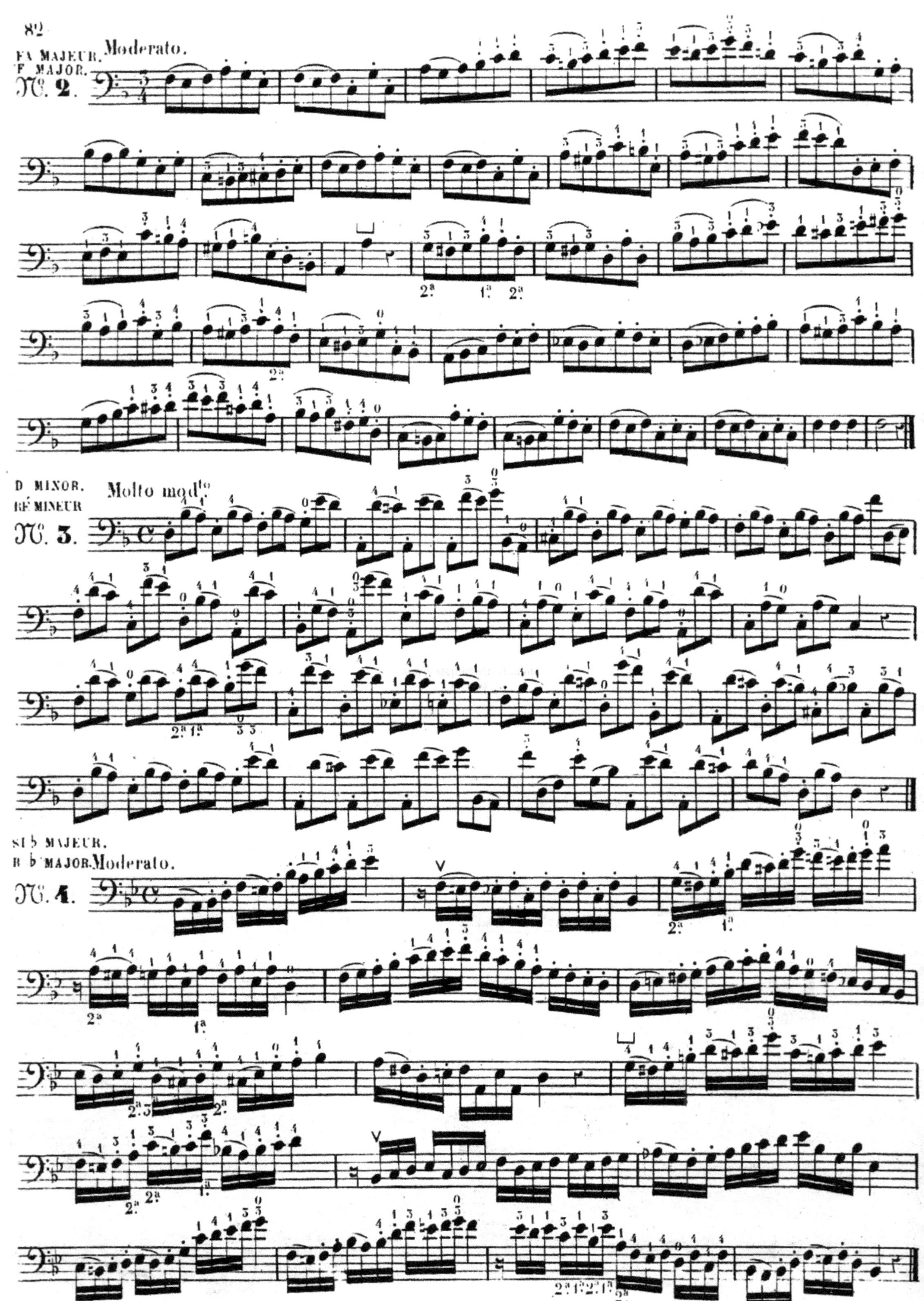
FA MAJEUR.
F MAJOR.
No. 2.
Moderato.
D MINOR.
RÉ MINEUR
No. 3.
Molto mod^to
SI ♭ MAJEUR.
B ♭ MAJOR.
Moderato.
No. 4.

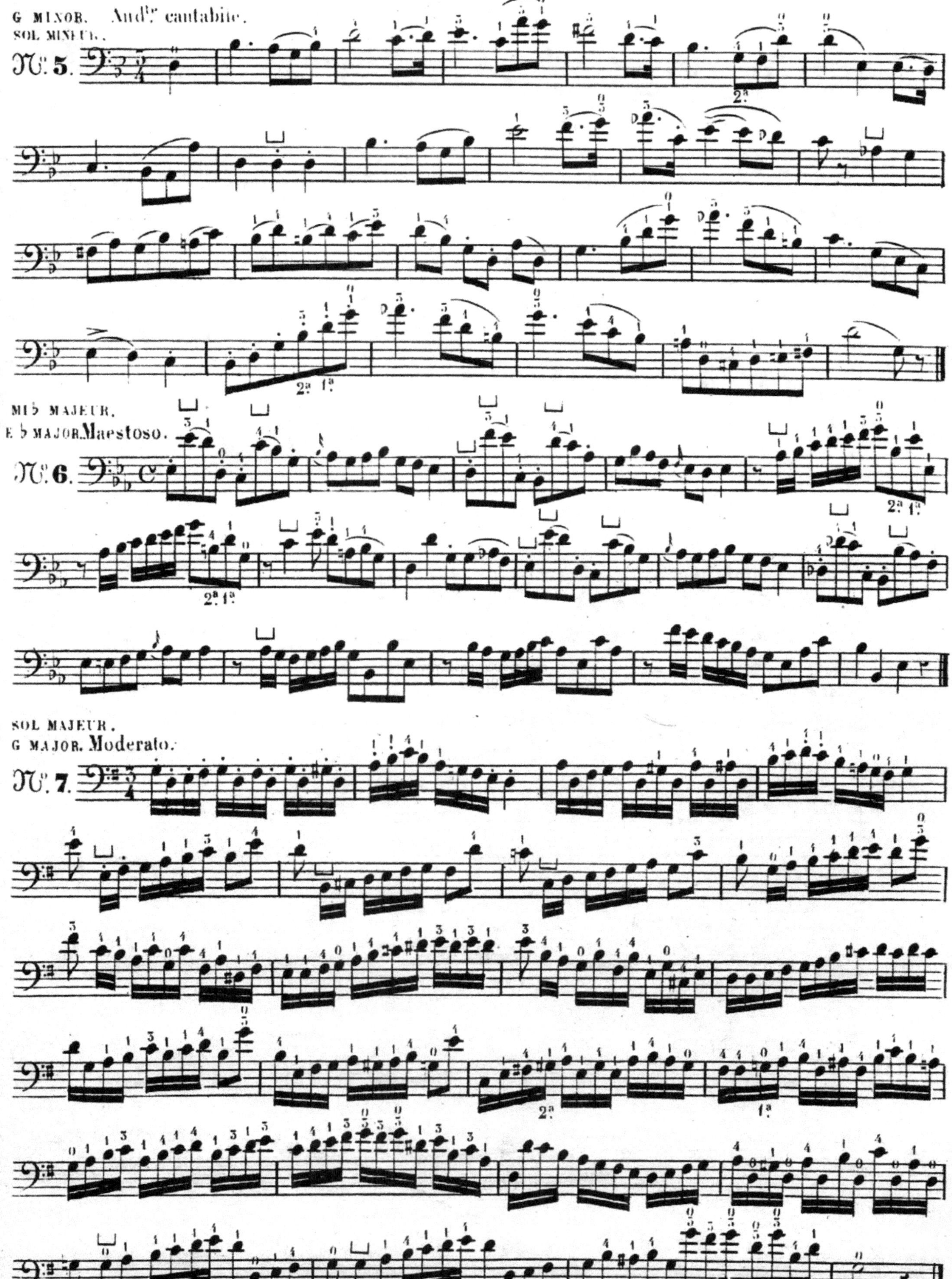

G MINOR. Andte cantabile.
SOL MINEUR.
No. 5.

MI♭ MAJEUR.
E♭ MAJOR. Maestoso.
No. 6.

SOL MAJEUR.
G MAJOR. Moderato.
No. 7.

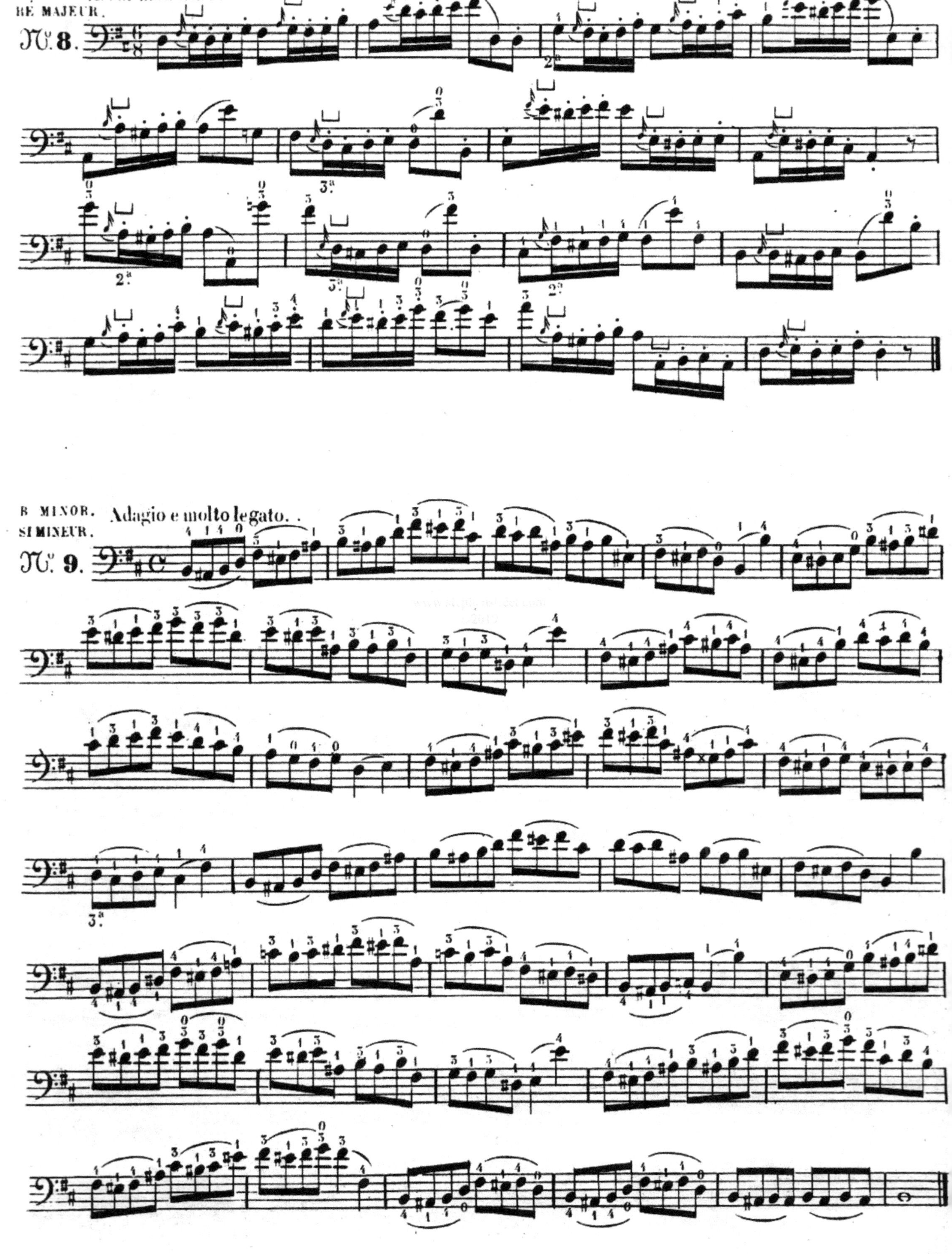
D MAJOR. Assai moderato.
RÉ MAJEUR.
Nº 8.
B MINOR. Adagio e molto legato.
SI MINEUR.
Nº 9.

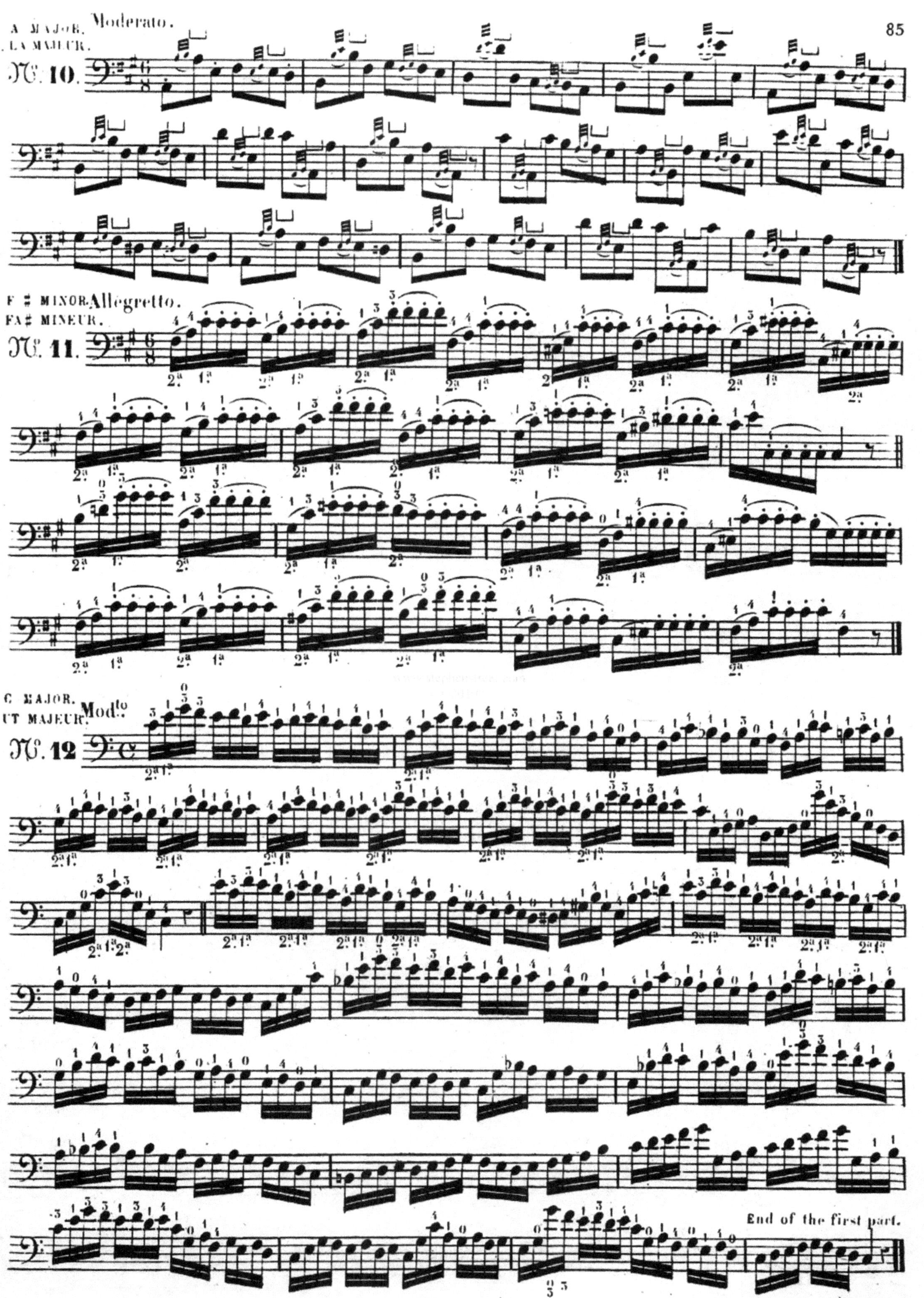

A MAJOR.
LA MAJEUR.
Moderato.
No. 10.
F ♯ MINOR.
FA♯ MINEUR.
Allegretto.
No. 11.
C MAJOR.
UT MAJEUR.
Modto
No. 12
End of the first part.

# SECOND PART.

## OF THE CONTRE BASSE CONSIDERED AS A SOLO INSTRUMENT.

As we have already mentioned we will, in this second part, write the notes without transposing them an octave higher. We shall avoid by that means a grave inconvenience: that of being obliged to use several Clefs, which, if inappropriately employed, complicate difficulties, embarrass the musician, and give rise to doubts. Thus although we give great compass to the solo Contre Basse we shall only require to use two clefs, by writing the note in its true place: the *G* clef and the *F* clef.

And now let us see the compass we can get on the Contre Basse, from the point of view of the Soloist.

### COMPASS OF THE CONTRE BASSE.

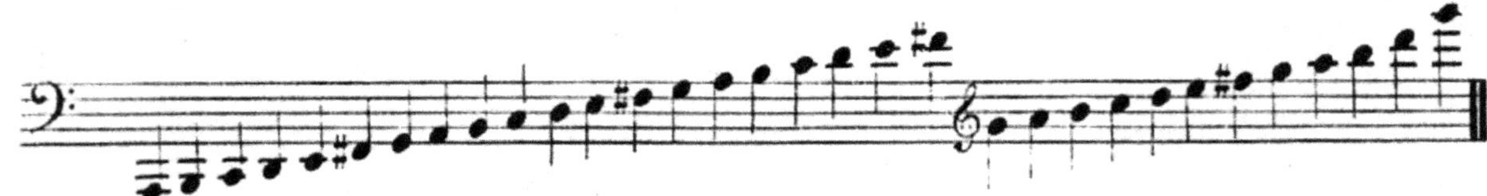

### HARMONIC SOUNDS.

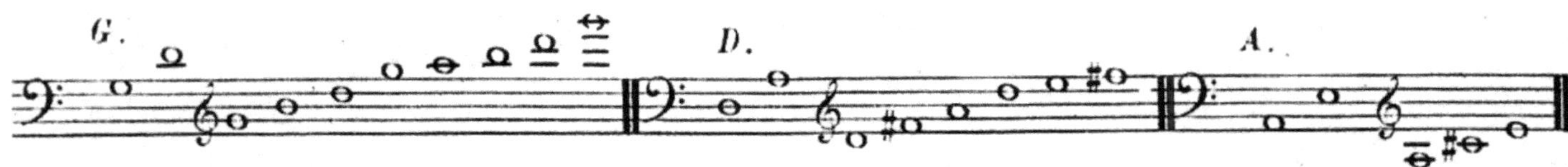


The harmonics drawn from a good Contre Basse by a vigorous pressure of the Bow, produce an excellent effect, for they adapt themselves to the character of the Instrument and in an equal manner. To obtain this equality the musician must have the tact to choose the most suitable music. The greatest difficulty of the Soloist is that of equalising the sounds spread over the full extent of the Contre Basse, an instrument which, despite its imperfections, is capable of excellent results. Laying aside the Harmonics, which I have been said to misuse, it cannot be denied that the Contre Basse has made a great advance, if it can play the Violoncello part exactly as it is written in a Quartett of Beethoven, by employing occasionally a few harmonics, which by their sensitive nature will bear comparison with any other instrument.

We commence then by giving numerous examples which in accordance with those we have seen in the first part of this Method will facilitate the pupil's perfection.

Take for Base the scale of *C*.

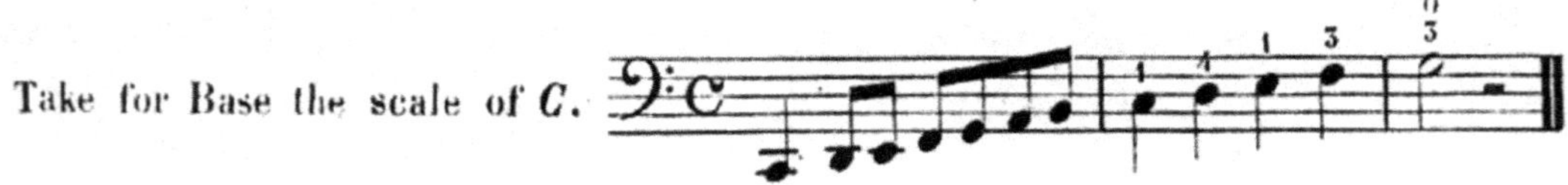

The little cross above the *G* denotes that the Thumb must serve as a stop; the other fingers are represented by the figures 1. 2. 3. 4. the open string by a 0. (See plate figure Nº 6.)

### EXAMPLES.

Upon the *G* string.

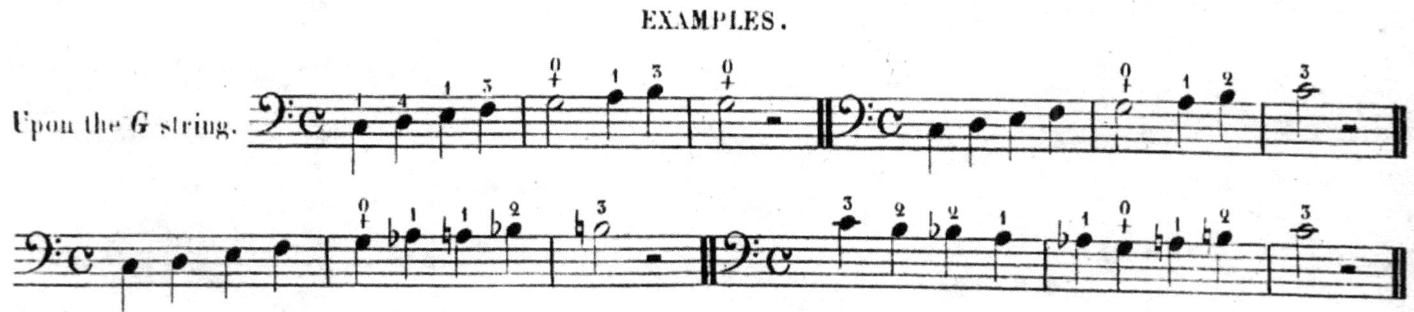

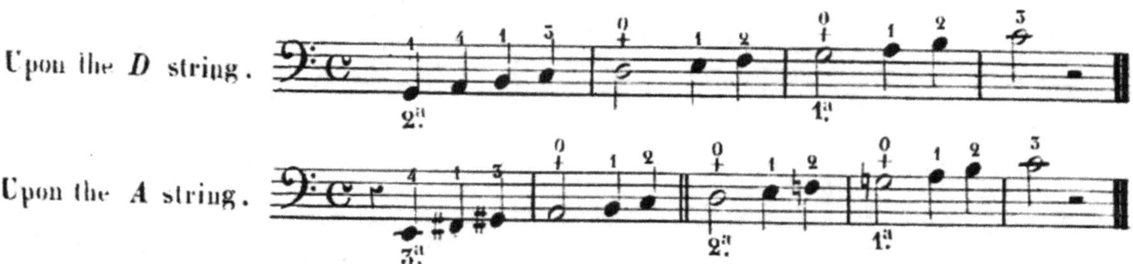


It follows from these examples that we can get the full scale of *C* with the use of the thumb for a stop.

EXAMPLE.

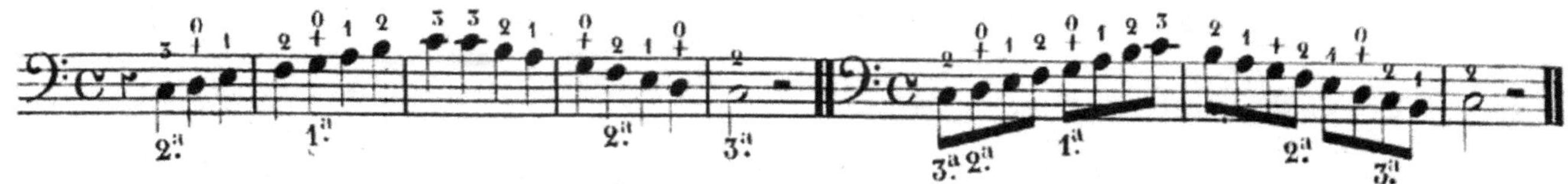

The hand well brought round, and equally over the three strings. This must be well practised.

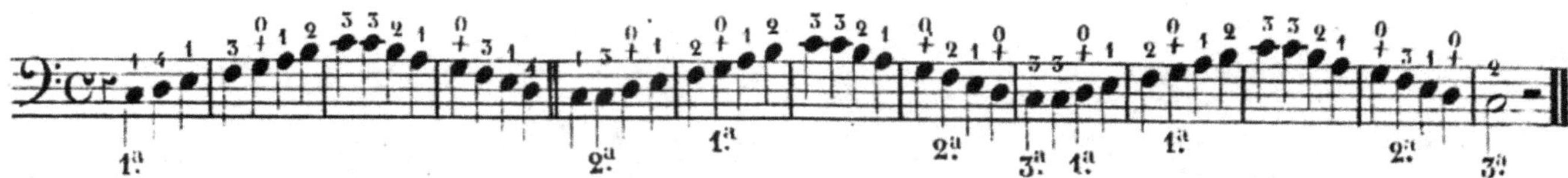

When the pupil has mastered this position, he can begin the following exercises.

1.

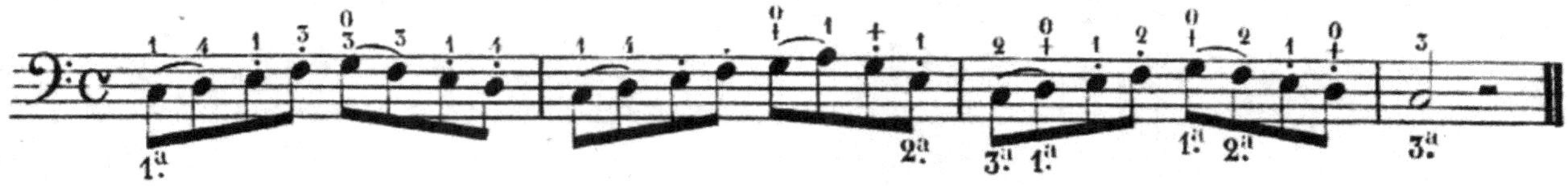

2.

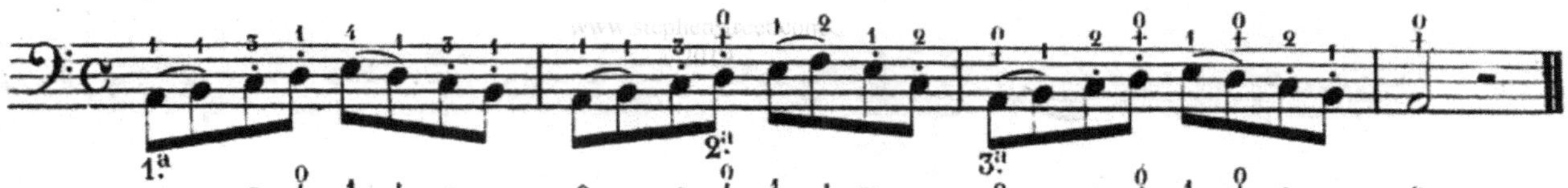

3.

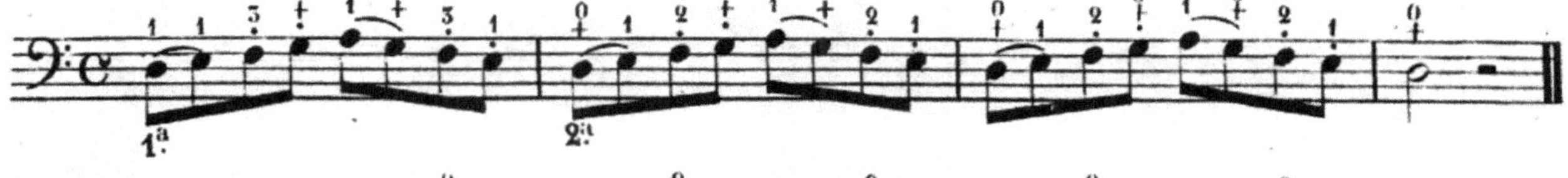

4.

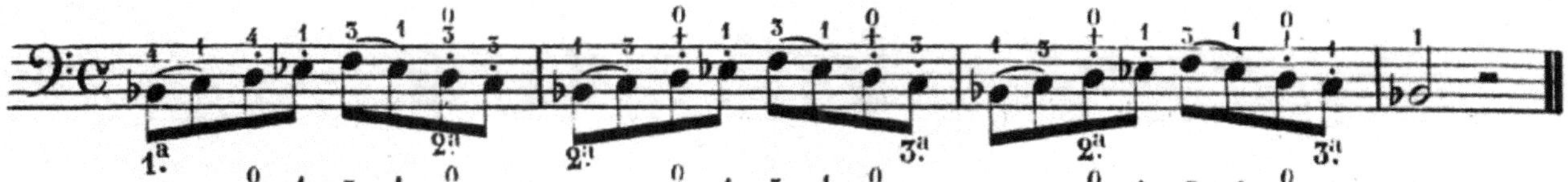

5.

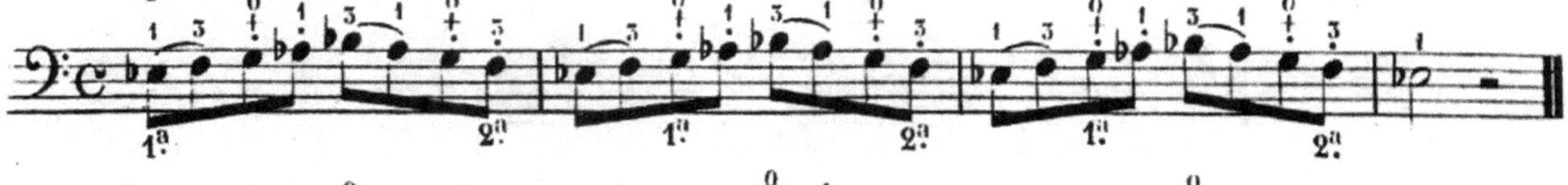

6.

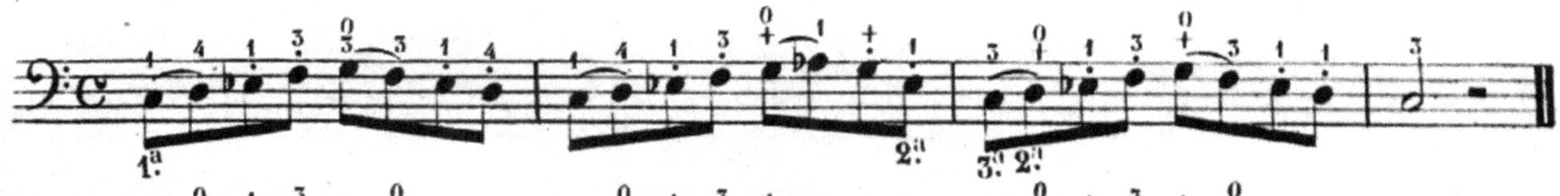

7.

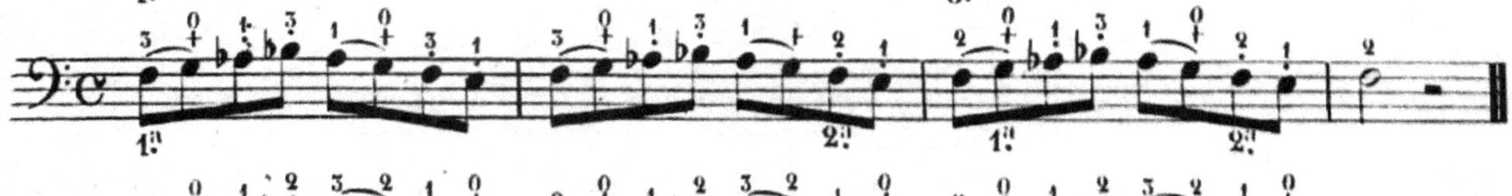

8.

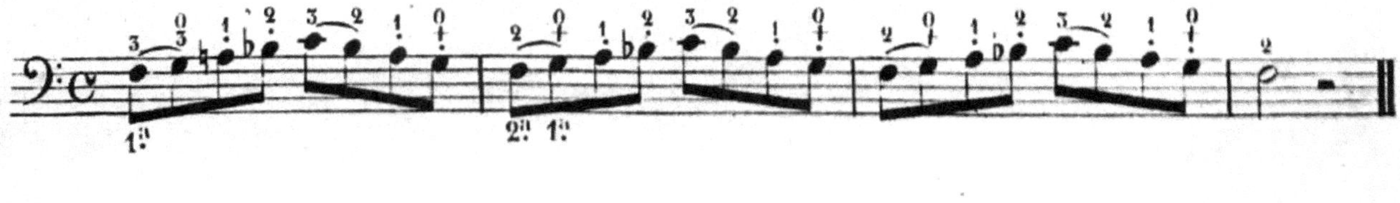

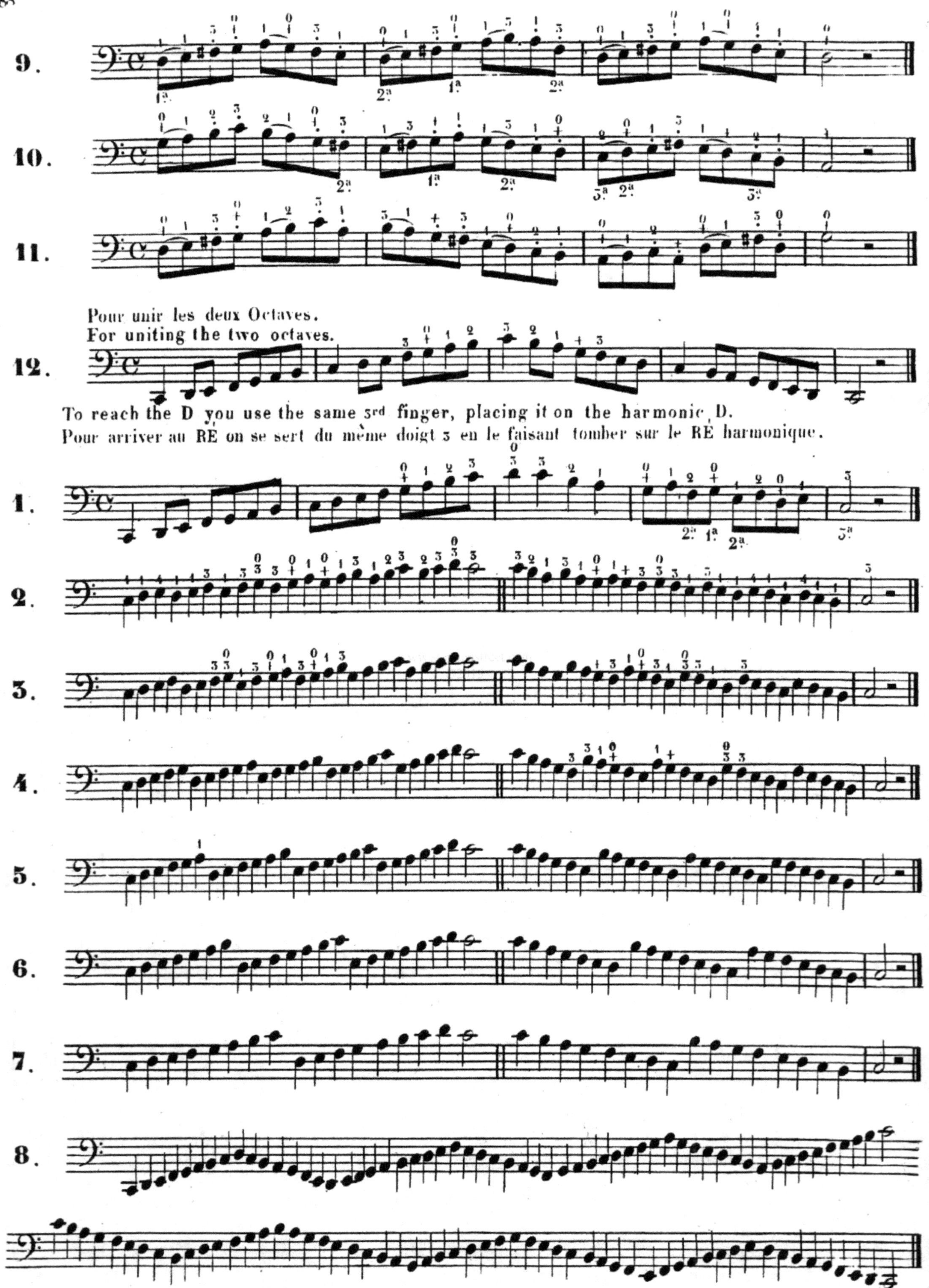
9.
10.
11.
Pour unir les deux Octaves.
For uniting the two octaves.
12.
To reach the D you use the same 3rd finger, placing it on the harmonic D.
Pour arriver au RÉ on se sert du même doigt 3 en le faisant tomber sur le RÉ harmonique.
1.
2.
3.
4.
5.
6.
7.
8.

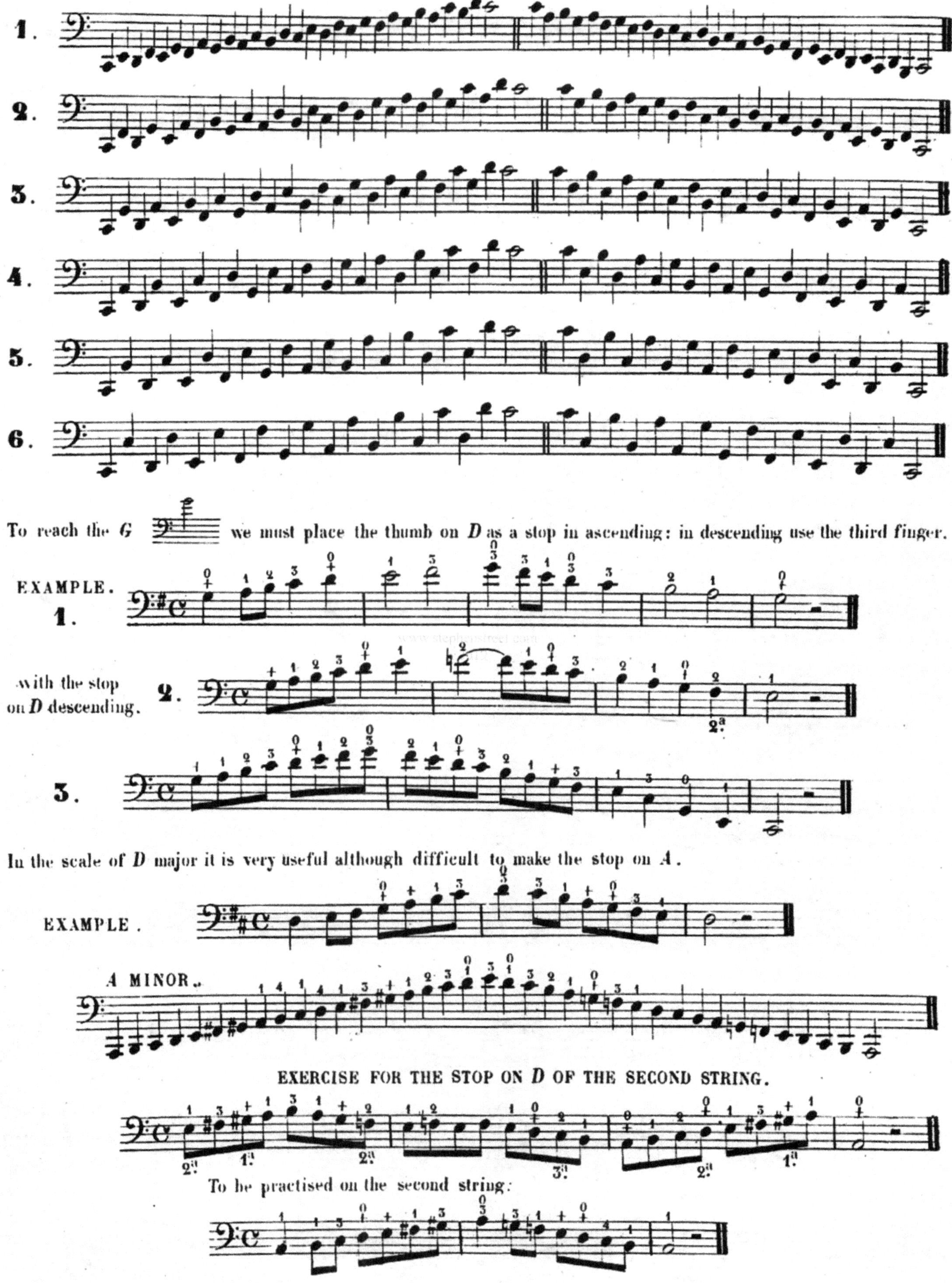
1.
2.
3.
4.
5.
6.
To reach the G we must place the thumb on D as a stop in ascending: in descending use the third finger.
EXAMPLE.
1.
with the stop on D descending.
2.
3.
In the scale of D major it is very useful although difficult to make the stop on A.
EXAMPLE.
A MINOR.
EXERCISE FOR THE STOP ON D OF THE SECOND STRING.
To be practised on the second string.

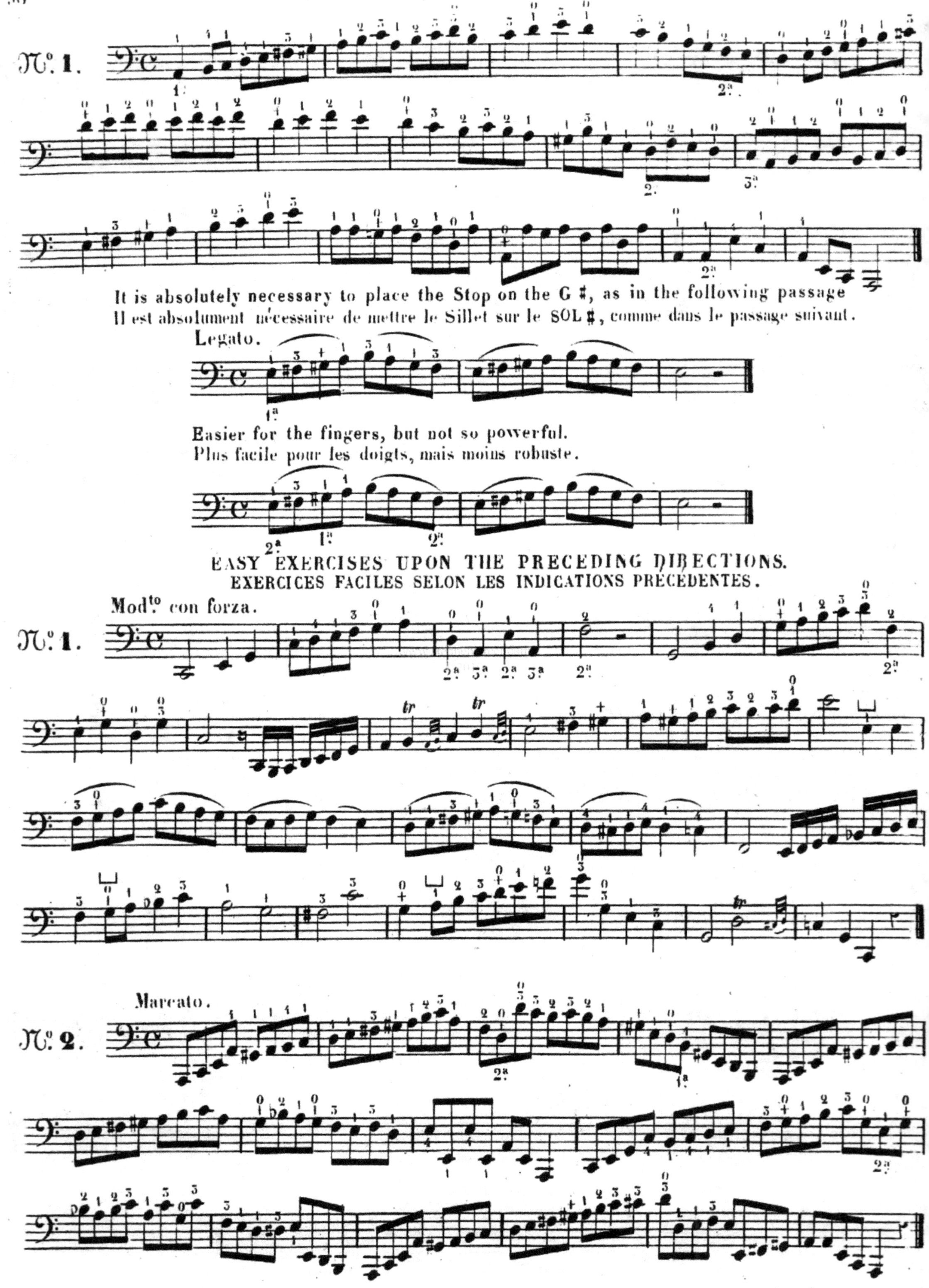
N° 1.
It is absolutely necessary to place the Stop on the G ♯, as in the following passage
Il est absolument nécessaire de mettre le Sillet sur le SOL ♯, comme dans le passage suivant.
Legato.
Easier for the fingers, but not so powerful.
Plus facile pour les doigts, mais moins robuste.
EASY EXERCISES UPON THE PRECEDING DIRECTIONS.
EXERCICES FACILES SELON LES INDICATIONS PRECEDENTES.
Mod.to con forza.
N° 1.
tr
Marcato.
N° 2.

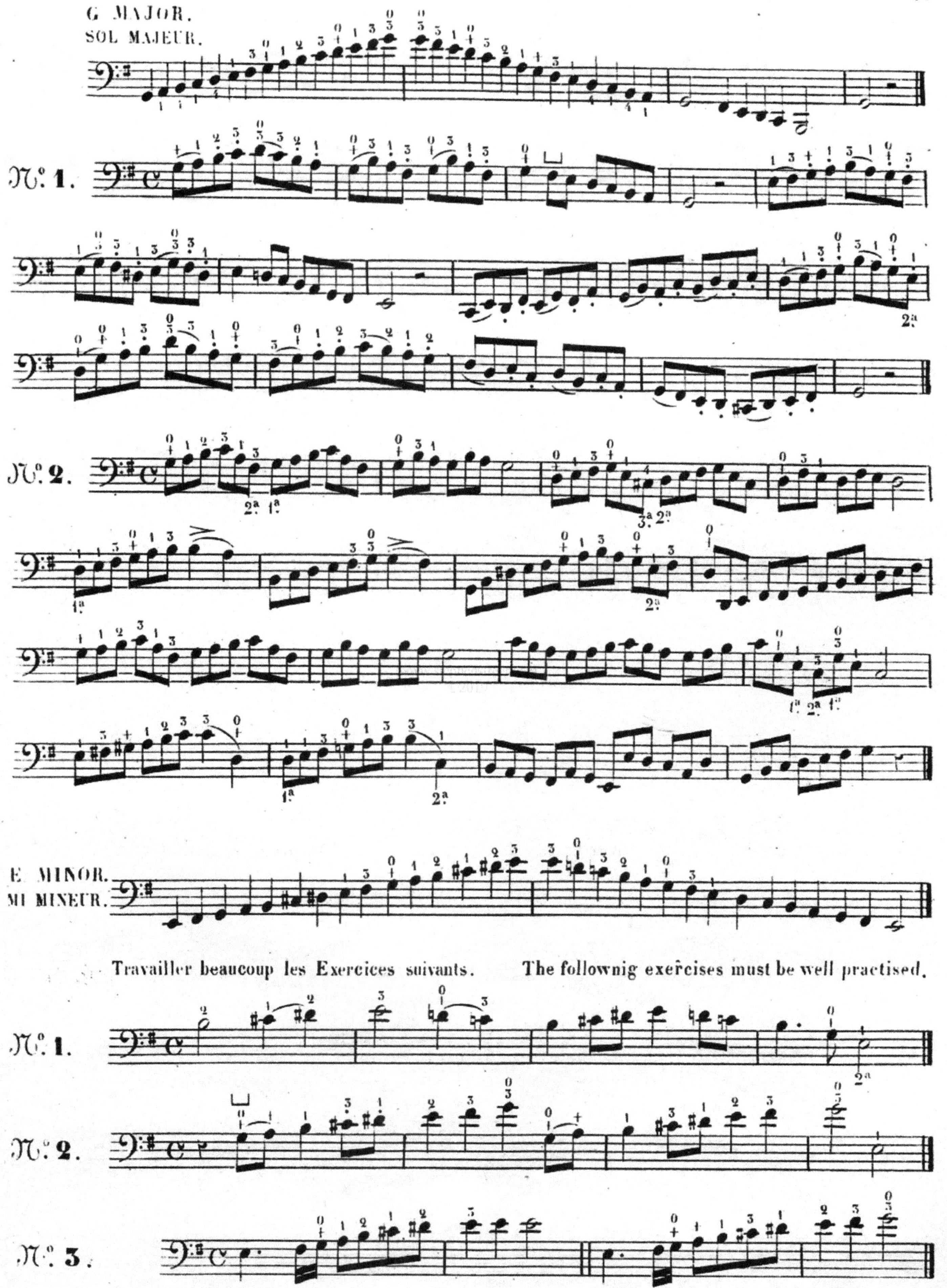
G MAJOR.
SOL MAJEUR.
Nº 1.
Nº 2.
E MINOR.
MI MINEUR.
Travailler beaucoup les Exercices suivants.
The followning exercises must be well practised.
Nº 1.
Nº 2.
Nº 3.

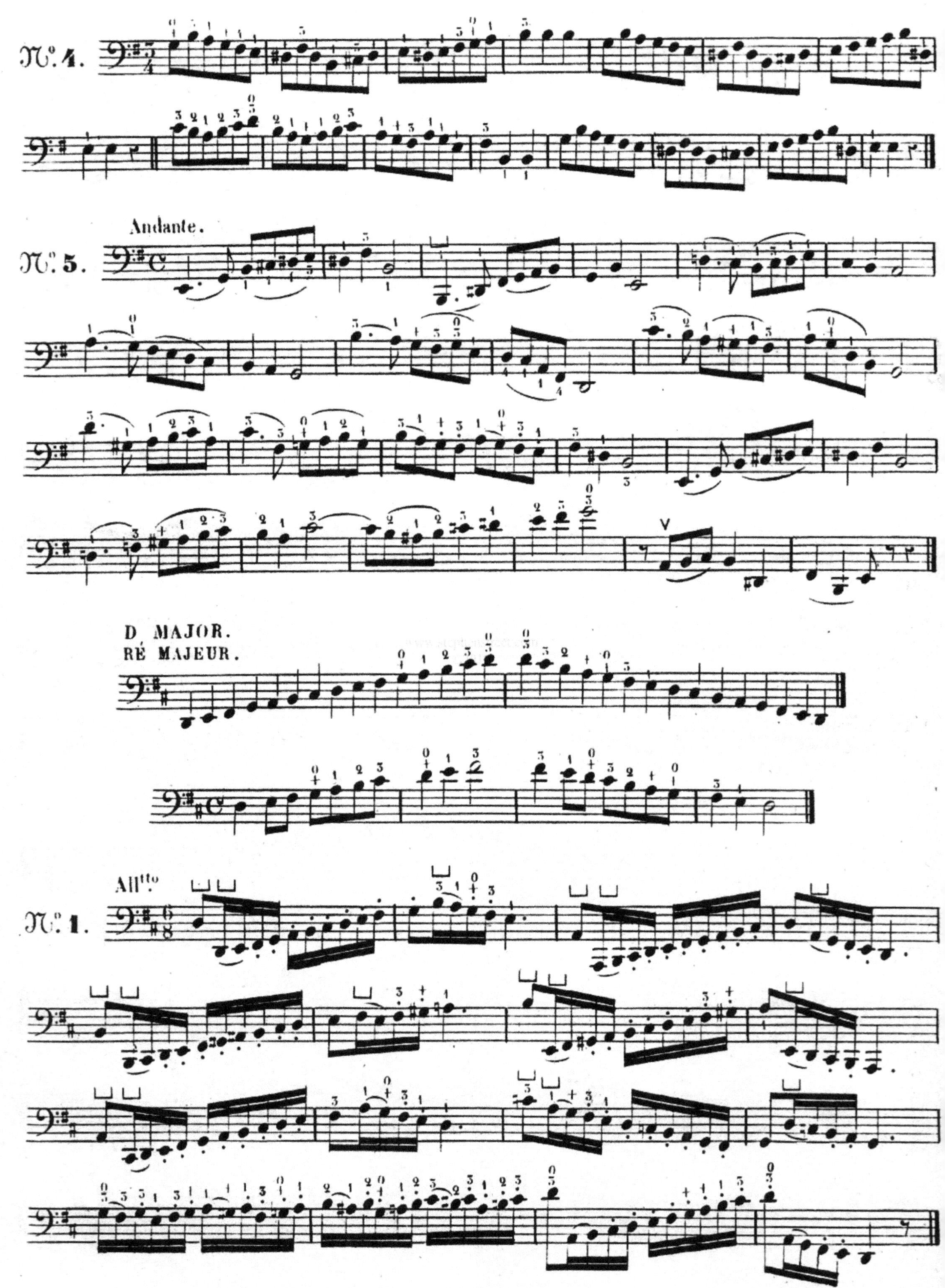

Nº. 4.
Andante.
Nº. 5.
D MAJOR.
RÉ MAJEUR.
All^tto
Nº. 1.

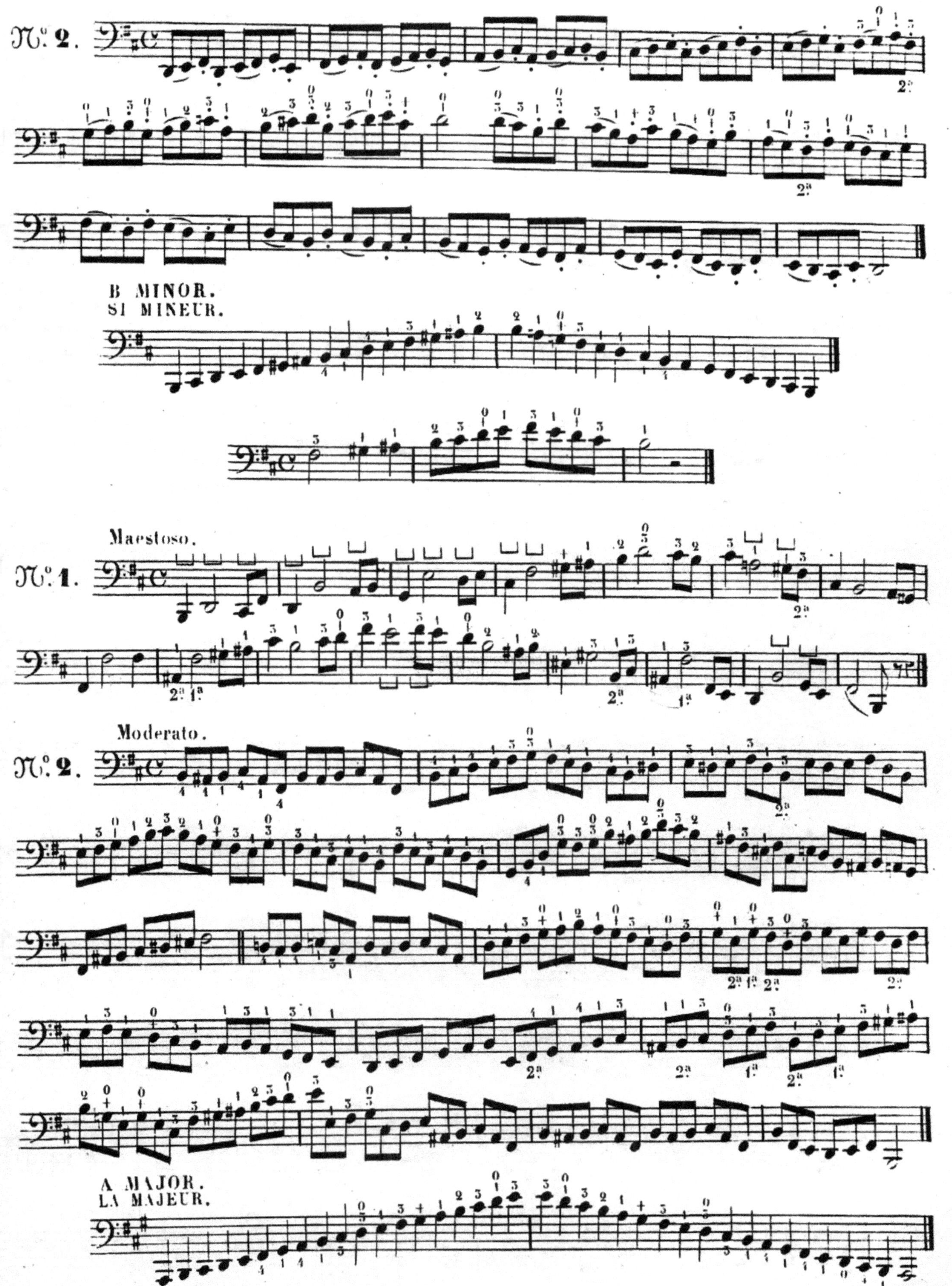

Nº 2.
B MINOR.
SI MINEUR.
Maestoso.
Nº 1.
Moderato.
Nº 2.
A MAJOR.
LA MAJEUR.

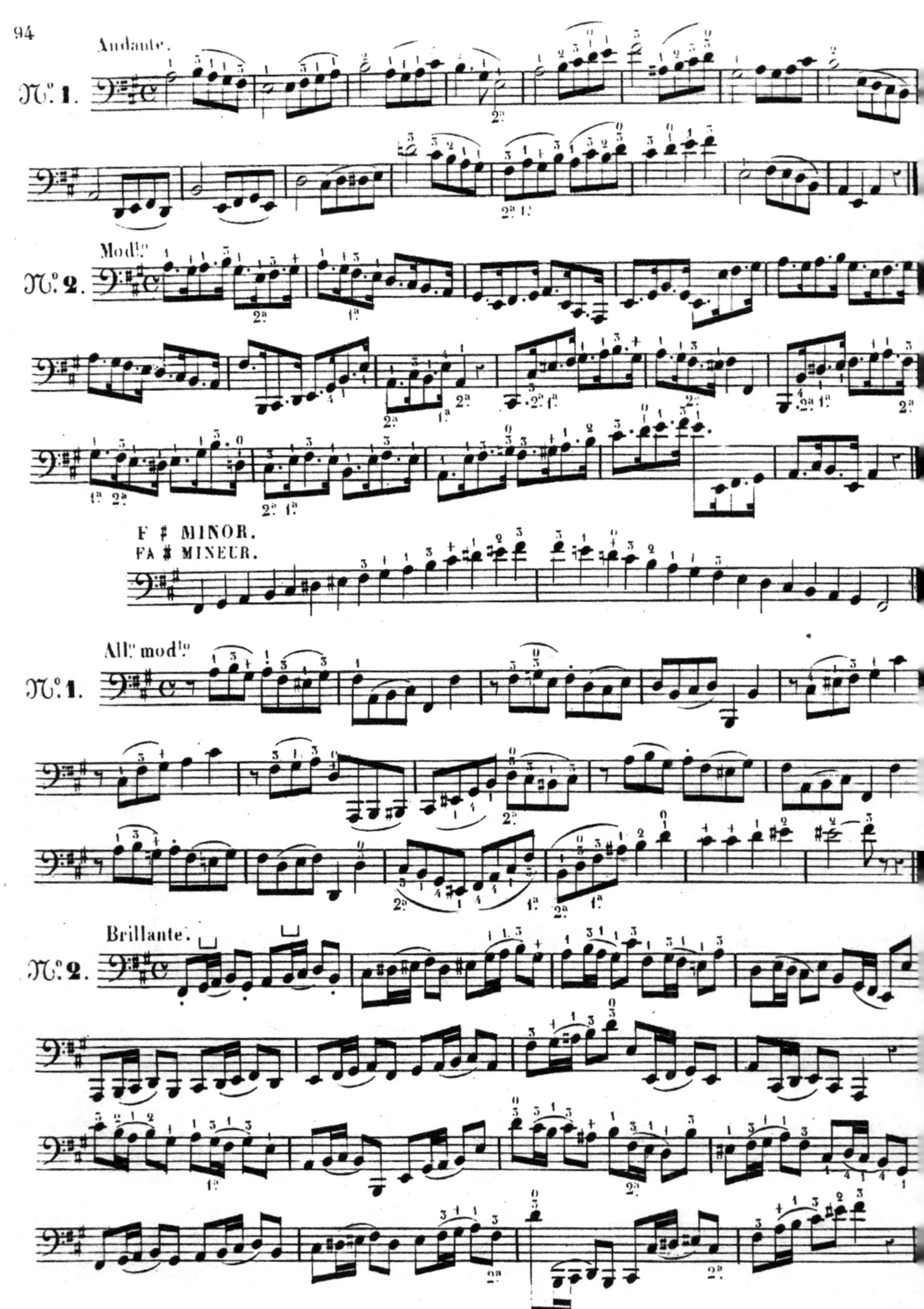
Andante.
Nº 1.
Modto
Nº 2.
F ♯ MINOR.
FA ♯ MINEUR.
Allº modto
Nº 1.
Brillante.
Nº 2.

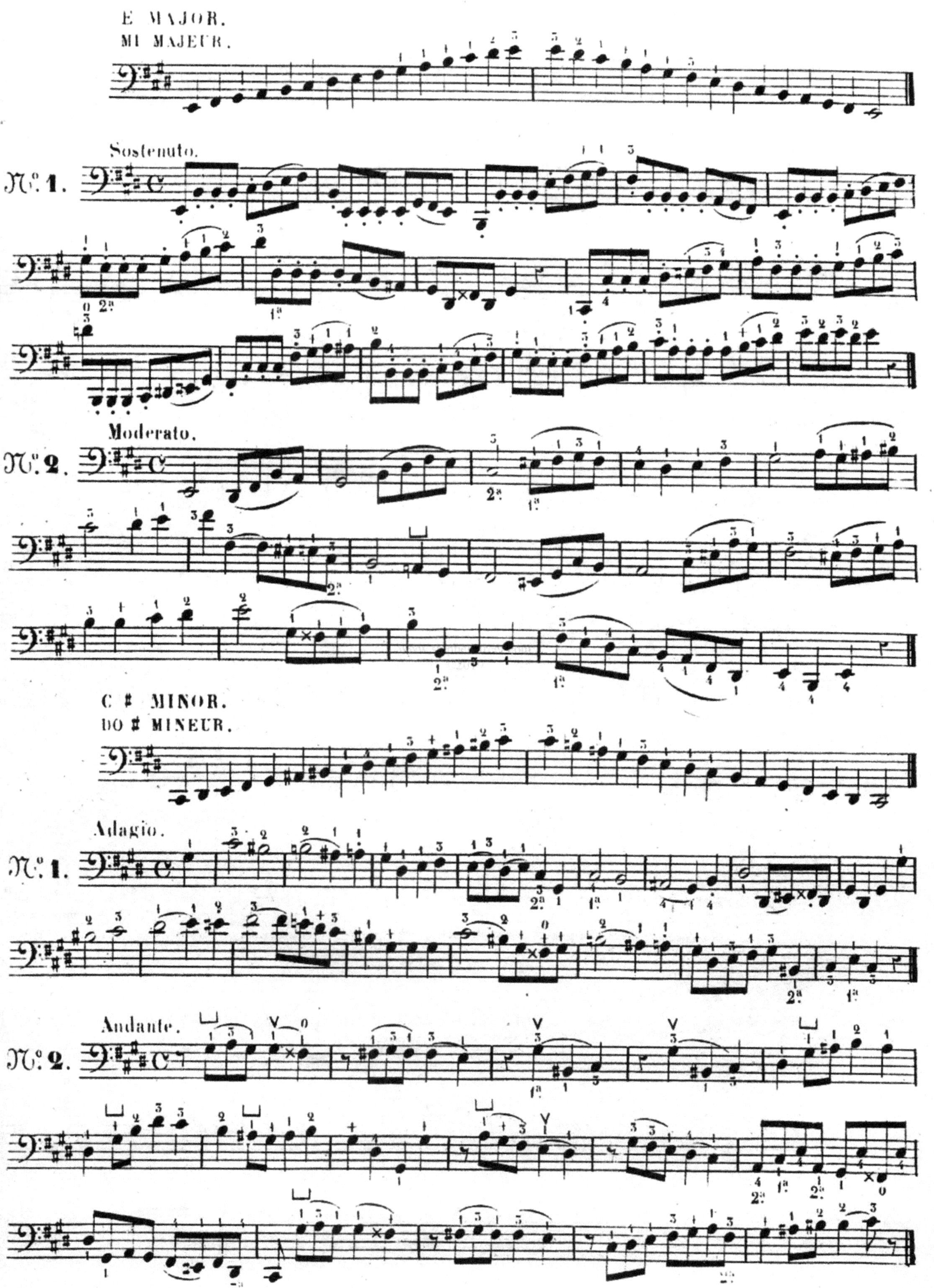
E MAJOR.
MI MAJEUR.
Sostenuto.
No. 1.
Moderato.
No. 2.
C ♯ MINOR.
DO ♯ MINEUR.
Adagio.
No. 1.
Andante.
No. 2.

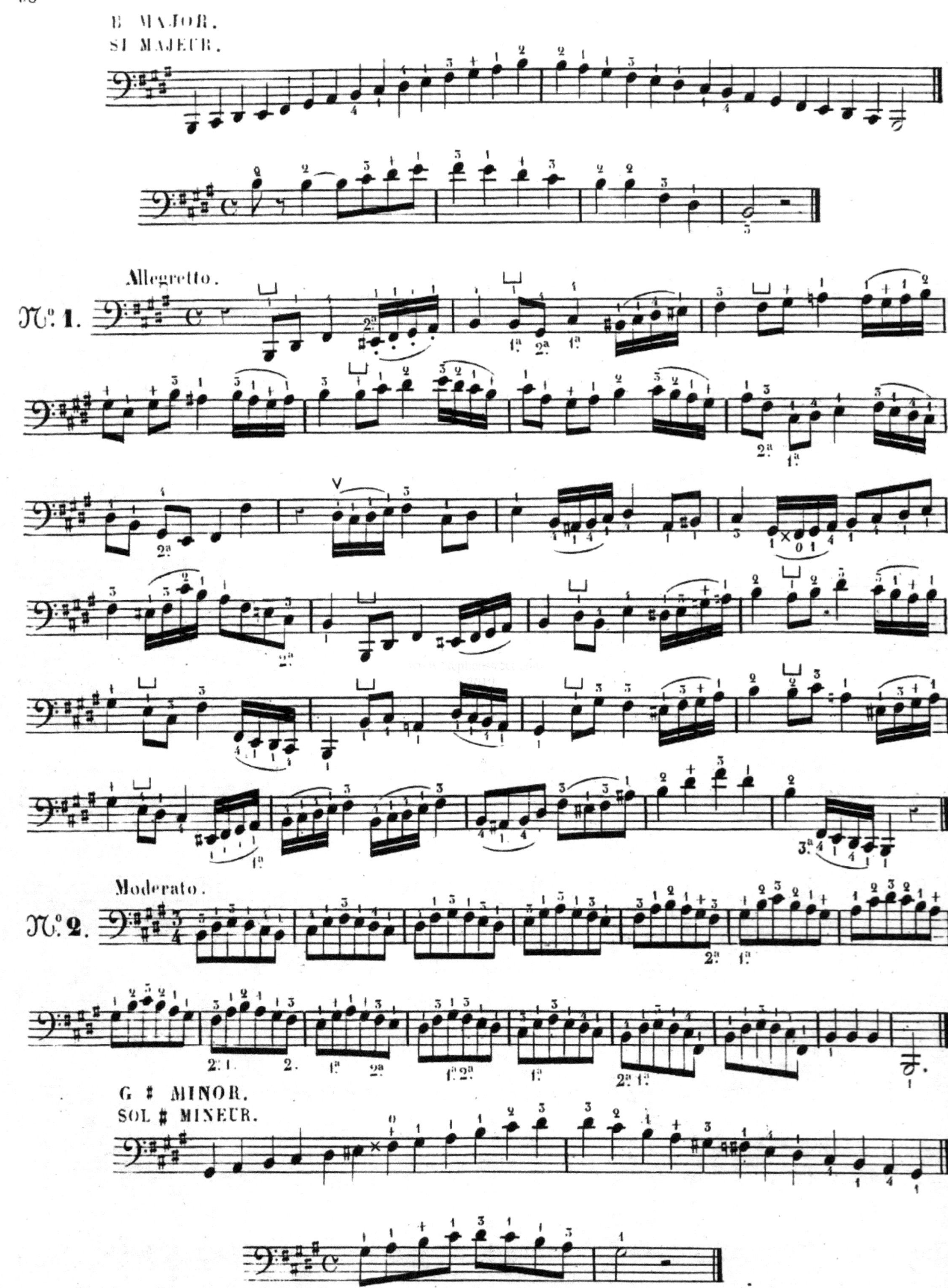

B MAJOR.
SI MAJEUR.
Allegretto.
Nº 1.
Moderato.
Nº 2.
G # MINOR.
SOL # MINEUR.

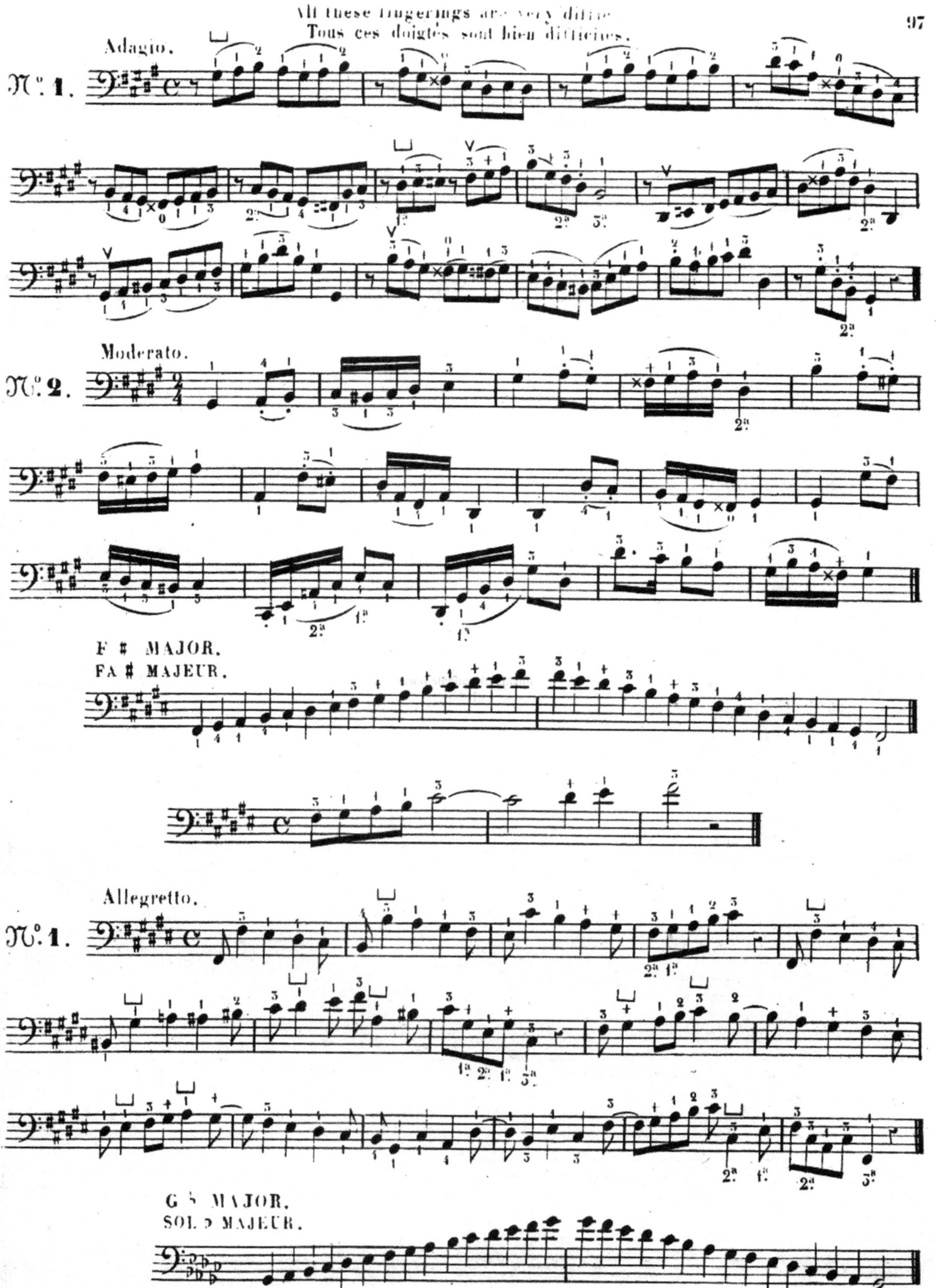
All these fingerings are very diffic
Tous ces doigtés sont bien difficiles.
Adagio.
N°. 1.
Moderato.
N°. 2.
F ♯ MAJOR.
FA ♯ MAJEUR.
Allegretto.
N°. 1.
G ♭ MAJOR.
SOL ♭ MAJEUR.

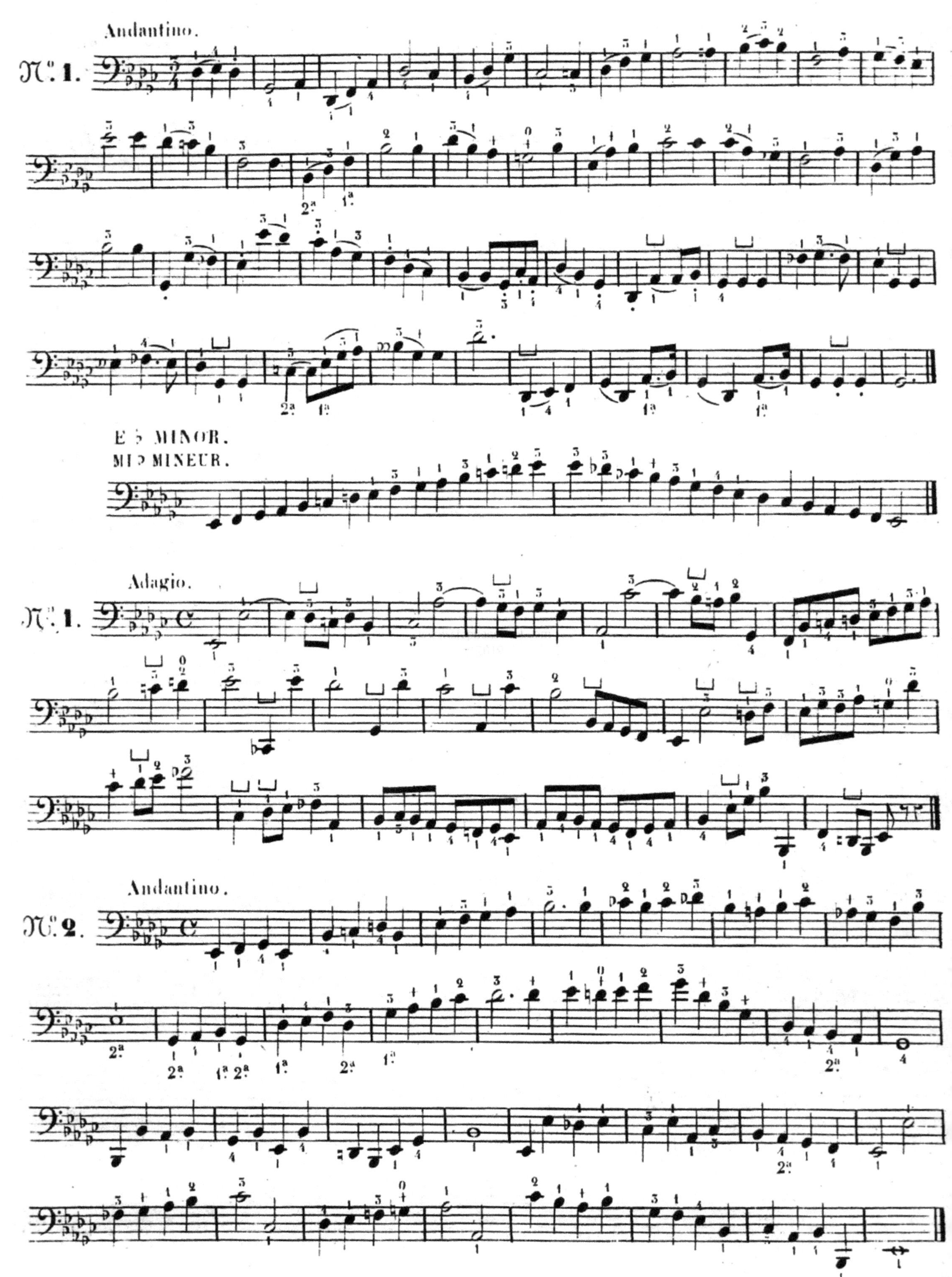
Andantino.
Nº 1.
E ♭ MINOR.
MI ♭ MINEUR.
Adagio.
Nº 1.
Andantino.
Nº 2.

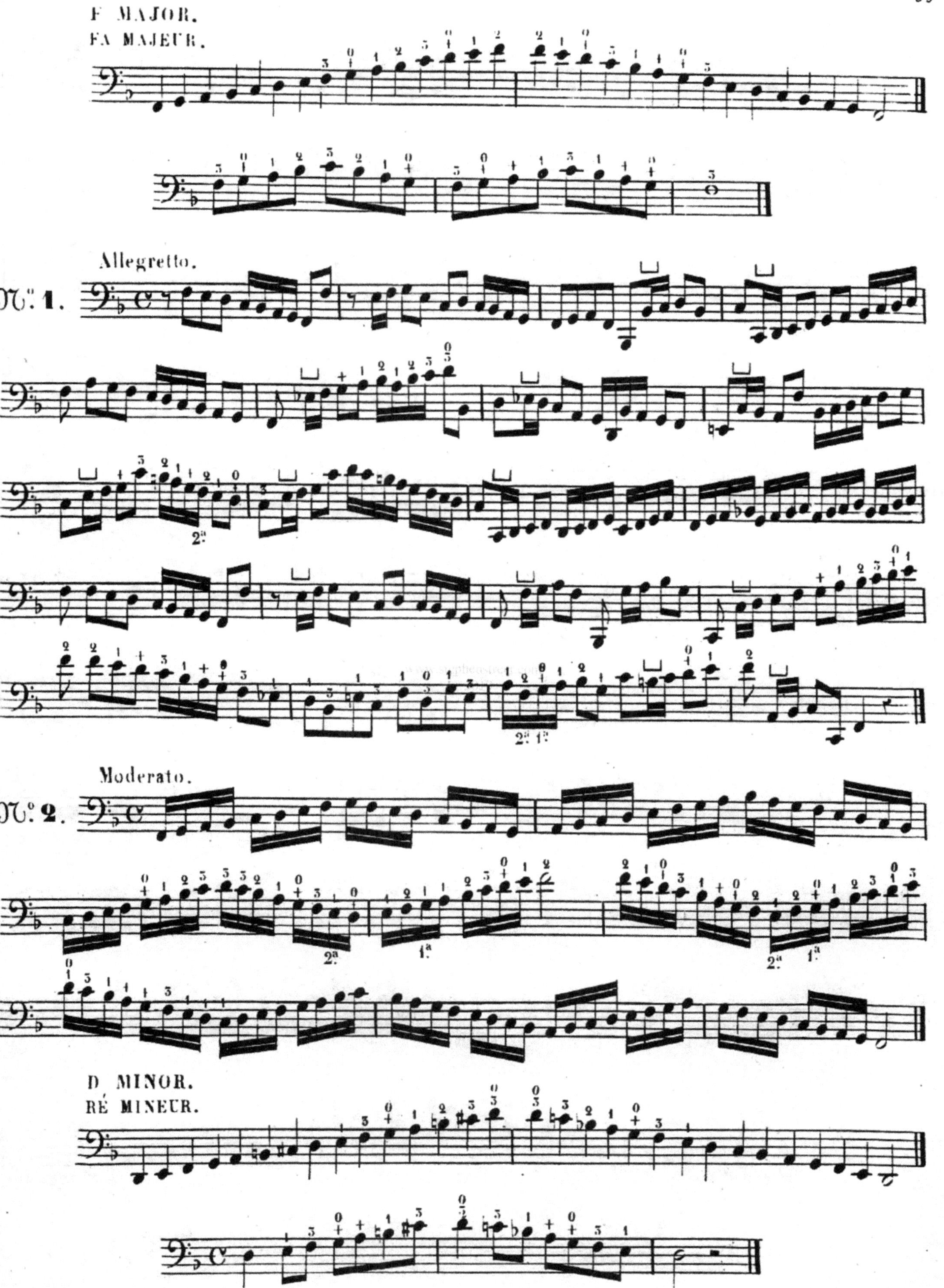
F MAJOR.
FA MAJEUR.
Allegretto.
No. 1.
Moderato.
No. 2.
D MINOR.
RÉ MINEUR.

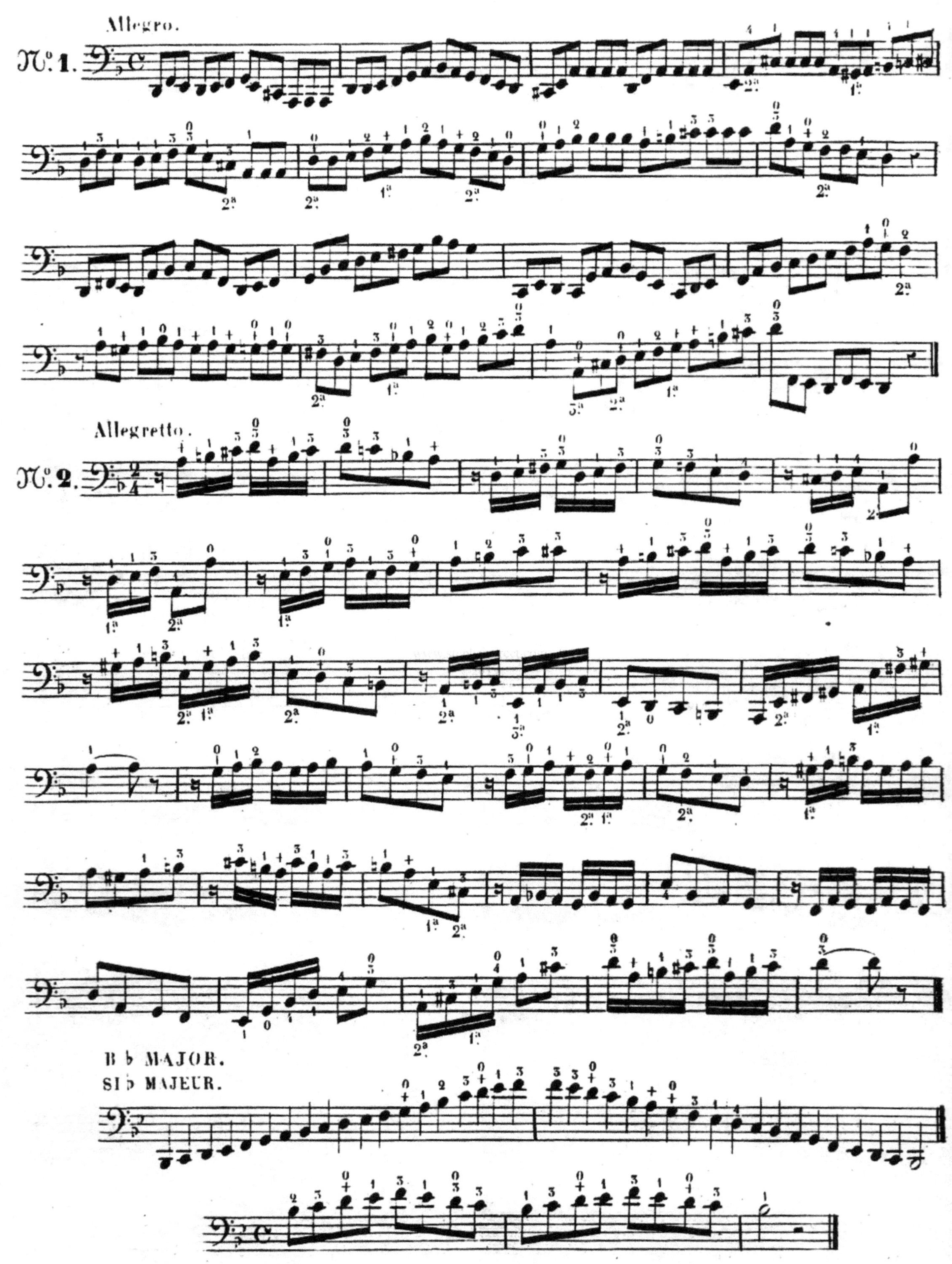
Allegro.
Nº 1.
Allegretto.
Nº 2.
B ♭ MAJOR.
SI ♭ MAJEUR.

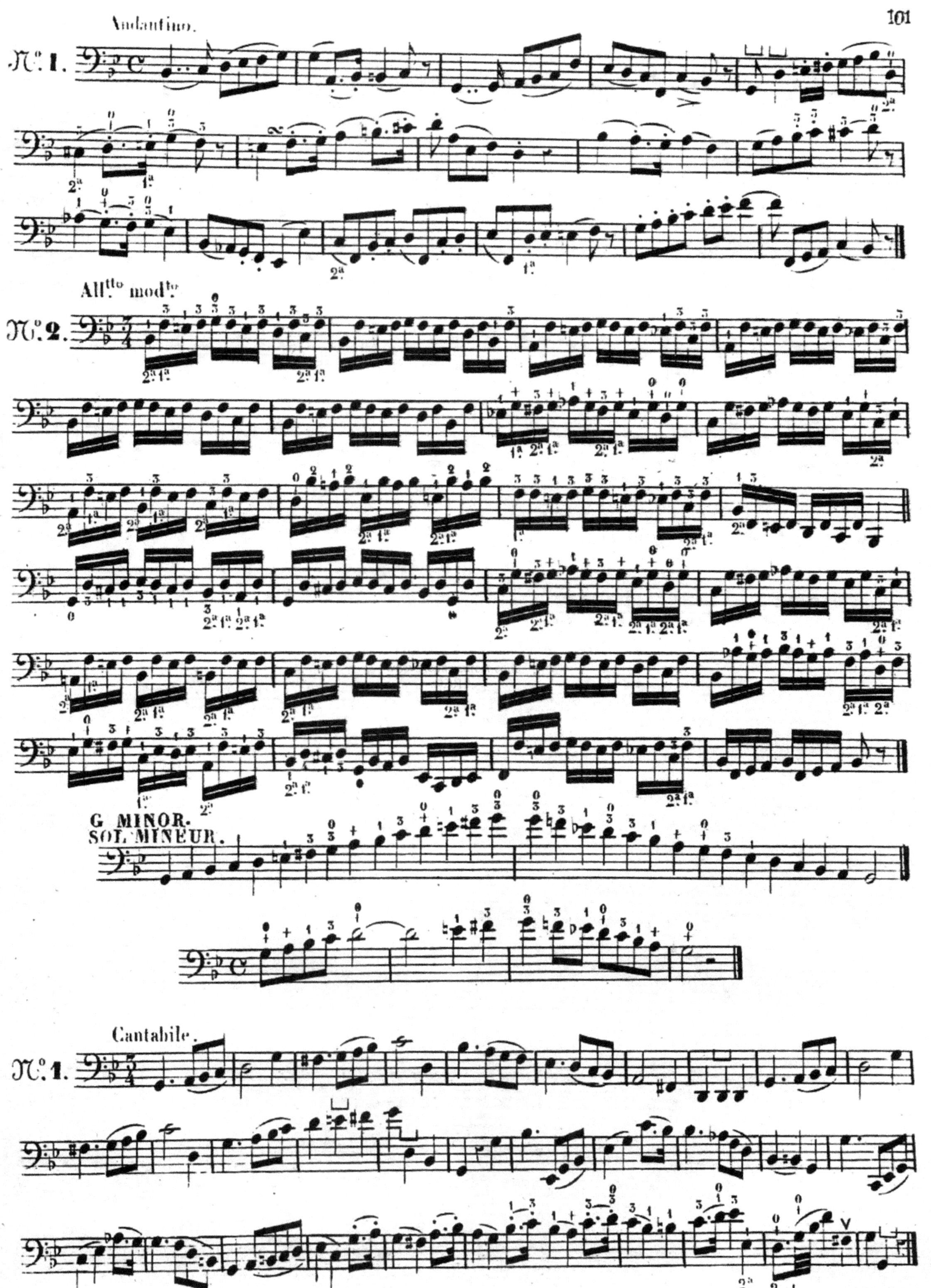
Andantino.
Nº. 1.
Allᵗᵗᵒ modᵗᵒ
Nº. 2.
G MINOR.
SOL MINEUR.
Cantabile.
Nº. 1.

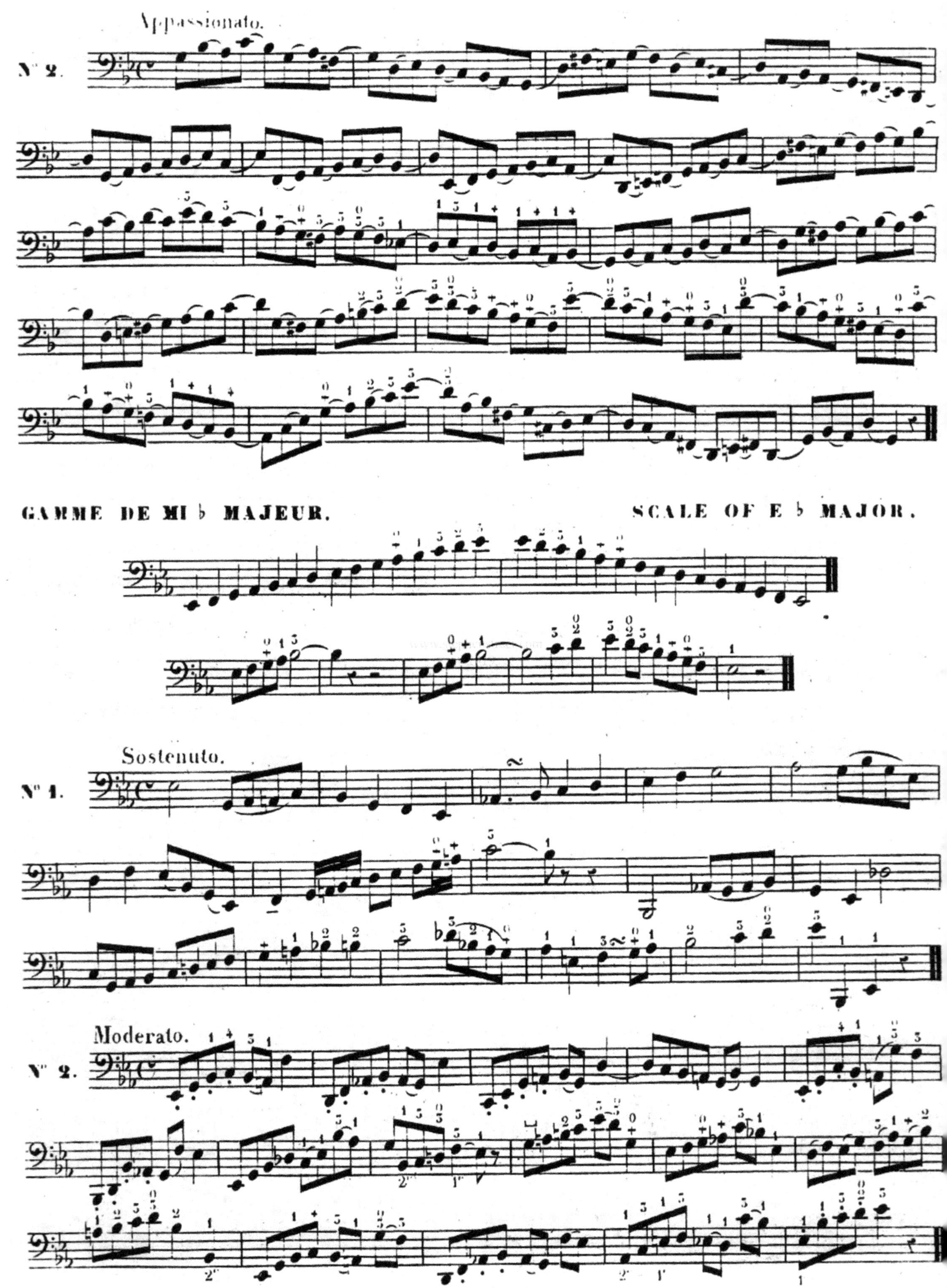
Appassionato.
Nº 2.
GAMME DE MI ♭ MAJEUR.
SCALE OF E ♭ MAJOR.
Sostenuto.
Nº 1.
Moderato.
Nº 2.

GAMME DE DO MINEUR. SCALE OF C MINOR.

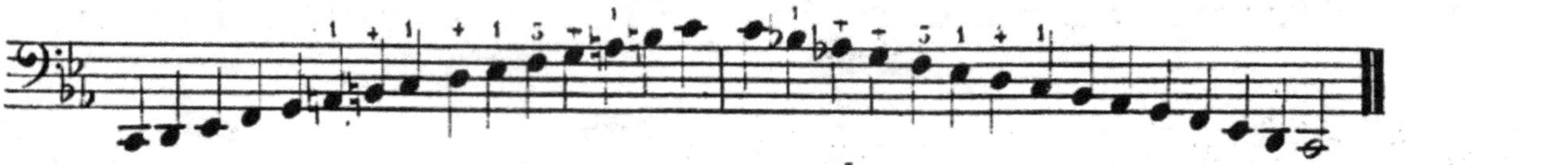

Adagio.

Nº 1.

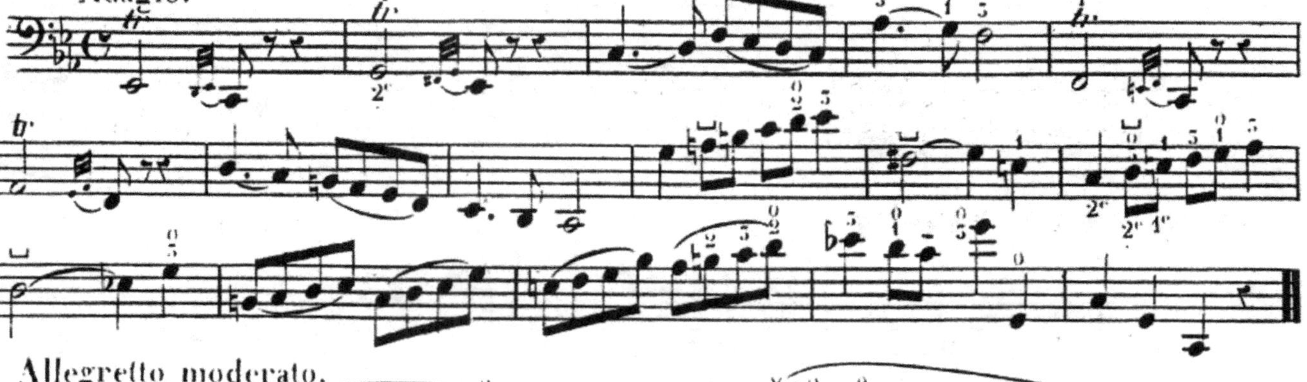

Allegretto moderato.

Nº 2.

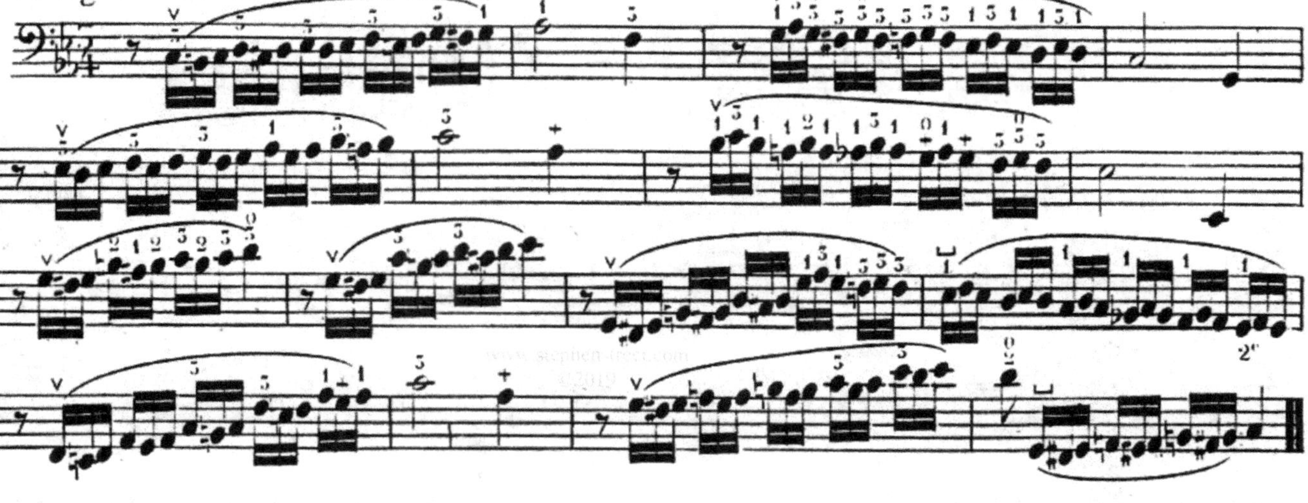

GAMME DE LA ♭ MAJEUR. SCALE OF A ♭ MAJOR.

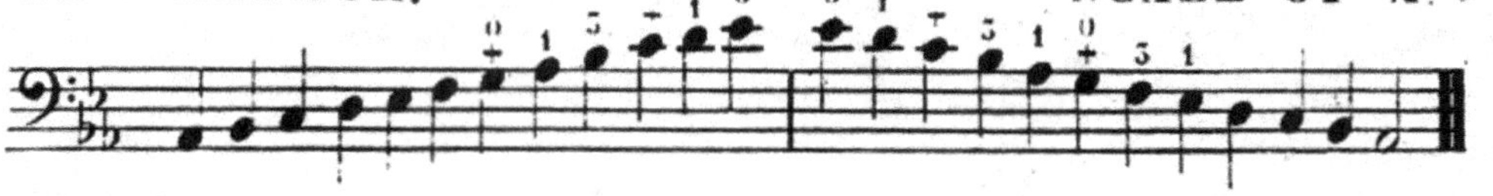

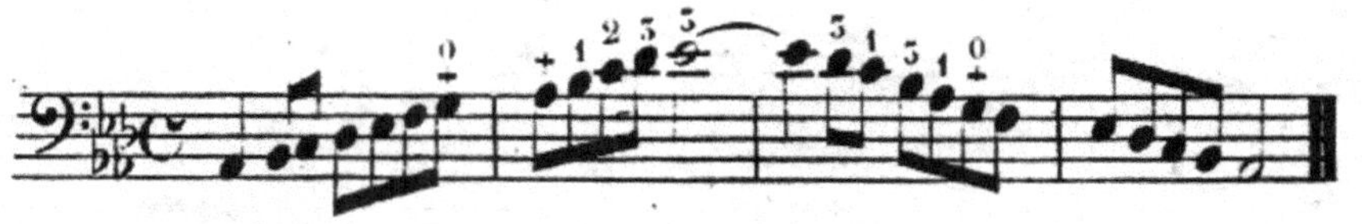

Allegretto.

Nº 1.

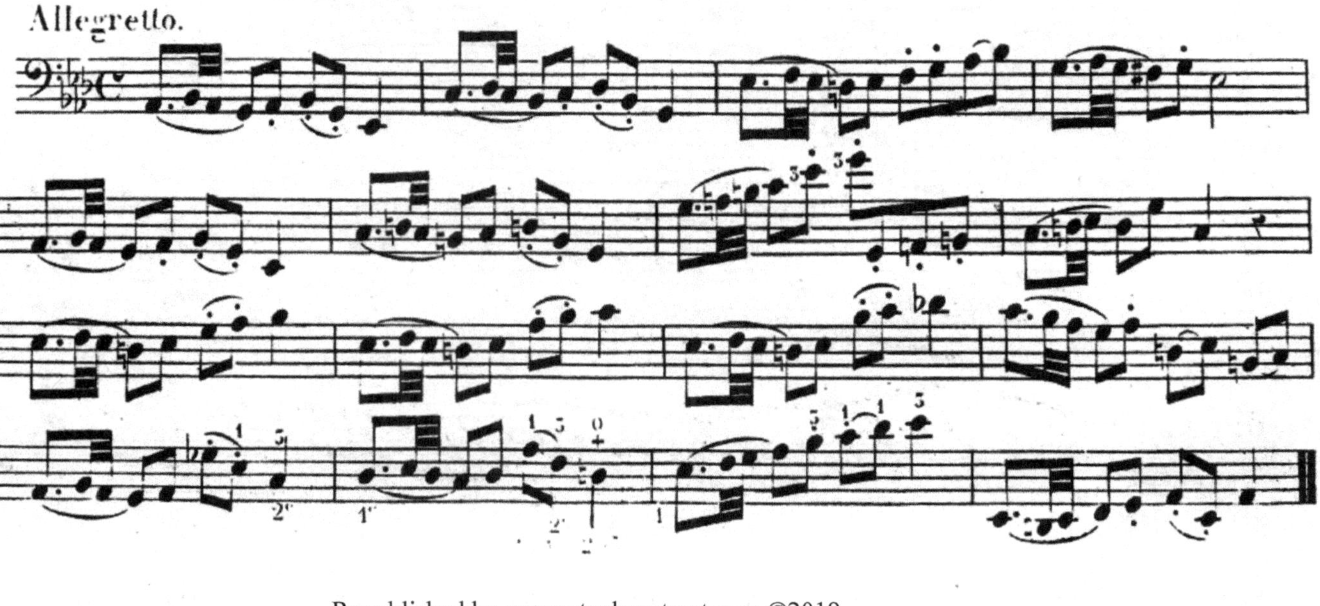

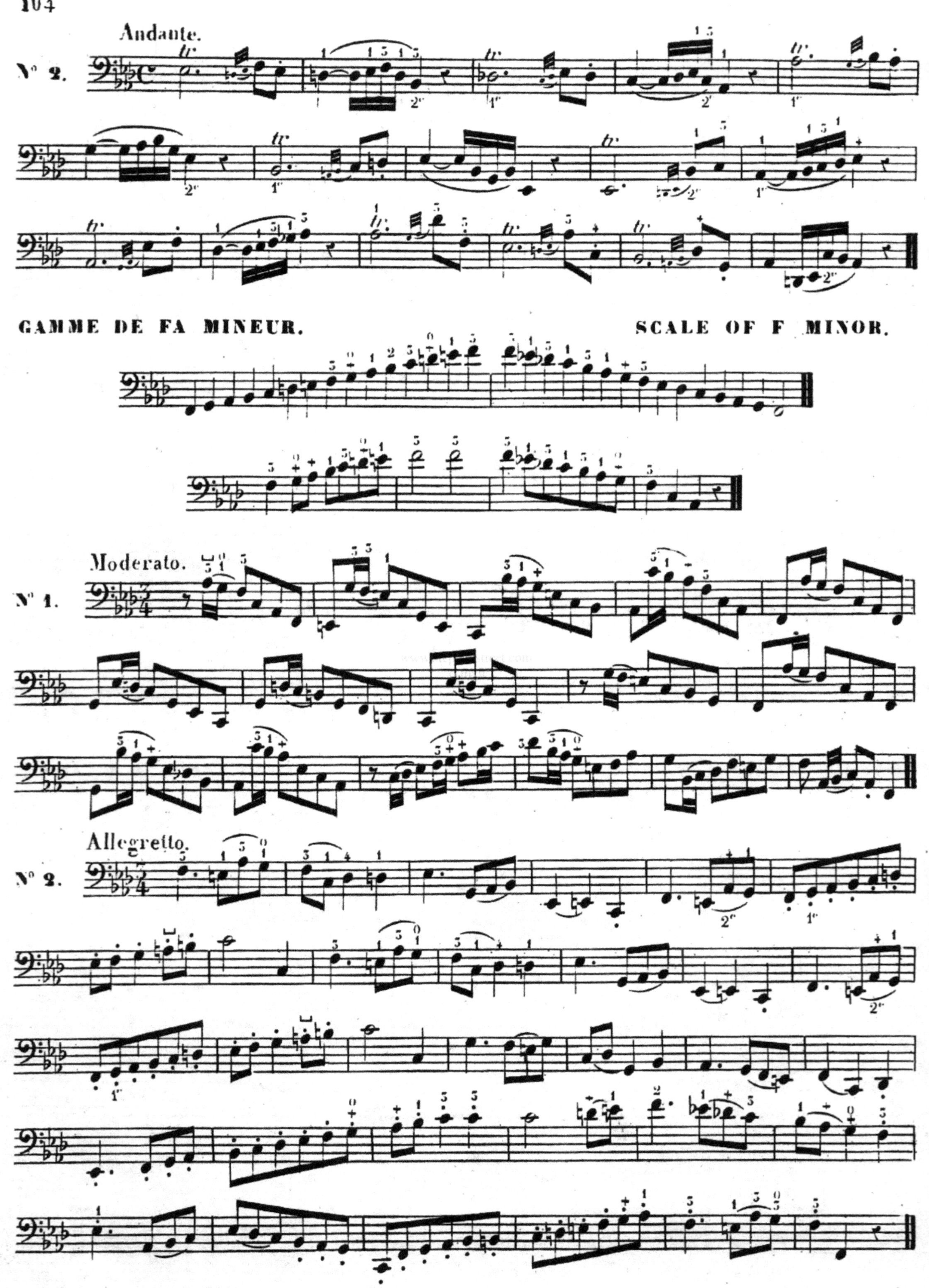
Andante.
Nº 2.
GAMME DE FA MINEUR.
SCALE OF F MINOR.
Moderato.
Nº 1.
Allegretto.
Nº 2.

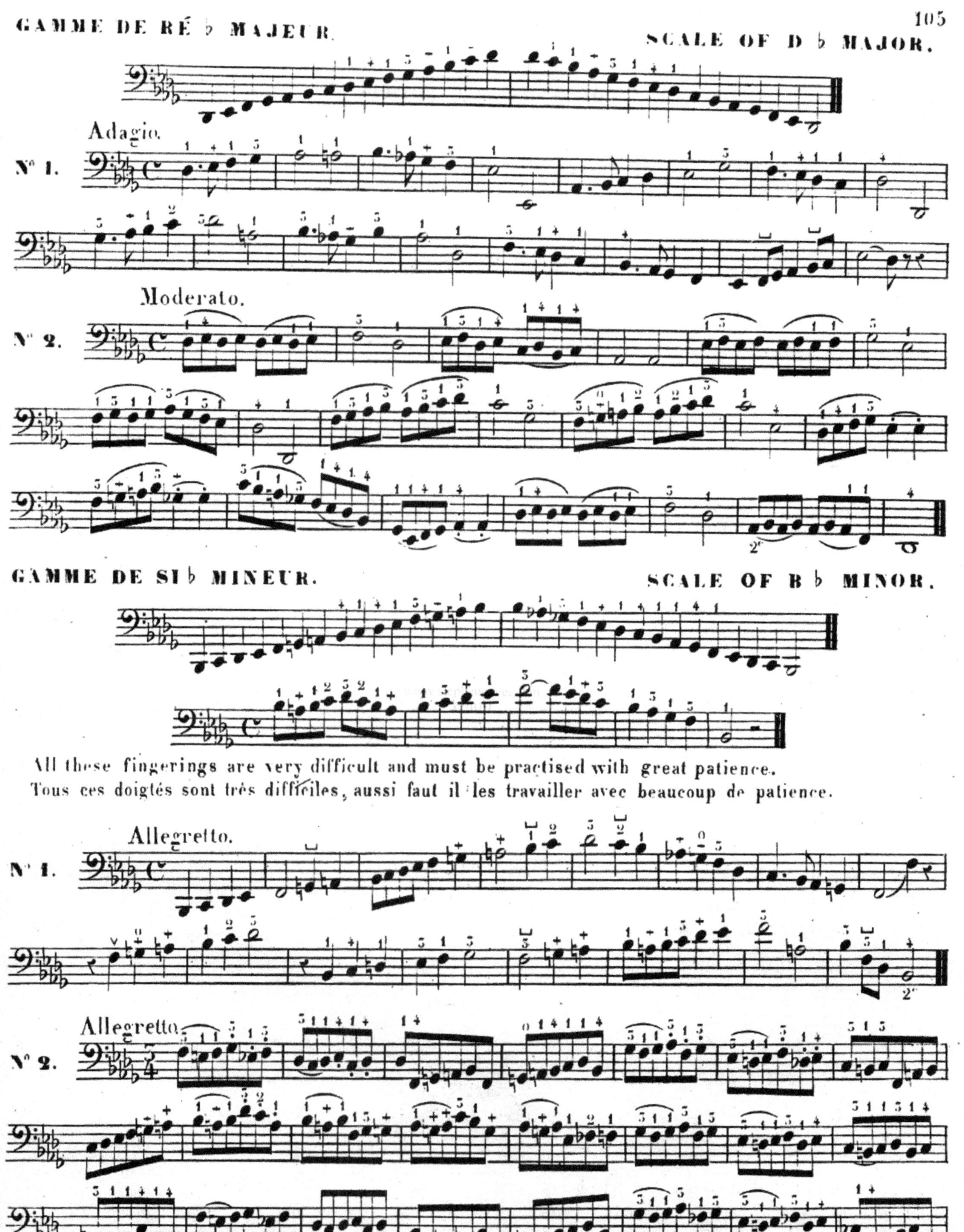
GAMME DE RÉ ♭ MAJEUR.
SCALE OF D ♭ MAJOR.
Adagio.
Nº 1.
Moderato.
Nº 2.
GAMME DE SI ♭ MINEUR.
SCALE OF B ♭ MINOR.
All these fingerings are very difficult and must be practised with great patience.
Tous ces doigtés sont très difficiles, aussi faut il les travailler avec beaucoup de patience.
Allegretto.
Nº 1.
Allegretto.
Nº 2.

## OF HARMONIC SOUNDS.

The following represents an extended string, which, as we know gives the octave at the middle, its central point, starting from whence, both ascending and descending, the string gives out always the same harmonic sounds.

### *G* STRING.

| | | |
|---|---|---|
| Nut........ | .... | *G* |
| | ........................................ | *G* |
| | ........................................ | *D* |
| | ........................................ | *B* |
| | ........................................ | *A* |
| | ........................................ | *G* |
| | ........................................ | *D* |
| | ........................................ | *B* |
| | ........................................ | *G* |
| | ........................................ | *D* |
| Middle of the string, Octave or 8ve.................. | Octave or 8ve.................................... | *G* |
| 2 thirds, Octave of the fifth or 12th................ | Octave of the fifth or 12th....................... | *D* |
| 3/4ths double Octave or 15th......................... | Double Octave or 15th............................. | *G* |
| 4/5ths double Octave of the third or 17th major........ | 17th............................................. | *B* |
| 5/6ths double Octave of the fifth or 19th............. | 19th............................................. | *D* |
| 7/8ths triple Octave or 22nd......................... | 22nd............................................. | *G* |
| 23rd................................................ | 23rd............................................. | *A* |
| 24th................................................ | 24th............................................. | *B* |
| 26th................................................ | 26th............................................. | *D* |
| 29th................................................ | 29th............................................. | *G* |
| Bridge....... | | |

We think it useless to notice the 21st (octave corresponding to *F*,) for this reason; that being the seventh of *G* and therefore defective, it is but exceptionally used and only as a passing note. The following examples will sufficiently demonstrate this.

For the position of the hand in making harmonics. (See the plate figure 7)

# VARIETIES OF FINGERING.

We shall not use the sign (o) The *G* clef indicates harmonic sounds.

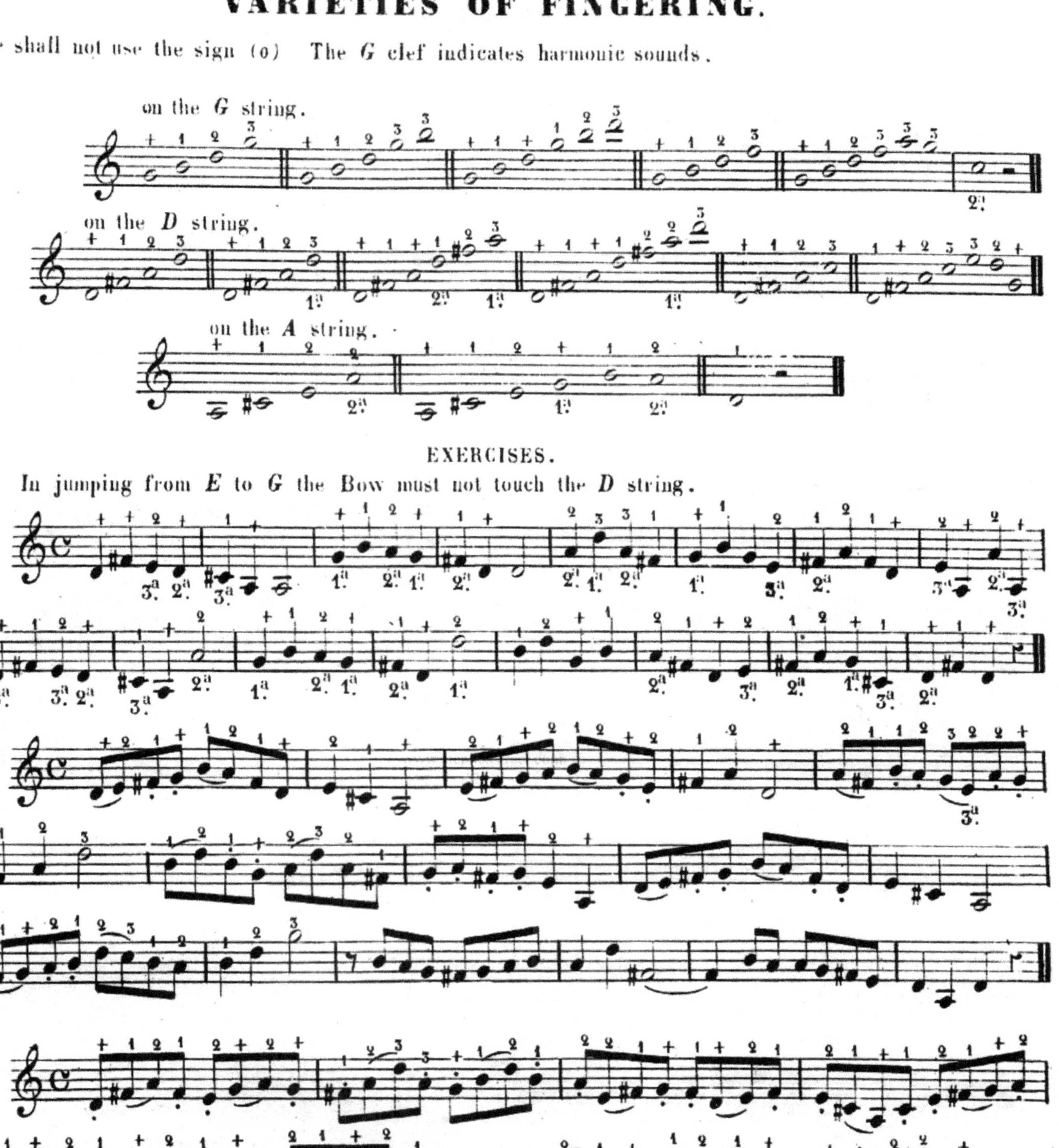

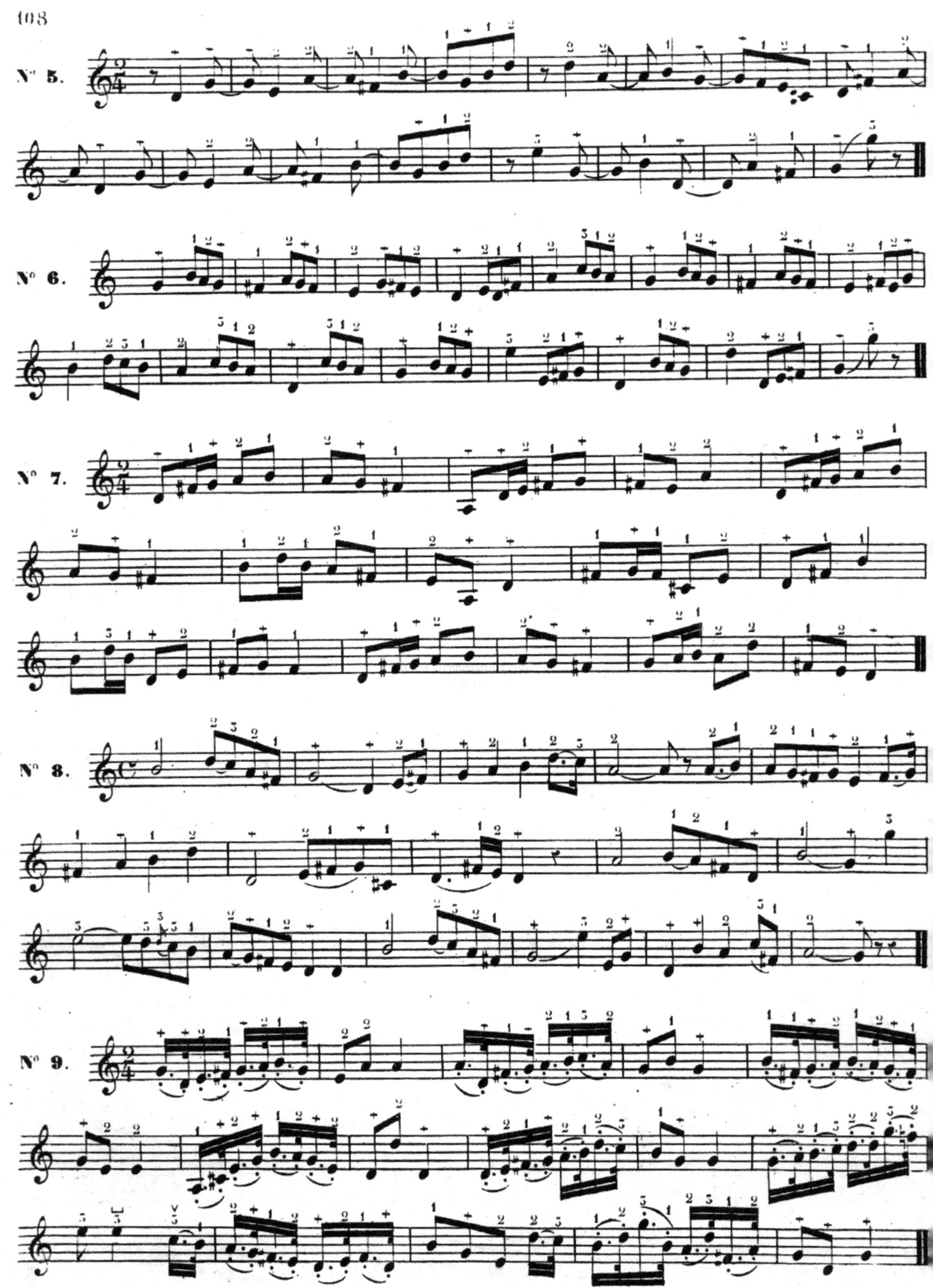
Nº 5.
Nº 6.
Nº 7.
Nº 8.
Nº 9.

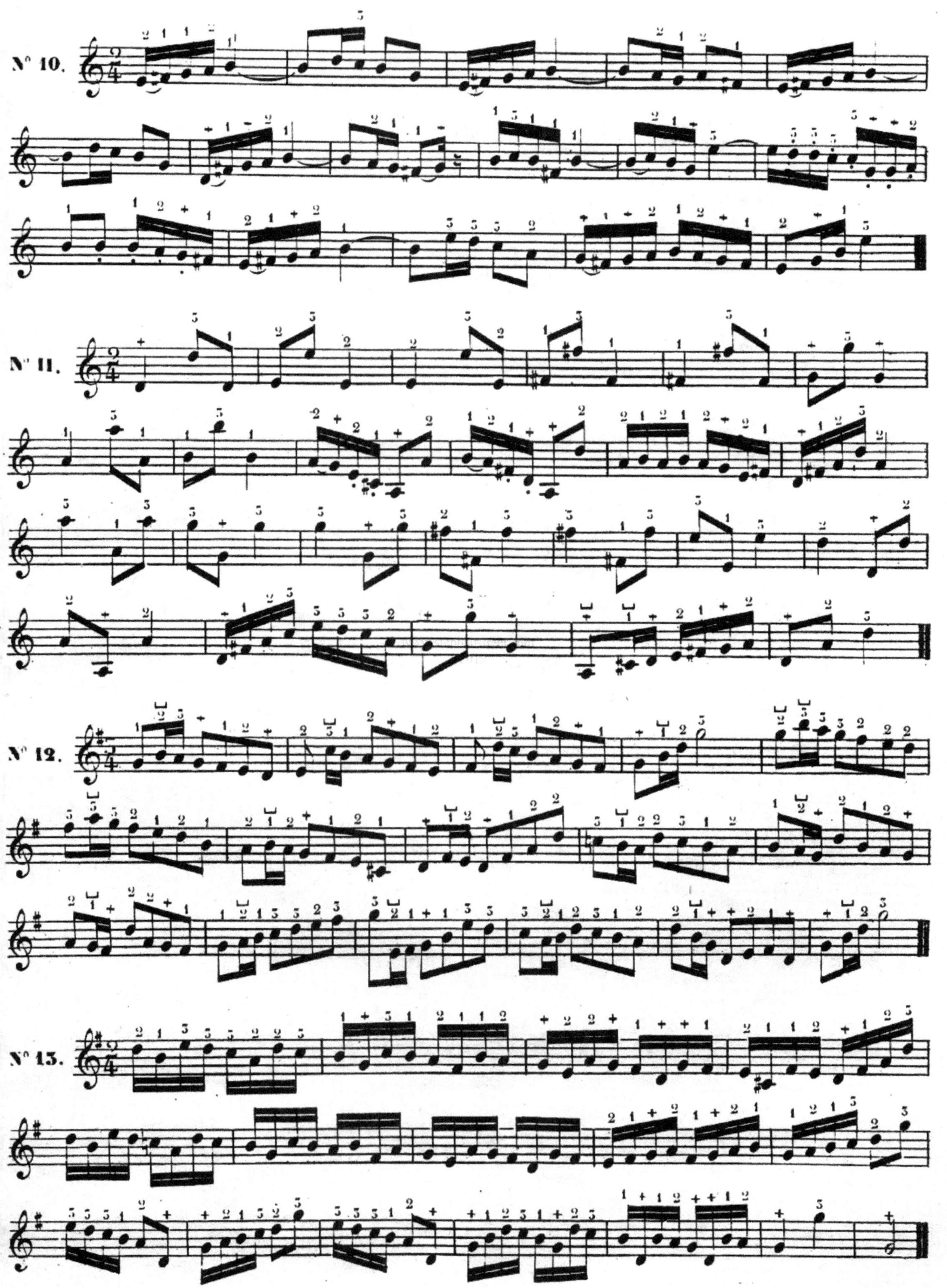
Nº 10.
Nº 11.
Nº 12.
Nº 13.

The preceding exercises enable us to understand the resources of the harmónics. The difficulty consists in uniting the stopped notes of the octave below, or rather of the whole instrument with the harmonic sounds.

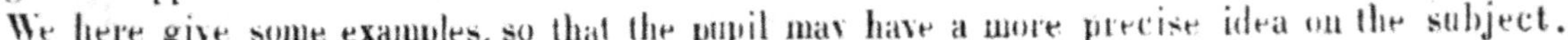

We here give some examples, so that the pupil may have a more precise idea on the subject.

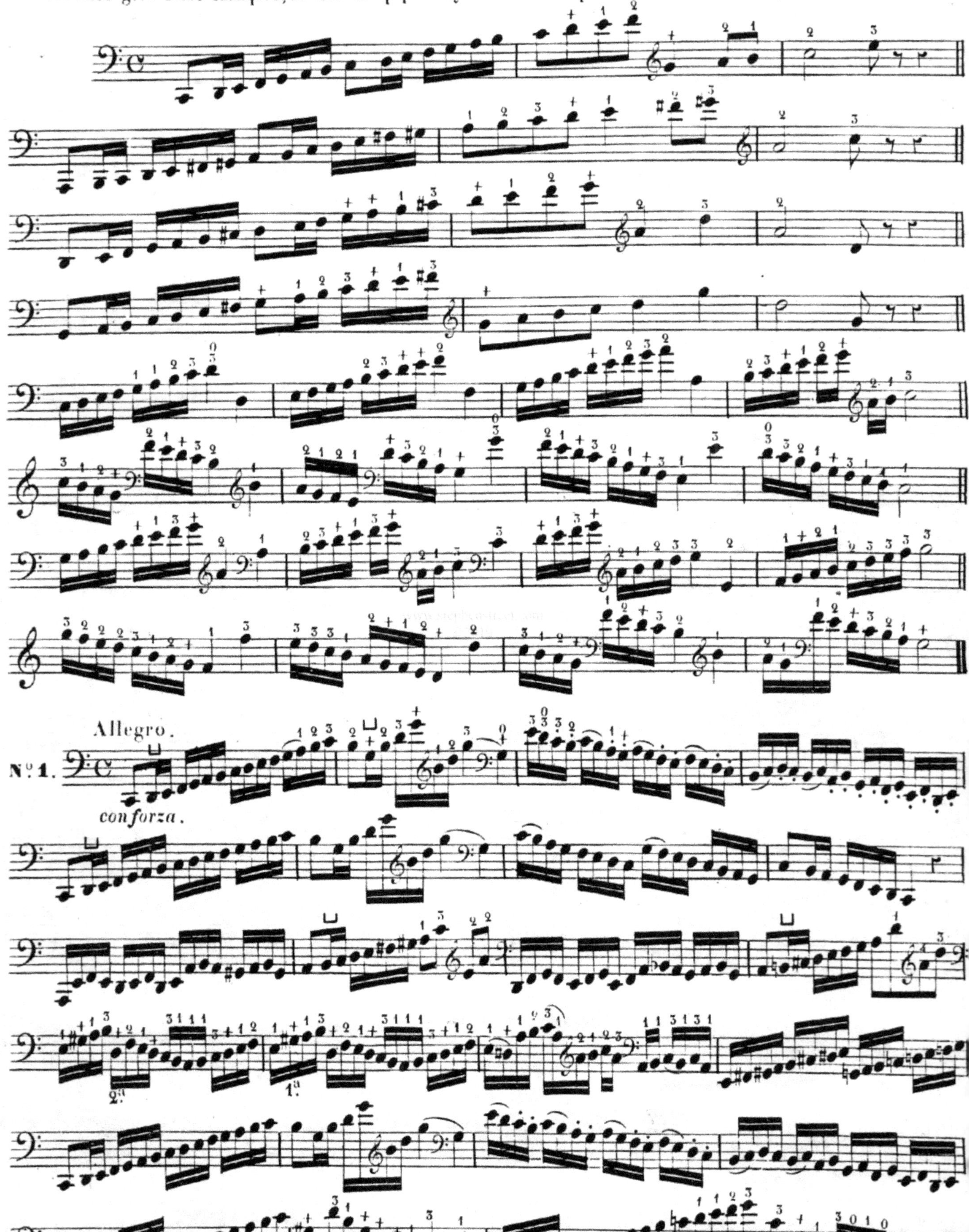

Allegro.

Nº 1.

con forza.

I. F. 3170.

Allegro moderato.

N° 2.

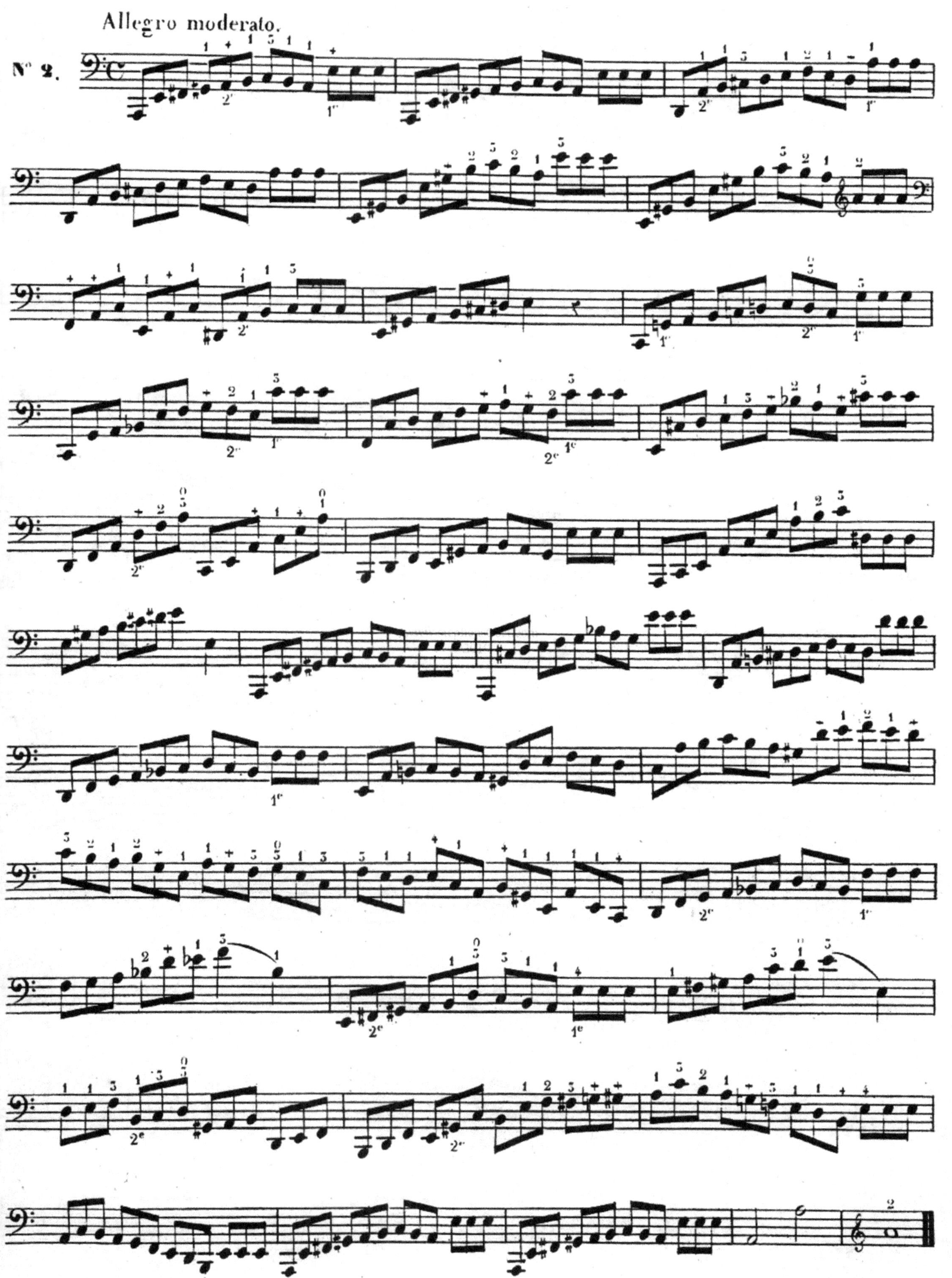

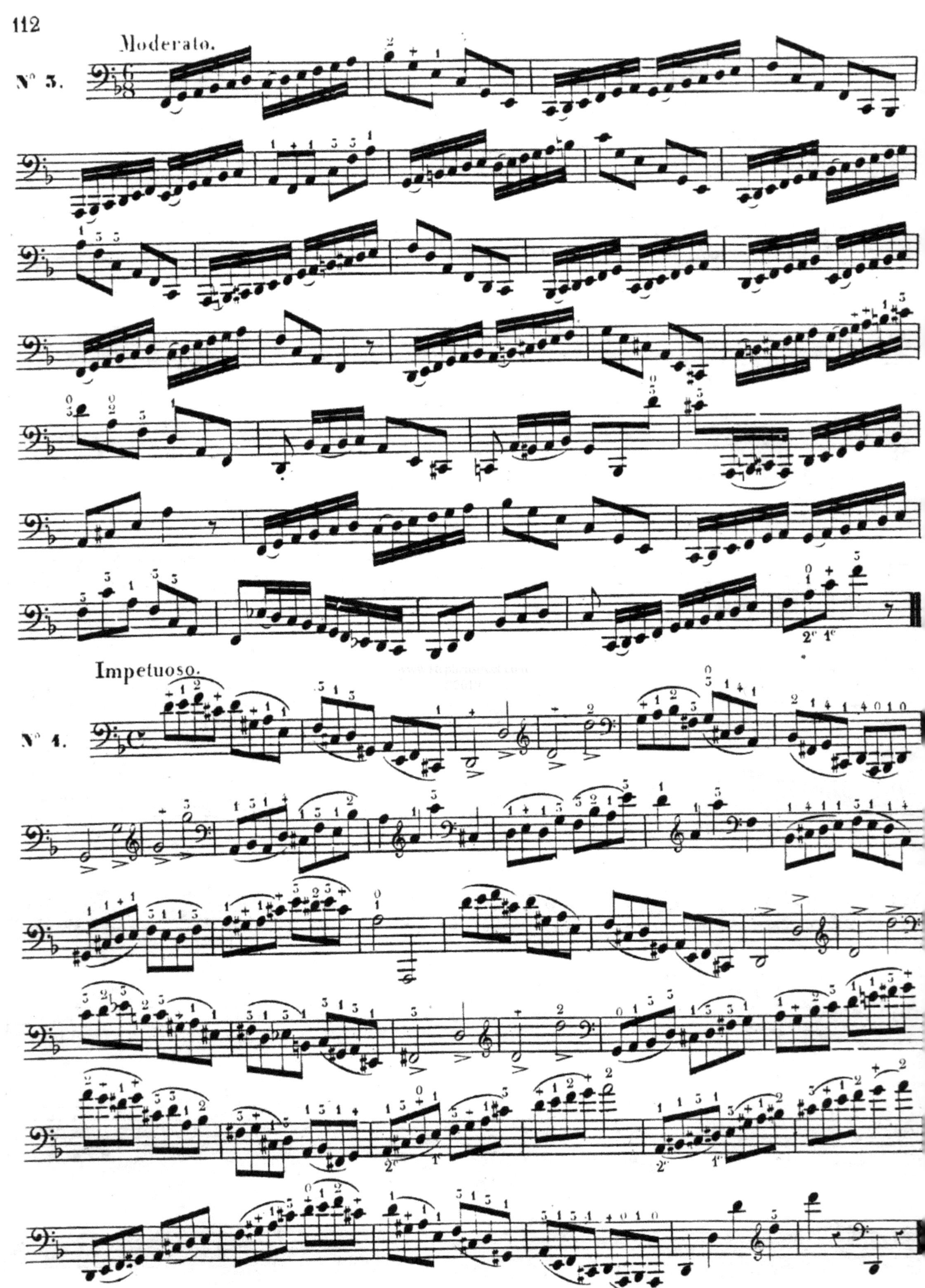
Moderato.
Nº 3.
Impetuoso.
Nº 4.

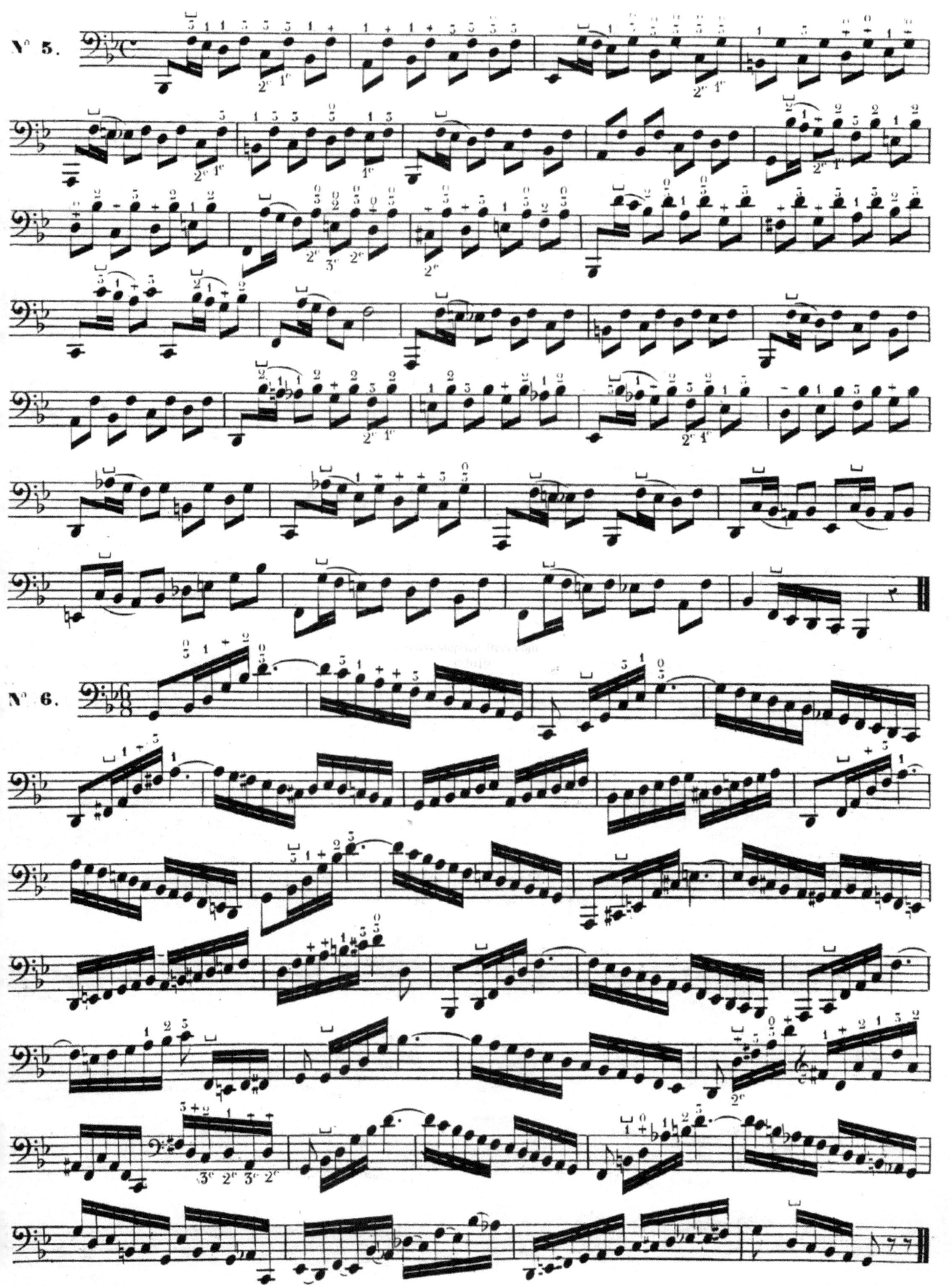
Nº 5.
Nº 6.

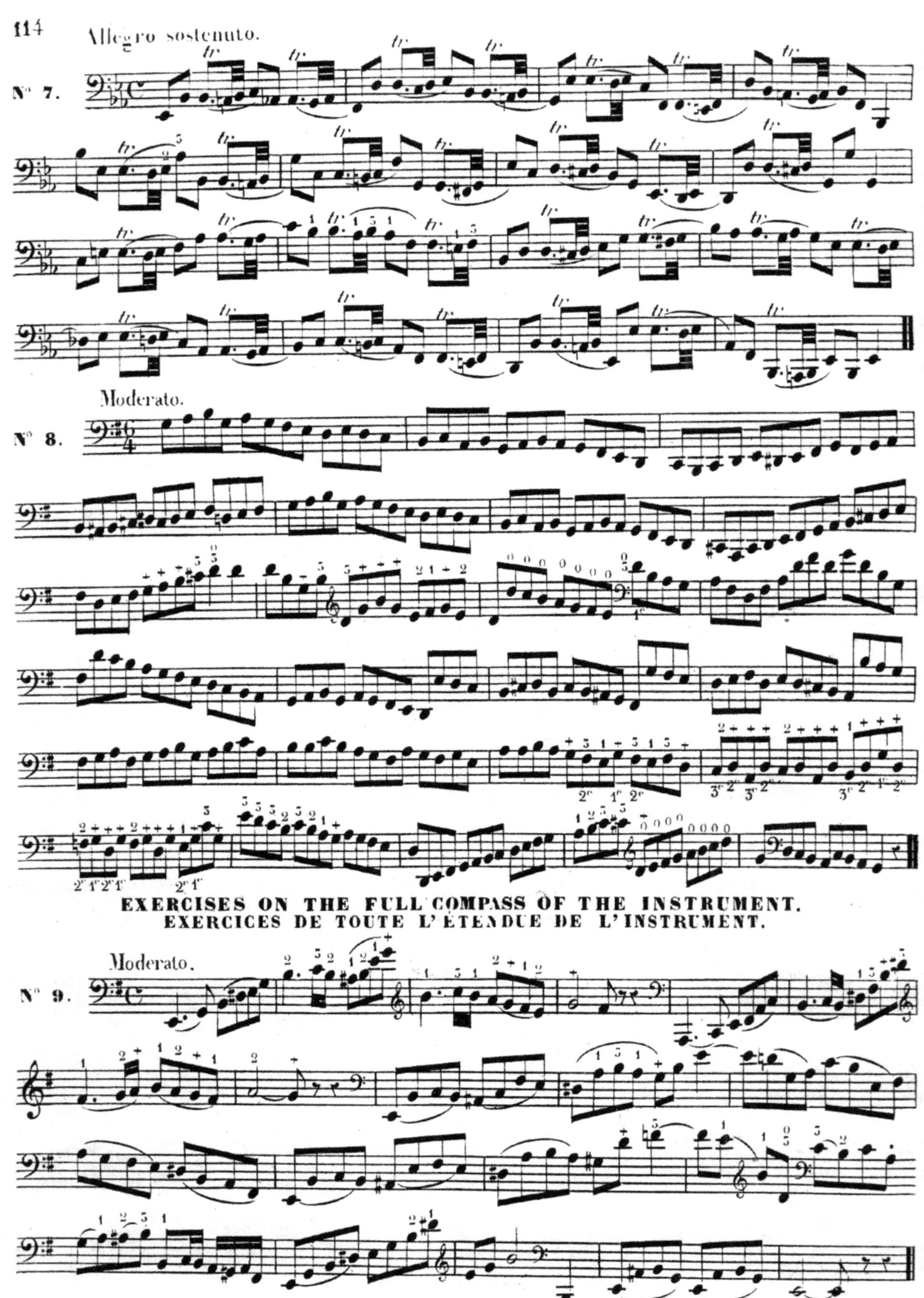
Allegro sostenuto.
Nº 7.
Moderato.
Nº 8.
EXERCISES ON THE FULL COMPASS OF THE INSTRUMENT.
EXERCICES DE TOUTE L'ÉTENDUE DE L'INSTRUMENT.
Moderato.
Nº 9.

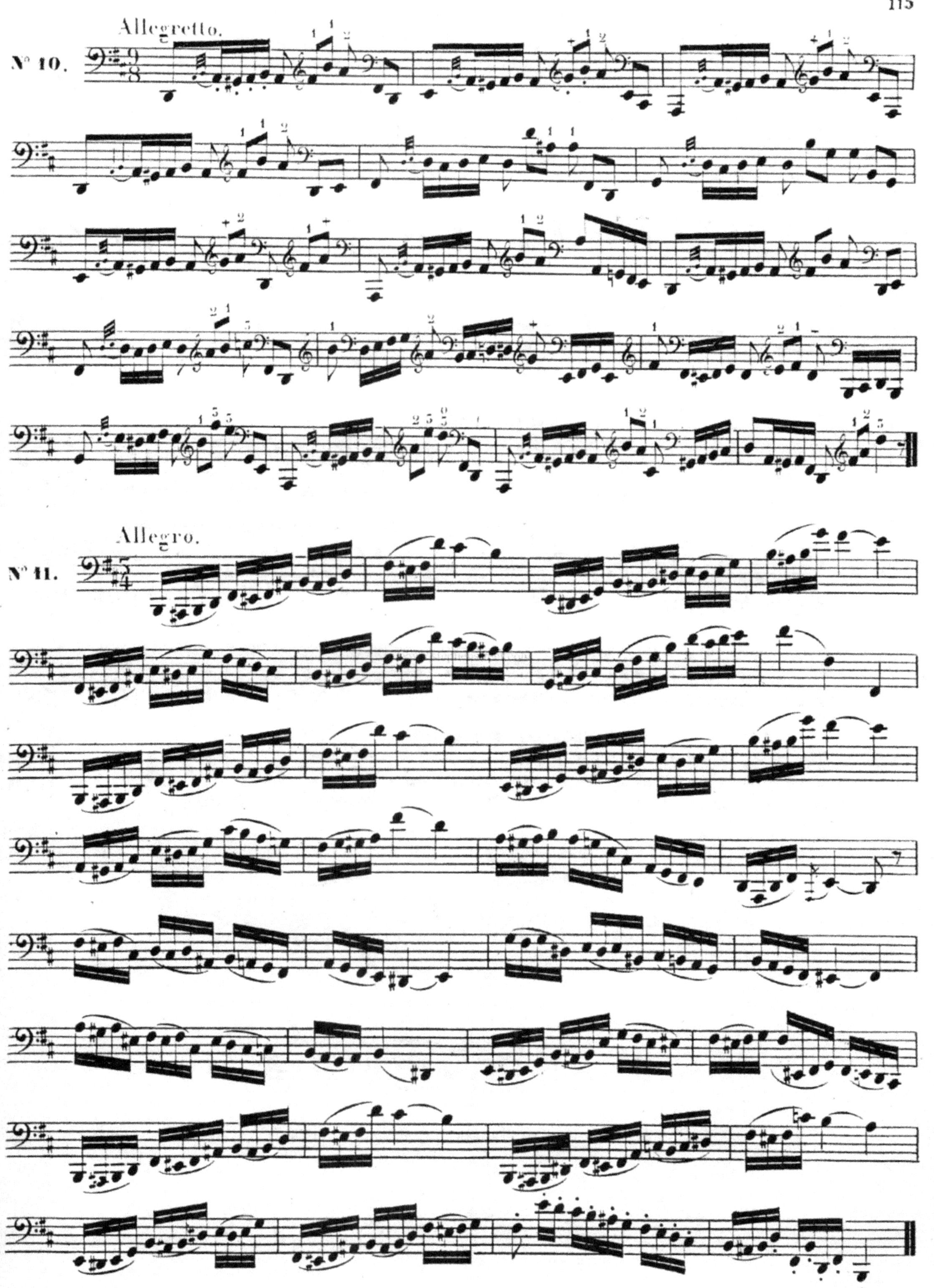
Allegretto.
Nº 10.
Allegro.
Nº 11.

## MANNER OF USING WITH LEAST DIFFICULTY THE SMALL NUMBER OF DOUBLE NOTES

TO BE OBTAINED ON THE INSTRUMENT.

No 12. Andante.

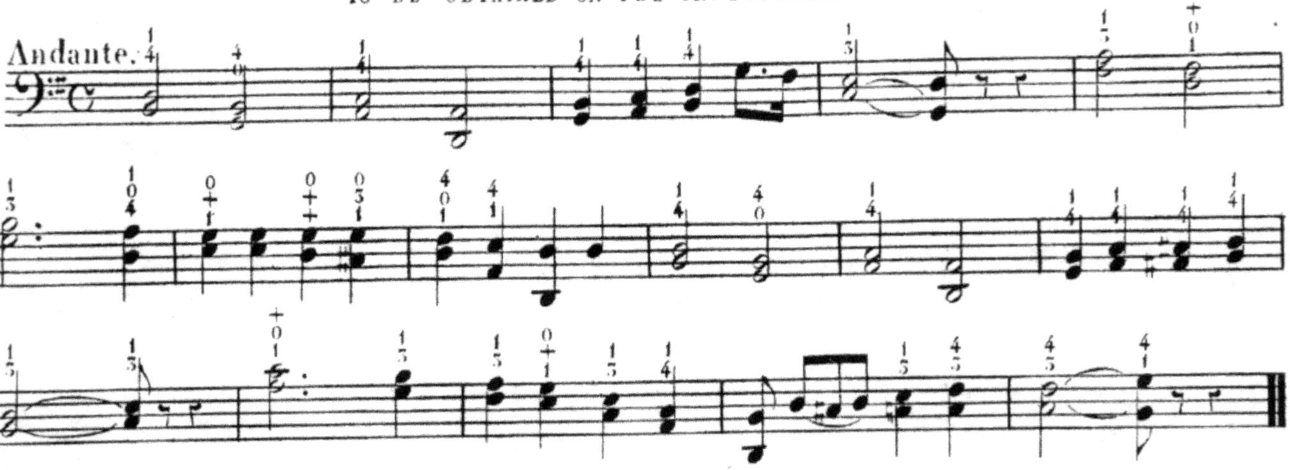

Arpeggio.

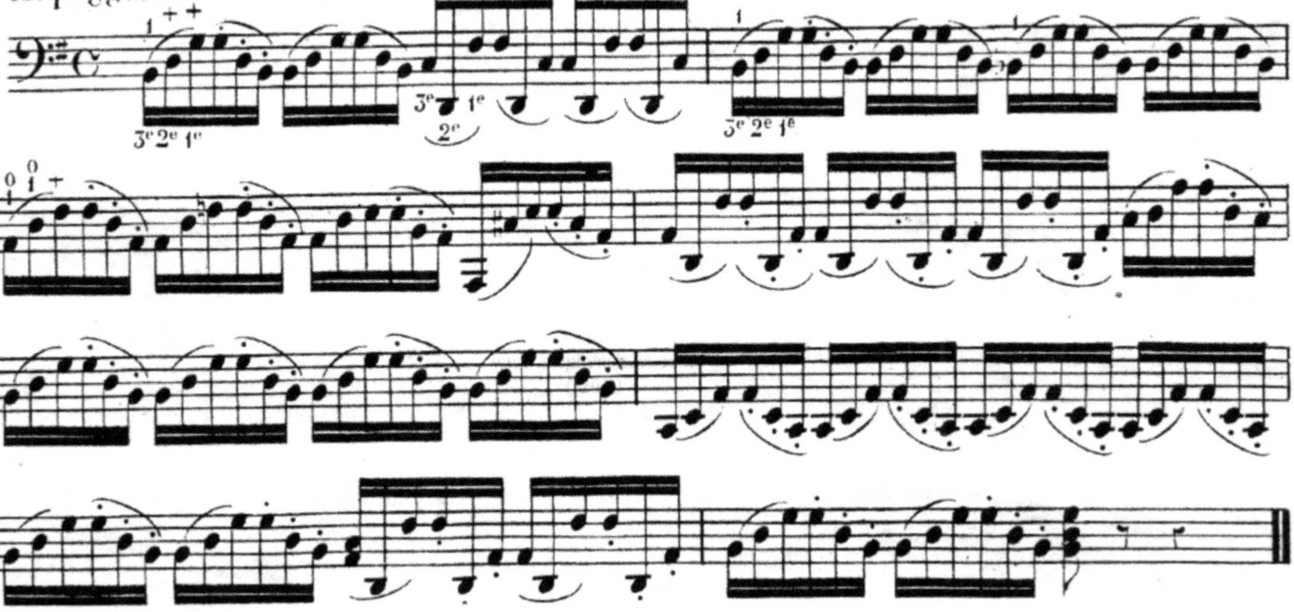

EXAMPLE FROM A PASSAGE OF ONE OF MY CONCERTOS.

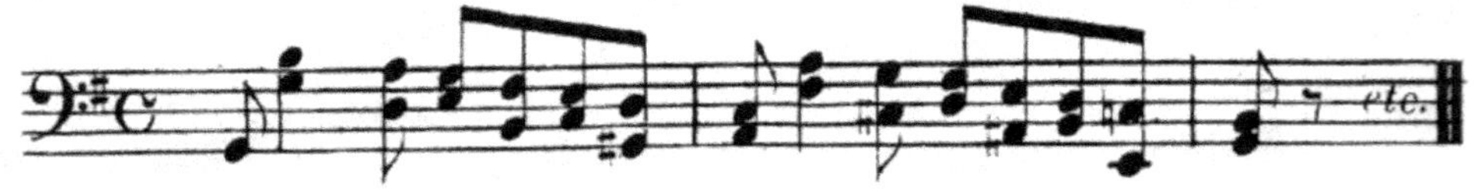


In the scale of D with harmonics we must strongly apply the 2nd finger on the C♯.

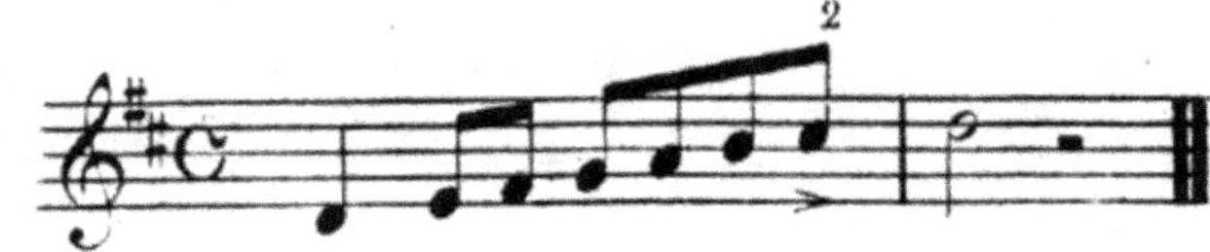


The A♯ upon the first string is obtained by taking the string vigorously between the thumb and first finger.

Adagio.

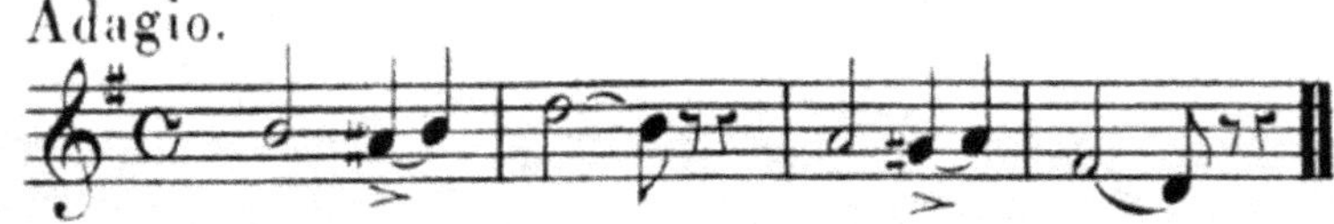

# ÉTUDES MÉLODIQUES

avec accompagnement de Piano.

## ÉLÉGIE.

BOTTESINI.

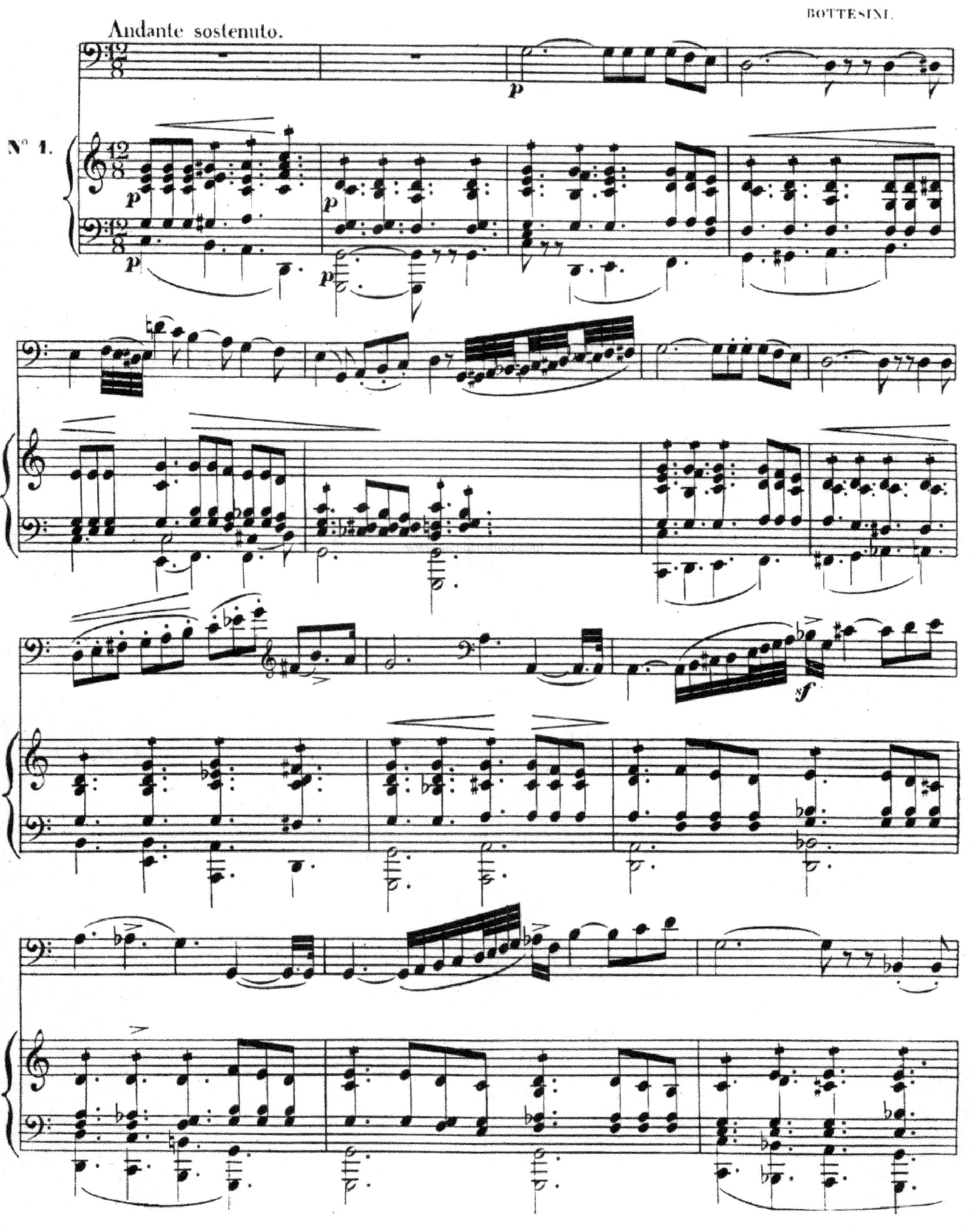

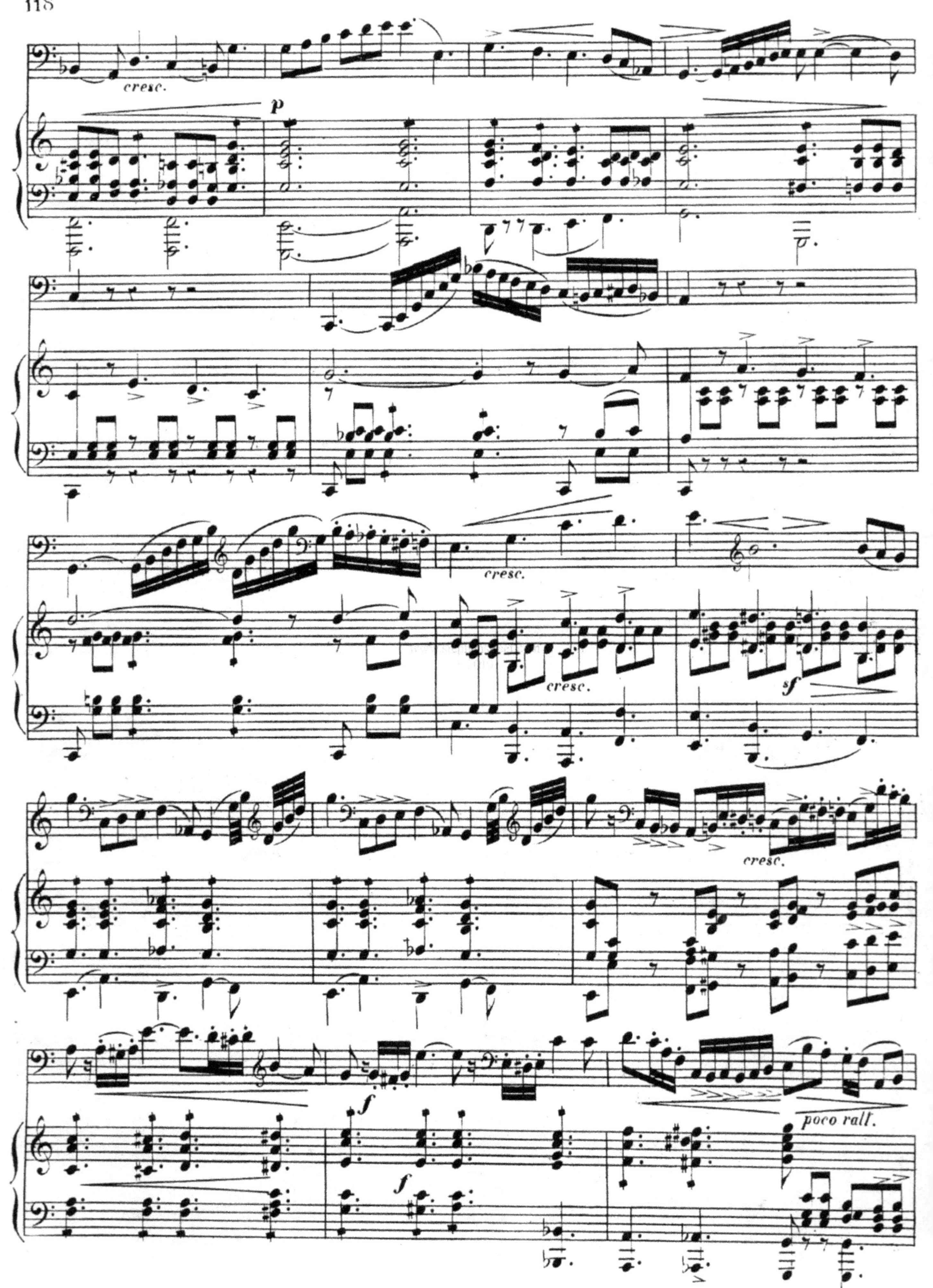
cresc.
p
cresc.
cresc.
sf
cresc.
f
f
poco rall.

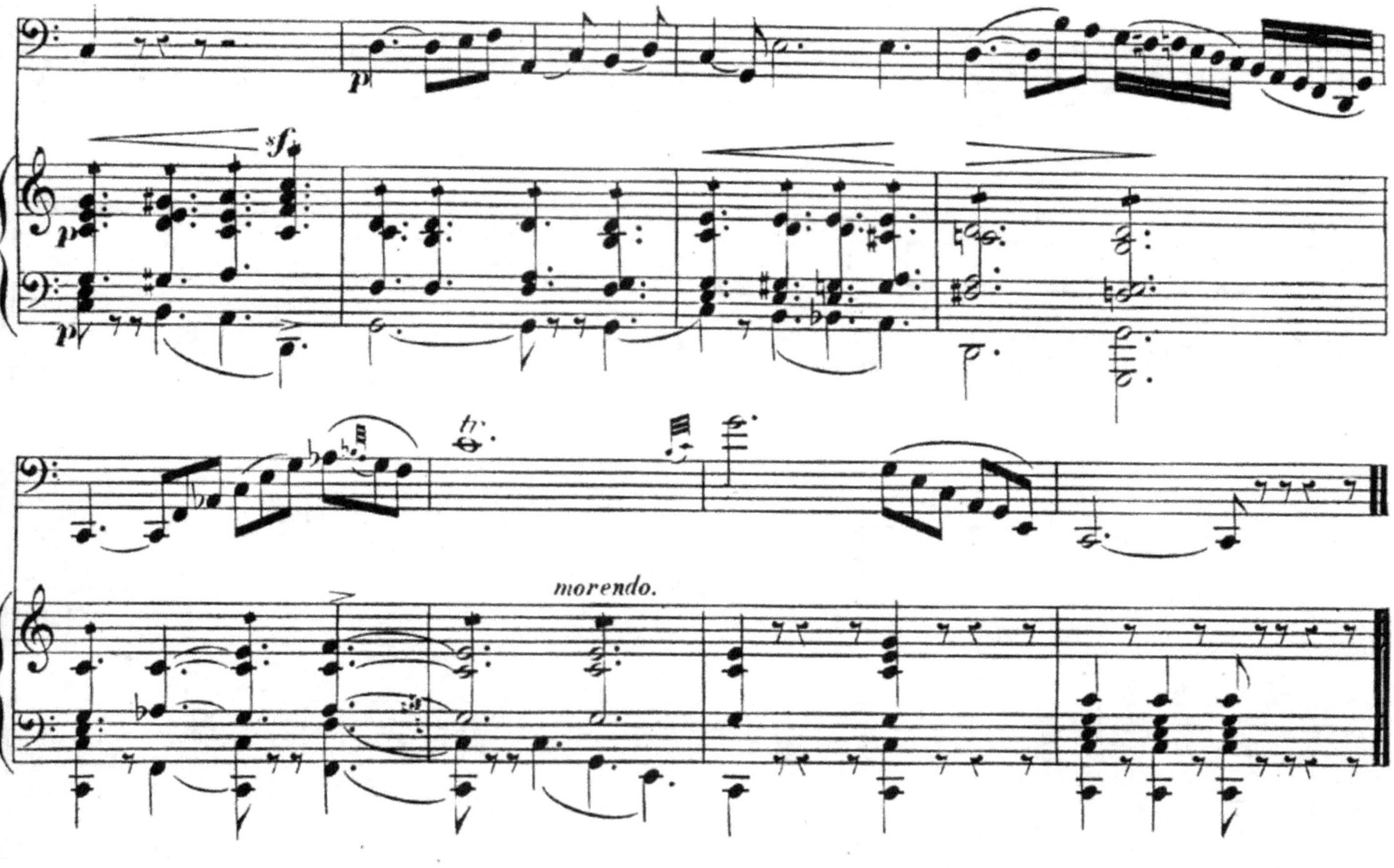

*sf*

*p*

*p*

*tr.*

*morendo.*

## FINAL DE LA SOMNAMBULE.

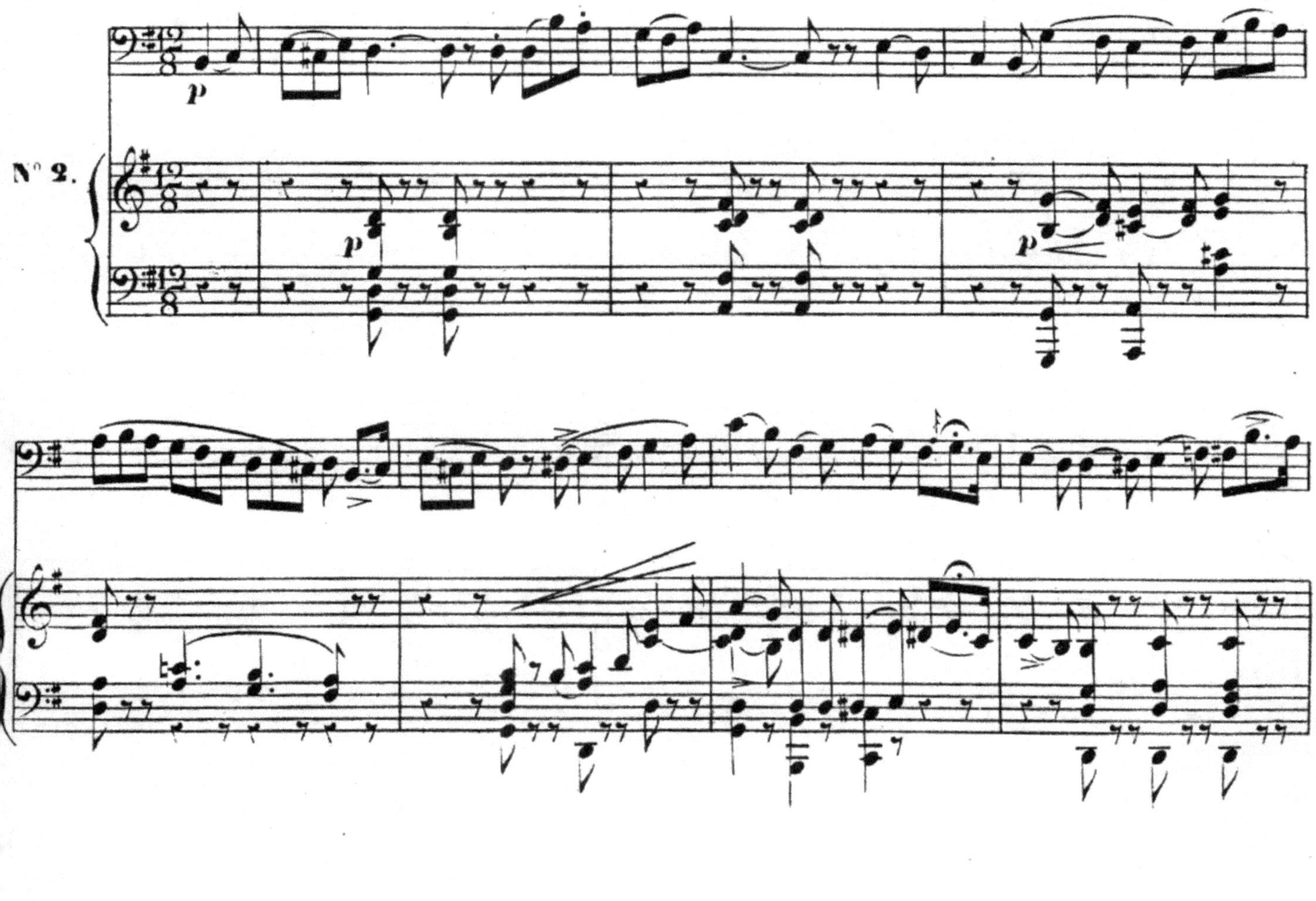

BELLINI.

Nº 2.

*p*

*p*

*p*

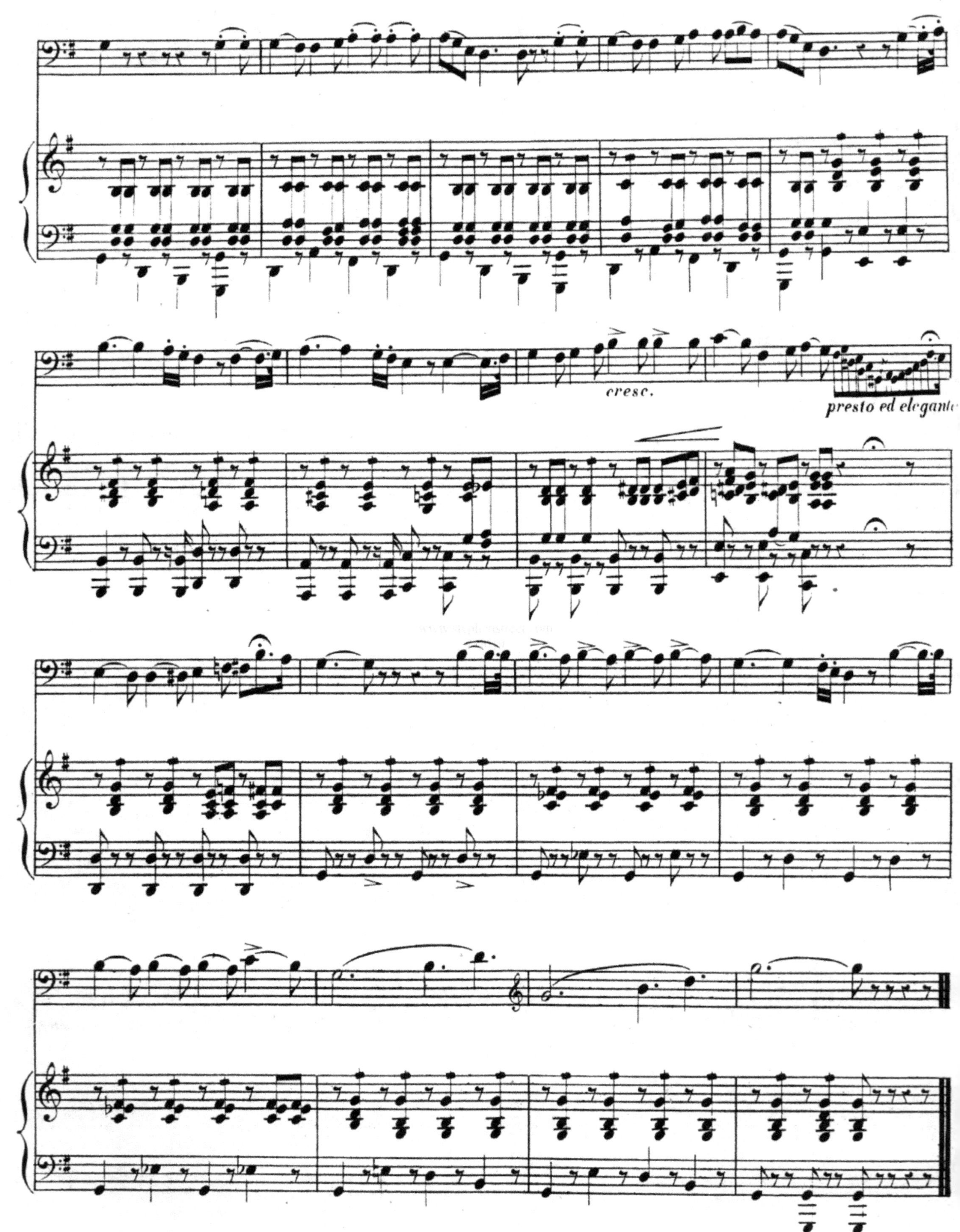
cresc.
presto ed elegante

# SÉRÉNADE DU BARBIER DE SÉVILLE

ROSSINO.

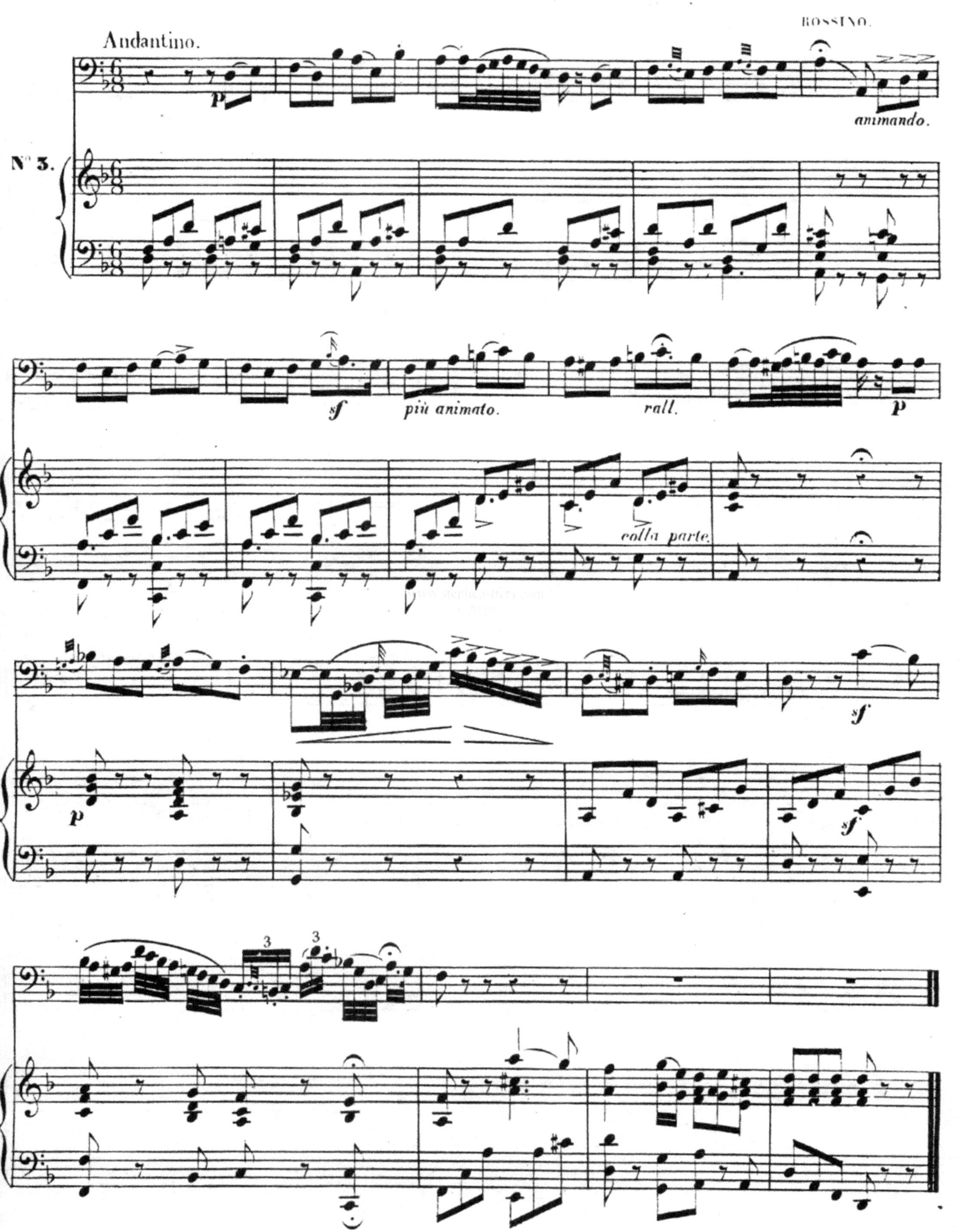

## AIR D'IL TROVATORE.

VERDI.

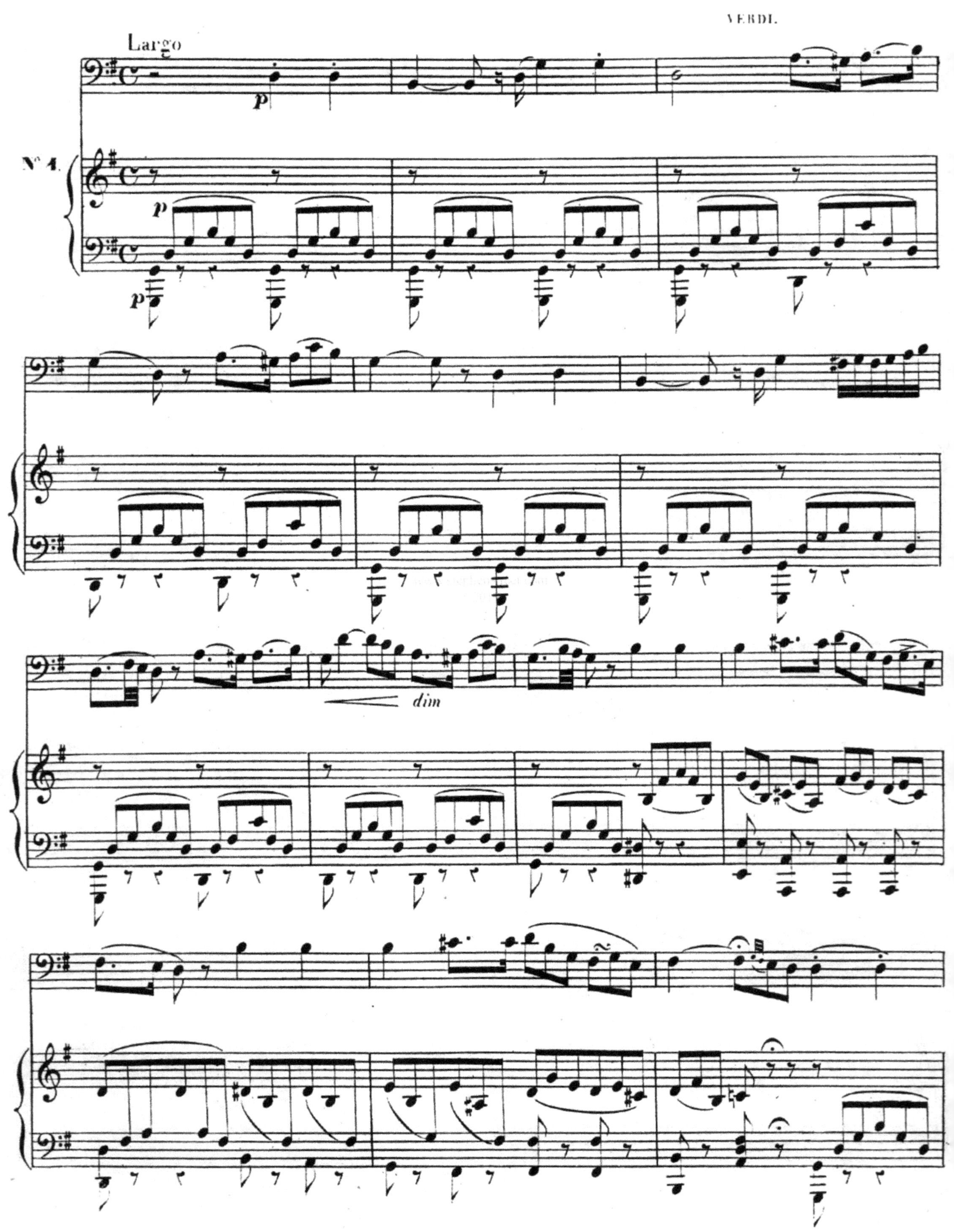

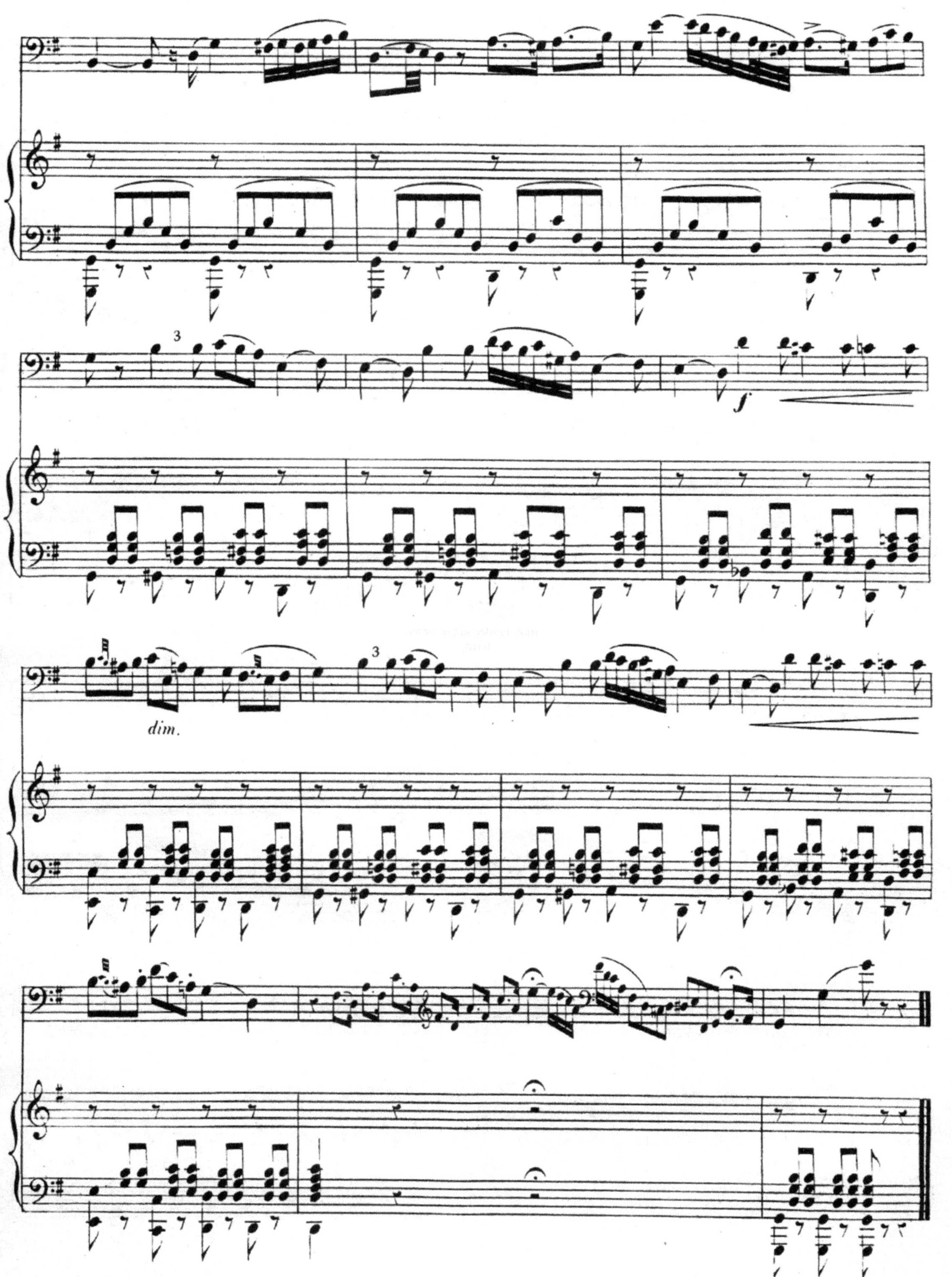

3
*f*
*dim.*
3

# ROMANCE DE L'ÉLIXIRE D'AMORE.

DONIZETTI.

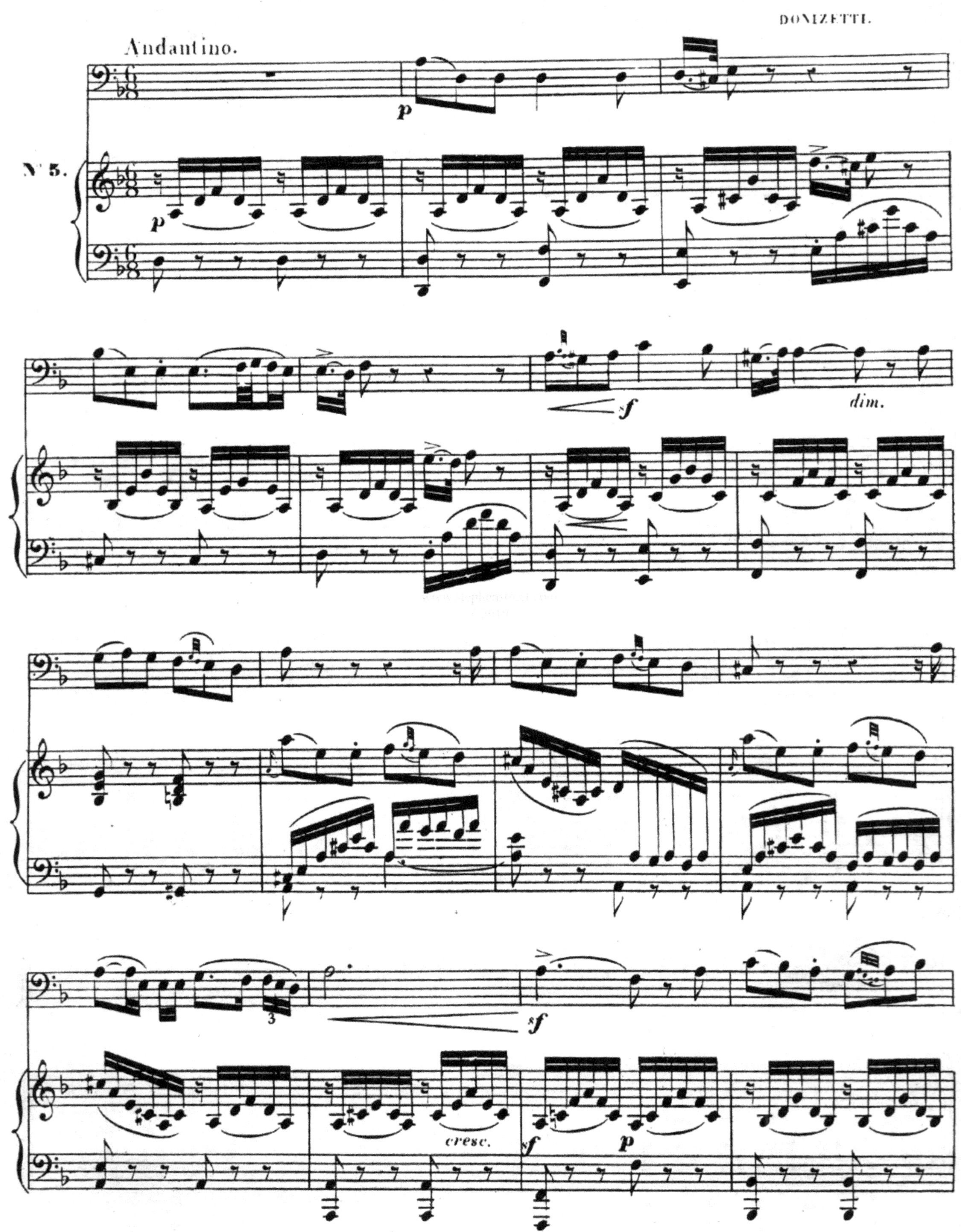

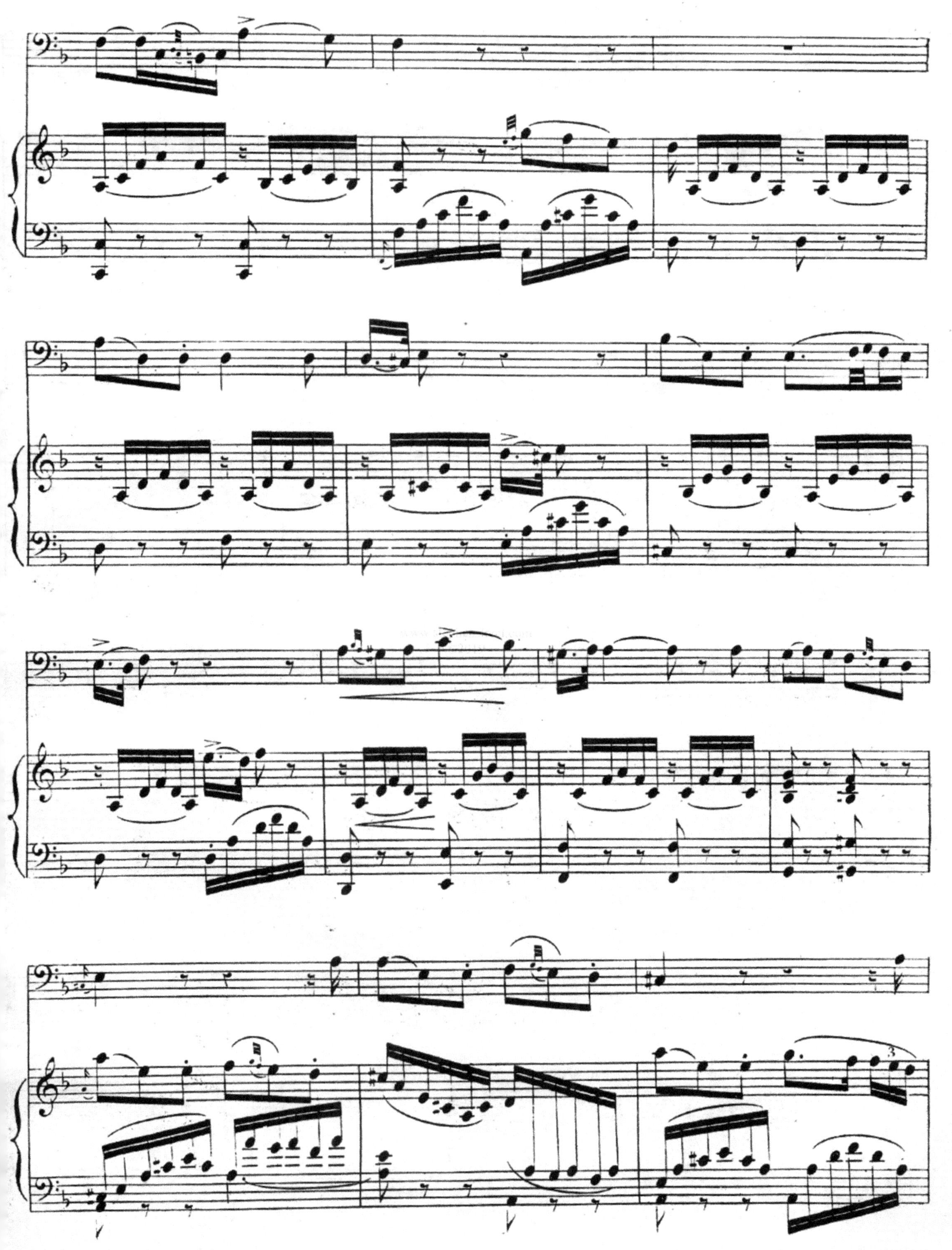

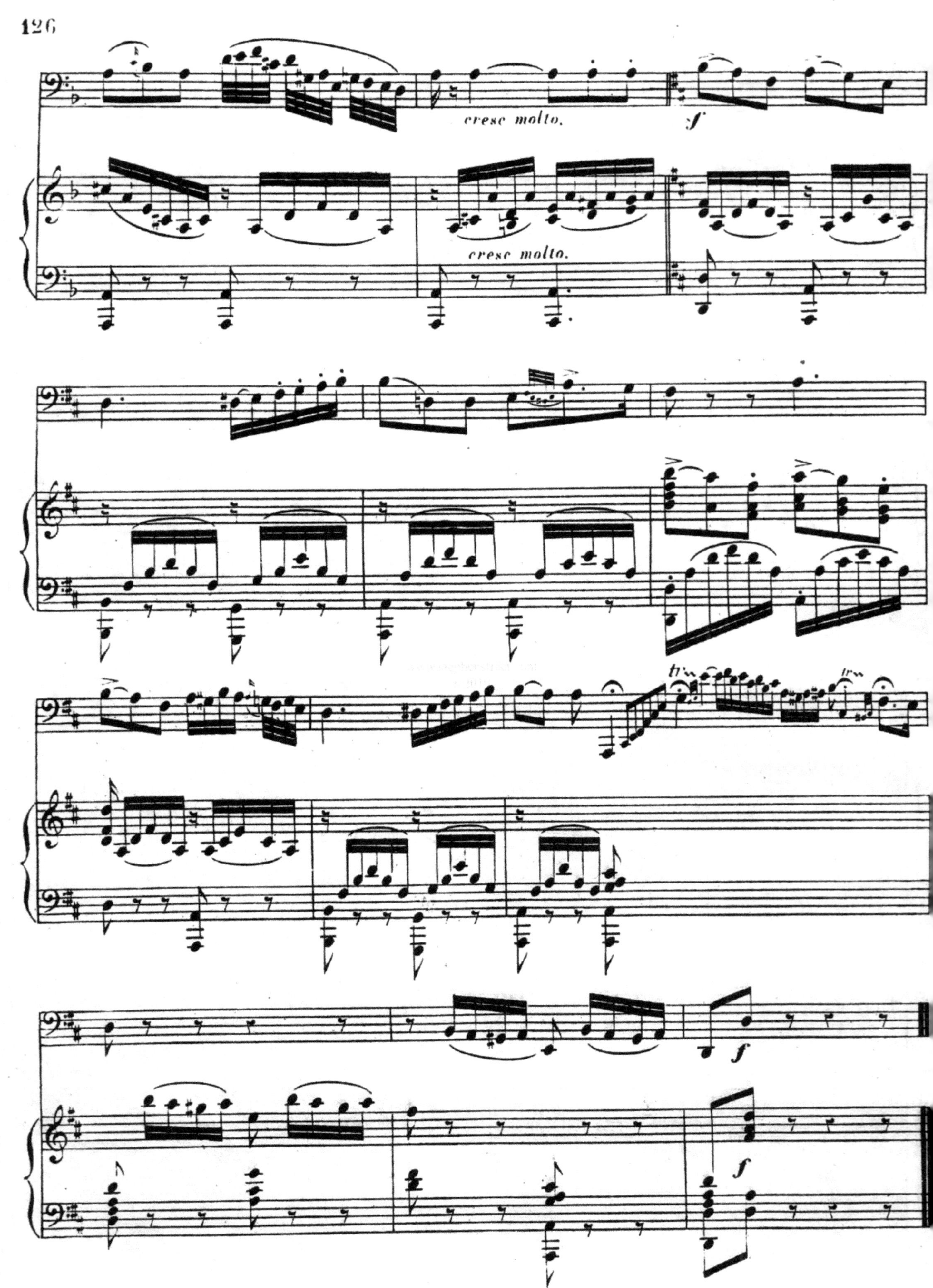
cresc molto.
cresc molto.

# CARNAVAL DE VENISE.

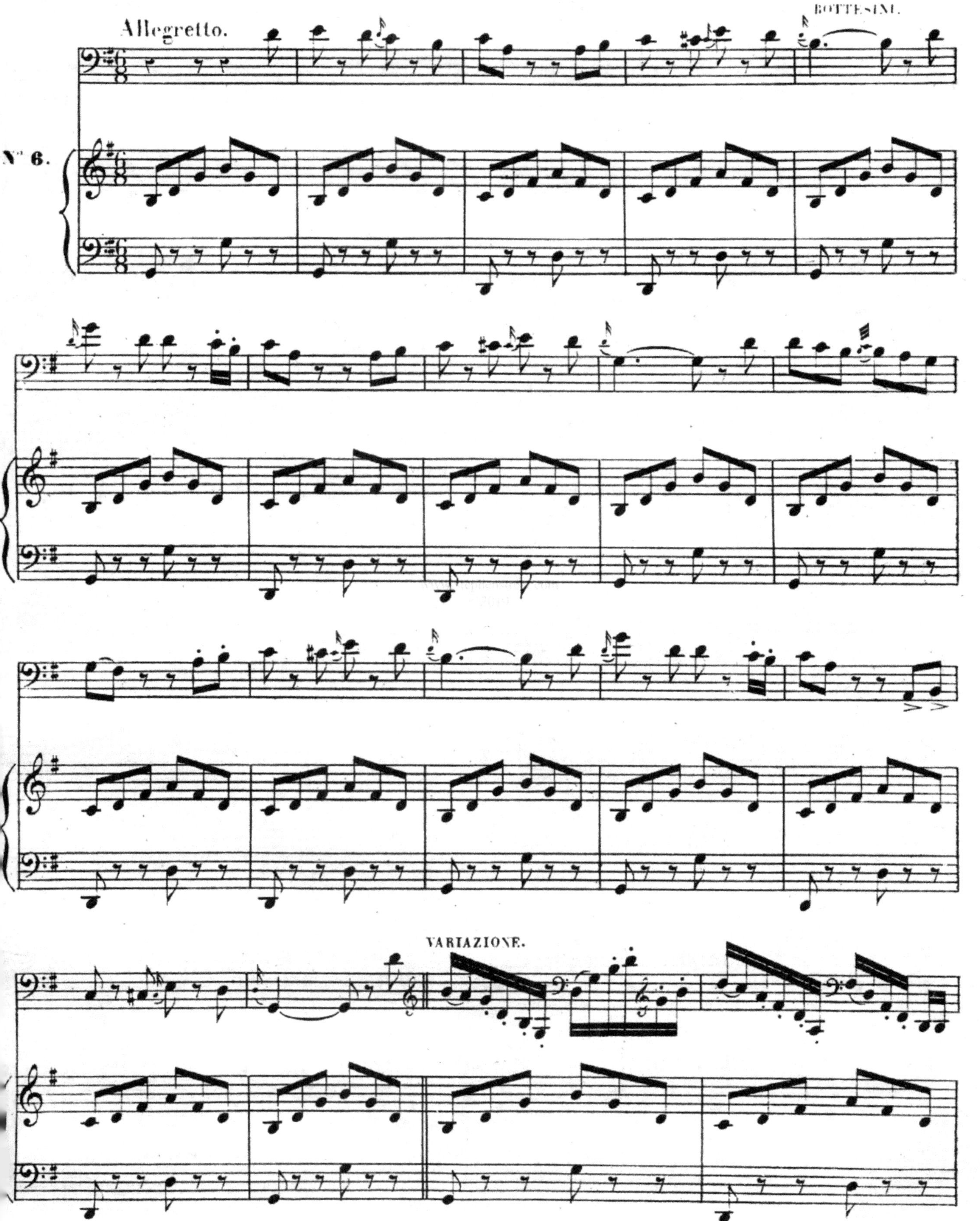

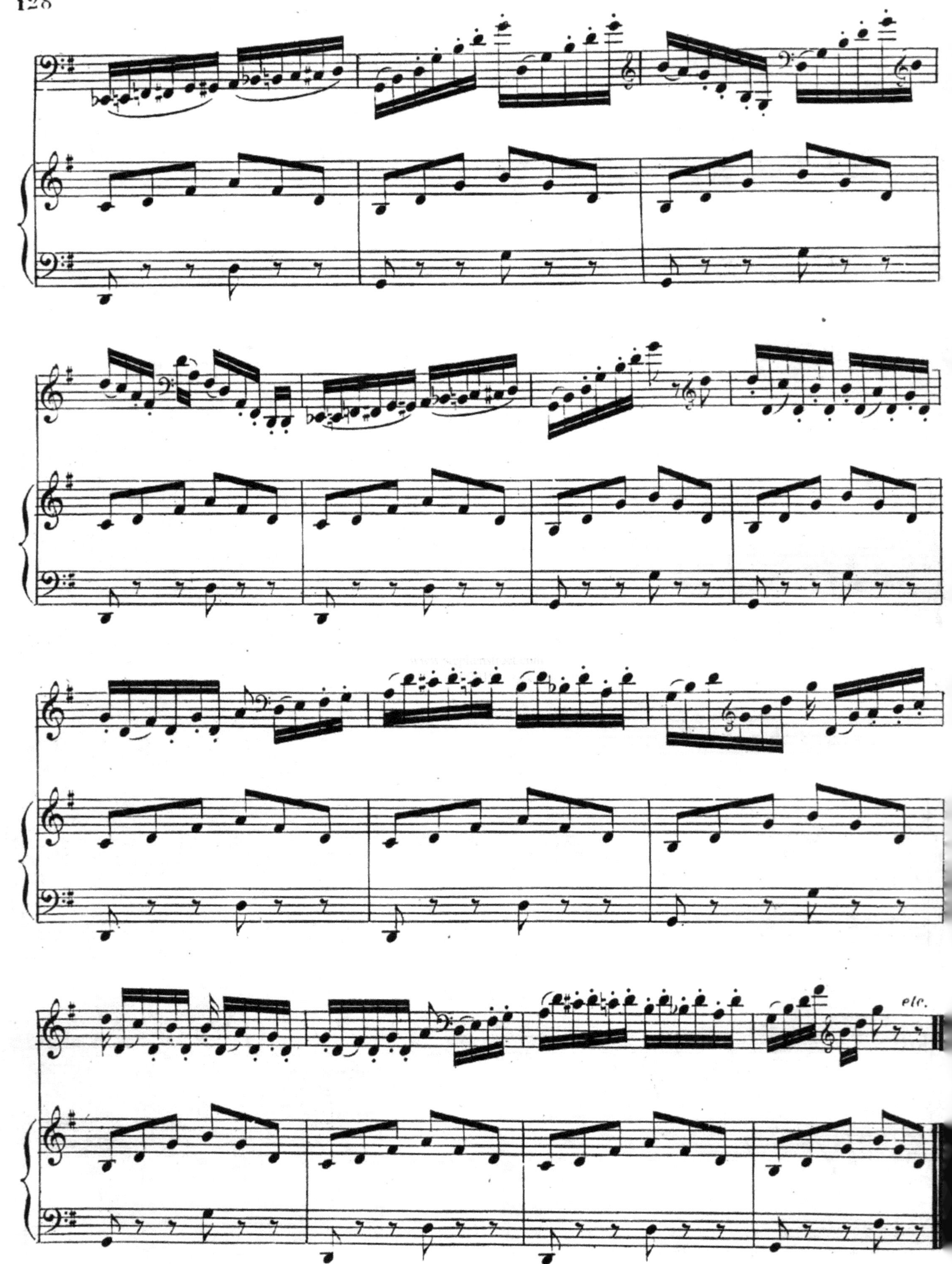
etc.

# INDEX.

## FIRST PART.



## SECOND PART.

www.ingramcontent.com/pod-product-compliance
Lightning Source LLC
LaVergne TN
LVHW081150110826
845149LV00008B/1612
* 9 7 8 1 9 9 9 8 6 6 4 5 7 *